THE CHEESE BOARD

THE CHEESE BOARD
COLLECTIVE WORKS

by the CHEESE BOARD COLLECTIVE   Foreword by Alice Waters

bread • pastry • cheese • pizza

TEN SPEED PRESS
BERKELEY | TORONTO

**DEDICATED TO OUR DEVOTED COMMUNITY OF CUSTOMERS
AND TO ALL COLLECTIVE WORKERS, PAST, PRESENT, AND FUTURE.
IN MEMORY OF TESSA.**

Ten Speed Press
Box 7123
Berkeley, California 94707
www.tenspeed.com

Distributed in Australia by Simon & Schuster Australia, in Canada by Ten Speed Press Canada, in New Zealand by Southern Publishers Group, in South Africa by Real Books, and in the United Kingdom and Europe by Airlift Book Company.

Cover and text design by Toni Tajima

Library of Congress Cataloging-in-Publication Data

Cheese Board Collective.
  The cheese board : collective works: bread, pastry, cheese, pizza / by the Cheese Board Collective; foreword by Alice Waters.
    p. cm.
Includes bibliographical references and index.
  ISBN 1-58008-419-2
  1. Baking. 2. Baked products. 3. Cheese Board Collective. I. Title.

TX765 .C465 2003

641.8'15--dc22

                                        2003014546

Printed in the United States
First printing, 2003

2 3 4 5 6 7 8 9 10 — 07 06 05 04 03

Contents

Acknowledgments vi

Foreword viii

Preface ix

Introduction 1

The Basics: Equipment, Ingredients, and Methods 17

CHAPTER ONE / THE MORNING BAKERY: SCONES, MUFFINS, AND MORE 35

CHAPTER TWO / YEASTED BREADS 73

CHAPTER THREE / SOURDOUGH BREADS 87

CHAPTER FOUR / RYE BREADS 117

CHAPTER FIVE / HOLIDAYS 127

CHAPTER SIX / THE CHEESE COUNTER 145

CHAPTER SEVEN / THE PIZZERIA 195

Source List 222

Bibliography 223

Directory of Cooperative / Collective Organizations 224

Index 225

Acknowledgments

THE COLLECTIVE WORKS is truly a collective project. While a small group of us worked on the book steadily for the past three years, its existence is entirely due to the support of all the Cheese Board Collective members. Cheese Boarders contributed to the project in so many ways: they tested and developed recipes; substituted on shifts, freeing up time for others to work on the cookbook; contributed artwork and photography; critiqued text; and supported the lengthy work that has gone into writing this book. We heard a collective sigh of relief at our monthly meeting when it was announced that the manuscript had finally been handed in.

The challenge of taking bakery-sized recipes and reducing them to recipes to be used by the home cook kept us busy. Our families and housemates were exceedingly patient about coming home time and again to discover the kitchen transformed into a test zone and plates and plates of delicious scones—but no hint of dinner. They complained only when we finished testing recipes and there were no more scones to taste!

Ten Speed Press is right in our backyard. Many of the staff are Cheese Board customers, which made it the perfect press to publish our book. They were patient and understanding when we explained that decisions would have to be agreed upon by our entire membership. Recently, when only two of us showed up for a meeting at Ten Speed (we usually travel in groups of six), Aaron, our editor, asked us twice if we were really the only ones coming.

Grateful thanks to the following people for their contributions to this project: Mark Anderson, our first contact at Ten Speed; Joshua Apte, photography; Mike Apte, kitchen cleanup, lunches, editing, and computer support; Oliver Apte, recipe tasting; Zac Apte, recipe tasting and computer support; Ann Arnold, artwork; Tina Birky, artwork, support, and information; Carrie Blake, recipe development and testing, information, and support; Lisa Bruzzone, recipe development and testing, editing, and writing; Rosalind Bruzzone, recipe testing; Brad Bunnin, legal advice and handholding; Mateo Chavez, recipe development, information, and support; Ken Della Penta, indexing; Arthur Dembling, writing, editing, support, and information; Lynne Devereaux of the California Milk Advisory Board, cheese information; Suzanne Doyle, recipe testing; Pam Erenberg, recipe development, editing, information, and support; Dan Falsetto, recipe testing, information, and support; Bruce Freedman, support, recipe tasting, and information; Charles Frizzell, photography, writing, and editing; Helen Gaffney, recipe testing; Cathy Goldsmith, recipe development and testing, editing, and writing; Joel Goldsmith, recipe tasting; Samuel Goldsmith, recipe tasting; Steve Goldsmith, support, kitchen cleanup, recipe tasting, and editing; Mariano Gonzalez, cheese-aging information; Reuben Hale, inspiration for steaming techniques; John Harris, encouragement, support, and information; Linda Hawkins, editing and advice; Arayah Jenanyan, recipe testing, information, and support; Alice Kahn, writing, support, and information; Suzanne Kiihne, recipe testing; Laurel Koledin, cheese information; Beverly Kraut, recipe development; Dave Magtanong, recipe testing, support, and information; Kirsty Melville, belief in the project; Carolyn Miller, copyediting; Jacinta Monniere, manuscript cleanup; Daphne O'Regan, editing and support; Jonas Osmond, poetry; Deborah Quick, writing, information, and support; Gary Salzman, artwork, recipe testing, information, and support; Ursula Schulz, recipe development and testing, editing, and writing; Jasmine Star, proofreading; Steve Sutcher, editing, writing, information, and support; Toni Tajima, our designer; Steve Upstill, recipe testing; Willa Walter, recipe development, recipe testing, and editing; Alice Waters, support and writing; Aaron Wehner, our patient editor; Victoria Wise, support and writing; Phil Wood, belief in the project; and Olivia Yee, recipe testing, information, and support.

And thanks to the following people for their information and support they provided: Bruce Aidells, Francisco Alonso, Nancy Austin, Cristina Barras, Paul Bellman, Carole Bidnick, Charlie Bonkofski, Sylvan Brackett, Martha Cornwall, Erin Crowe, Pat Darrow, Lourdes De Real, Frieda Dilloo, Kate Dowling, Arielle Eckstut, Julia Elliot, Stu Epstein, Gonzalo Ferreyra, Dwight Ferron, Sloan Fidler, Janet Fletcher, John Grau, Michael Helm, Darryl Henriques, Robert Jackall, Mollie Katzen, Adam King, Craig Knudsen, Artemio Maldonado, Michael McGee, Laura McNall, Jesus Mejia, Tessa Morrone, Giorgia Neidorf, Stephanie Pardee, Rafael Peña, Guillermo Perez, José Ruiz, Vicki Salzman, Cory Schreiber, Shehanna Stevenson, Yeshi Tenzin, Arturo Toczynski, Elizabeth Valoma (Avedisian), Lynn Ventresca, Michael Wild, David Weidenfeld, and Eric Wong.

Foreword

THE CHEESE BOARD is the one indispensable institution in the north Berkeley neighborhood where I live and work. It has created a community larger than itself, composed of the collective and all its former members, suppliers, customers, neighbors, and all the beneficiaries of its commonsense purity of motivation. And the Cheese Board has anchored and sustained this community by its uninterrupted practice of compassionate collectivism, expressed through food.

Where else but the Cheese Board could I walk through the door on a Saturday morning into a more or less orderly but still thrilling and lively throng of people, all drawn in by the irresistible good smells of baking bread? Inside there are warm loaves fresh from the ovens and huge cases filled with hundreds of cheeses. Everywhere there is greeting, gossiping, and babies crying. Right in plain view is an undisguised workshop: an open, no-nonsense kitchen and counter, with no high-concept merchandising, and nothing boutiquelike about it. And I can always count on a hug and a kiss from a friend behind the counter.

The Cheese Board was there, a hole-in-the-wall with a line out the door, before Chez Panisse was so much as a gleam in my eye. When the restaurant was conceived, I wanted it to be in north Berkeley so the Cheese Board would be nearby, because I knew I would be among friends. The Cheese Board was then a beacon of honesty, and it still is, although now it is also a central gathering place, cheese merchant, bakery, and pizzeria—and still with a line out the door. Its liberality and sheer political expressivity is an inspiration to us here across the street.

Knowing that the Cheese Board is nearby has helped save Chez Panisse from getting too expensive and exclusive, I think. I know I will never forget the astonishing night in the seventies when the merry collectivists, having stripped themselves naked, burst through our front door in the midst of the dinner service and streaked through the restaurant, the very embodiment of ecstatic, anarchic nature, if not anarchosyndicalism.

To have been their across-the-street neighbor for so long is to love the Cheese Boarders most of all for their generosity and kindness. For over thirty years the collective has been quietly teaching its patrons with authentic food and authentic politics. I'm very happy they are now expressing their passion in this book.

—Alice Waters

Preface

WHEN WE BEGAN THINKING ABOUT a Cheese Board cookbook, we knew that it would have to contain not only recipes, but also the multiplicity of voices that have been a part of the Cheese Board these past thirty years. A small group set out to interview past and present members about their experiences, and this resulted in an invaluable anecdotal archive of Cheese Board history. Since 1967, each decade has had its benchmarks: the moving of the store, the starting of the pizzeria, the spawning of new collectives. And with the passing of time, new voices joined the group, adding their creativity and helping the Cheese Board to grow.

The history of the Cheese Board is one of creativity, investigation, trial, and change. Someone gets an idea and throws it out there. Then we pool our knowledge; the idea grows and changes, profiting from the group's participation and experience. The experience of writing this book has mirrored this process. At first, it was an idea, then a small group of people gathered in support of this idea, the Cheese Board membership endorsed the project, and here we are. We have grown closer, eaten great food, and had a terrific time. And if we've learned anything from being Cheese Board collective members, it is that process and product can work together to create something new and worthwhile.

There are many excellent books that explain the science of bread baking. Our book does not go into those details; instead, we offer our years of baking experience. Please follow these recipes as we would: No instruction is carved in stone and no technique is a rule. You are the ultimate judge of what tastes good to you. Our philosophy is that preparing food should be joyous and fun.

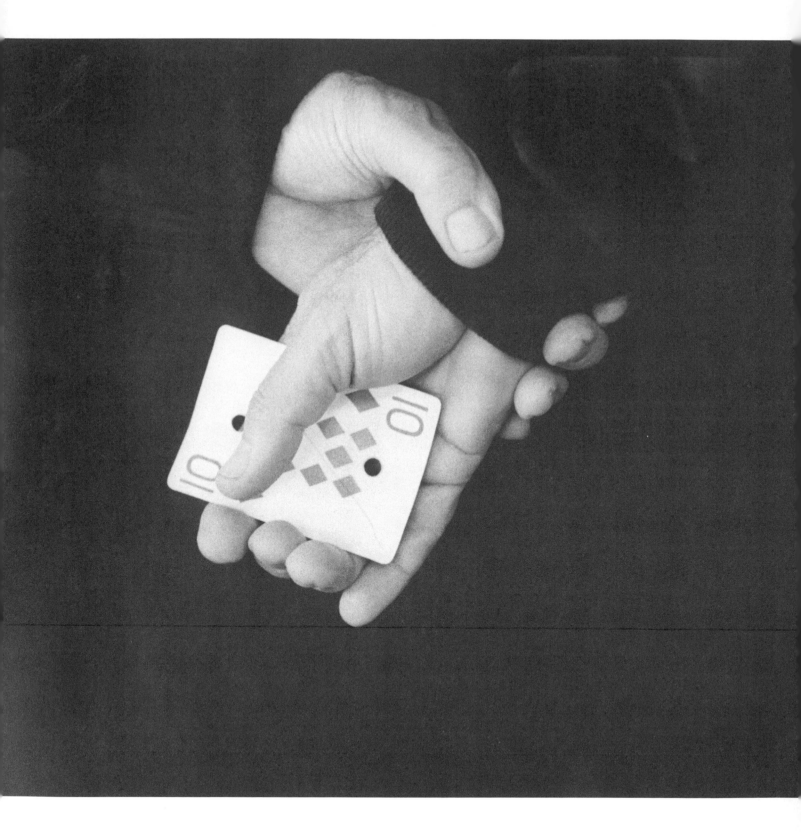

Introduction

Someone out on the street is always asking, "Who *really* is the boss?"

THE CHEESE BOARD COLLECTIVE is a neighborhood bakery, cheese shop, and pizzeria in Berkeley, California. Entering our store is initially overwhelming to some first-time customers. As you walk in, a multitude of sensations surrounds you: the aromas of fresh baguettes, hot cheese bread, and garlic oil from trays of focaccia. From the cheese counter comes the barnyard smell of goaty chèvres and the sharp tang of the blue cheeses. The open kitchen allows you to see the whole operation. Everything is in motion: in the front of the store, workers are selling cheese and customers are browsing and choosing breads and cheeses; in the back, workers are rolling and baking bread. The large selection of products can be confusing. There are forty feet of cases with over three hundred varieties of cheese from around the world. Sourdough products are a store specialty, as are hearty wheat breads, hefty scones, muffins, and savory breads. The varying daily bread schedule is complex enough that even the workers have difficulty remembering it. Customers seem to prize the store as a gathering place for social nourishment as much as a place to buy food. There is a loud party atmosphere of busy shoppers waiting for service and catching up with old friends. Instead of taking a number, you grab a playing card from a hook. When a cheese clerk calls out,

"Who's got the jack of hearts?" you know it's your turn. If you happen to draw the joker . . . well, you're in luck because jokers are wild.

HOW WE RUN OUR BUSINESS

The Cheese Board is worker-owned and -operated. We run our business without any formal hierarchy and in as egalitarian a fashion as possible. Regardless of seniority, every member is paid the same hourly wage. Everyone is encouraged to learn all the jobs. Some of the jobs, such as ordering, payroll, and bookkeeping, are held for several years and then rotated to a different member. Each member has equal voting power. Major decisions are made at the monthly meetings using a modified consensus process, while minor decisions are made by the shift at the time that they arise. There are quarterly meetings involving the entire membership to discuss issues that affect both the pizza operation and the cheese and bread operation.

We strive to produce good products with integrity, made by workers who have an investment in their workplace and community.

A few doors down from the bakery and cheese shop is the Cheese Board Pizzeria. The pizzas feature a crisp sourdough crust, Mozzarella, and different combinations of fresh seasonal produce and, of course, specialty cheeses for the topping. For the customer, the choice is easy—there is only one type of pizza each day. The toppings are changed to produce the flavor of the day, but the only choice you have is the number of slices or pies. Just as the hot pizzas are taken from the oven, garlic-infused olive oil is brushed over the crust, creating a heady scent. There is always live music—piano and stand-up bass, sometimes a drummer—and occasionally musician friends drop by and bring their horns, saxophones, guitars, and flutes. Jazz, the roar of the oven fans, aromas, and conversation fill the small space as customers wait in line for slices or whole pizzas. "For here or to go? For here or to go?"

Our History

It absolutely changes people to work here. You learn about yourself, you learn about trying to get along with people. Hopefully, before you die, you learn that these are the most important things in life.

—ART

We would never have survived the years of change if we hadn't laughed as hard as we did.

—CHARLIE

The basis of the Cheese Board is generosity and love. That was the original gift. A couple of people started it, and the people who work here today revel in that gift. The history is strong.

—LISA

"I've been shopping here since this was just a tiny store up on Vine Street." We hear this comment from our customers all the time. What does it mean? For the veteran collective member it is a reminder that we are friends, family, and community. For the newest members, it is an invitation to join the communal history. We are fortunate to have such loyal and involved customers. Through the years they have supported our alternative work style and joined us in our enthusiasm for and pleasure in food.

Getting our history to sit still on a piece of paper isn't easy. Since our fundamental spirit is the equality of all voices, it is especially difficult to translate our rich tradition of stories into a single narrative. While interviewing past members, sharing stories with customers, and laughing over experiences with each other, a strong sense of our collective past came through in the individual voices we heard. Here are some of those voices.

1967

One day, I came across Peet's coffee at Vine and Walnut, where I had a cup of coffee that I remember to this day—it was a Proustian flood of memory that took me back to Paris a year earlier. It was the first time I'd had French roast coffee in the United States. I had discovered something very European in Berkeley. Then I walked down the street and there was this little shop, and once again the cheeses were from France. Oh my God, I'd never seen anything like this: such an array of cheeses, there were maybe thirty or forty.

—JOHN HARRIS, FORMER MEMBER

Elizabeth and Sahag Avedisian first opened the doors of the Cheese Board in 1967. Their dream was to run a small specialty shop together and make use of slow moments to pursue their interests and studies. The location was a tiny, narrow storefront wedged into a converted alleyway on Vine Street, in north Berkeley. While south Berkeley and the university campus were often roiled by the political actions of the era, the Cheese Board's immediate locale seemed nothing more than a quiet corner of a small college town. The neighborhood had two gas stations, a drug store, and a small five-and-dime store. The laundromat on the corner was mostly deserted except for a cat sleeping in the window. The Berkeley Consumer Co-operative grocery store, a local meeting place for townspeople, was a block and a half away. Just up Vine Street was Peet's, a newly established European-style coffee shop that soon was vying with the Co-op as the place to run into friends.

The Avedisians selected the first cheeses for the store by randomly paging through a Domestic Cheese Company catalog. By reading and tasting, talking and sharing, they soon developed a sense for what they liked. By offering samples to customers they learned more about what was delicious and popular. Despite having no real retail experience and little knowledge of cheese, Sahag and Elizabeth soon had a steady business. Berkeley's large European community and well-traveled locals were thrilled to find a store that carried a variety of authentic, imported cheeses.

Within three months it became necessary to hire a few people to help out in the busy store. The first employees were hired because they were friends or frequent visitors to Vine Street. The new workers and the owners were an eclectic group, which created a vibrant and exciting atmosphere in the small store.

After about six months of talking and eating, and hanging out with Sahag and Elizabeth, I started working there.

—JOHN HARRIS

Well, I hadn't done that much retail. Being part of the Cheese Board was like being part of a family. I really liked everyone there. It was just fun, and you got paid for it—that was really something.

—TESSA MORRONE, FORMER MEMBER

Creativity and personal expression were supported by the staff and owners. Most people worked part-time in order to pursue their outside interests. The combination of the store's character, the appreciation of European culture, and the changing politics of the times created exactly the right environment to foster experiments in alternative work- and lifestyles.

We were not interested in becoming men in gray flannel suits. We wanted to live the free artistic life—we were after more personal expression and freedom.

—GIORGIA NEIDORF, FORMER MEMBER

Everyone had a main career goal or ambition, whether it was to be an artist, actor, politico, or whatever, and the Cheese Board was a supportive part-time gig.

—JOHN HARRIS

People began to drop by out of curiosity as well as for cheese.

I don't think that the customers were coming in just for the cheese. It was the atmosphere. It had something to do with what Berkeley was then and what we were. Sahag's ideals were seductive and wonderful; everybody was ripe for them, the customers and we who worked there. For example, he gave away free soup; the ideals embodied in this offering were right for the community. Those were the days when Berkeley got its reputation.
—PAT DARROW, FORMER MEMBER

THE COLLECTIVE

Arising from a deep belief that a more equitable distribution of wealth was necessary for a good and just society, and inspired by time spent on an Israeli kibbutz, Elizabeth and Sahag offered to sell the shop, at cost, to their employees. In 1971, the two owners and six employees formed a worker-owned collective.

I couldn't believe it when we collectivized. It seemed to me that Sahag and Elizabeth were just giving the place away. I had never heard of anything like that. It just seemed so extraordinarily unusual.
—TESSA MORRONE

Sahag and Elizabeth were instrumental in having this collective come into being. There it was, and there it still is. They had the chance to become serious capitalists and they turned it down for the benefit of the workers.
—DARRYL HENRIQUES, FORMER MEMBER

We were marching for peace, but we had not heard anyone say the owner should not make money off the workers. That was amazing to me!
—PAT DARROW

Originally, the change in status was not formalized on paper. Issues such as legal ownership were not as important to the group as the shift into a brand-new, democratically run business. The transformation from a small, privately operated store into a collective with a completely egalitarian pay structure was revolutionary. The generosity of this act has graced the workplace for succeeding generations of workers.

We still believe that everybody's time is worth the same amount of money. The quintessential element of the Cheese Board politics is that notion.
—MICHAEL

Trying to devise a legal entity that reflected the reality of the Cheese Board's structure wasn't a straightforward proposition.

We were trying to stay out of "the system" as much as possible. We were told we had to incorporate, but then we found out that there were no laws about collectives in the state of California. We decided to hire a lawyer to set something up.
—A LONGTIME MEMBER

To me the central issue was that we had figured out a way for the store to own itself and there were no people that actually owned the store. Your participation in the store had to do with the number of hours that you worked. It was critical that everybody made the same hourly wage no matter how long they had worked there.
—DARRYL HENRIQUES

The transition to a worker-owned and -operated cooperative relied upon a shared work ethic, high standards, and the strong emotional connections among the group. Decisions were made, after much debate, either on the shift or at the monthly meetings. The operation and management of the collective was, and is still, a constantly evolving process. Meetings in the first years were frequently loud, argumentative, and unstructured.

Things were different then. First of all, there were a lot of strong characters who had very fascinating and extreme personalities. In the beginning of the seventies, we didn't really believe in getting along so much. That wasn't the big principle—it was more express your emotions and let it all hang out.
—FRIEDA DILLOO, FORMER MEMBER

The politics of the traditional workplace had been turned on its head. The new owners shared a belief that the collective process would organically create a truly democratic society. Discussions were an exploration into limitless territory. The utopian vision was, however, firmly grounded in an everyday reality.

We succeeded as a business because we weren't doctrinaire; we were inclusive. We didn't choose people on the basis of their politics.
—FRIEDA DILLOO

During one member's job interview with the entire group, she asked, "Do I have to agree with all those posters and signs in the front window of the store in order for me to work here?" We all told her, "Of course not." She wouldn't have worked here with us unless we had said that.
—CRAIG KNUDSEN, FORMER MEMBER

We're still around because we paid attention to the business. Other collectives criticized us for being too bourgeois. Being a collective does not make you exempt from market forces. You still have to create a place customers want to shop in so that you can generate enough income to pay a living wage to your members.
—S. S.

I love saying to people that this seems like an impossible business model, but it works, and it works very well.
—CHARLIE

BREAD

Daily work at the Cheese Board consisted of waiting on customers, cleaning, cutting cheeses, sweeping the floors, and paying the bills. The introduction of bread for sale, like so many changes at the Cheese Board, wasn't planned. One day friends of the store brought by a loaf of whole-wheat rye as a gift. With its hearty crust and dark crumb, it couldn't have been more different from sliced white bread. Inspired, the members invited the friends to bake loaves to sell alongside the cheeses. The loaves were baked in a single oven in the cramped kitchen space. Bread making was seductive—it was a hands-on, tactile experience that was deeply satisfying. On a political level, it was an honest handmade product. Customers loved the bread, and the new product added variety to the store, inspiring members to develop recipes for other breads.

I simply put everything I could think of that was good into the honey egg bread! It was such a rich bread.
—PAT DARROW

The collective was expanding in a new direction, slowly evolving into more than just a cheese shop. But not all the members were excited by this new direction.

I wasn't that interested in the breads—I think that I rolled out a bread once. The main thing that I wanted was the social relationship with the community. I wanted to stand at the counter and talk to people and sell cheese. It was like a cabaret; the public was the audience and we were the performers.
—JOHN HARRIS

SHATTUCK AVENUE, 1975

With a steadily growing business in cheese and the development of new breads, the Vine Street store was bursting at the seams.

It was tight on Saturdays in the old store on Vine Street. There were four of us behind the counter and there was only one scale and two cutting spaces. We had to move around each other. The line went out the door on Saturdays.

—A LONGTIME MEMBER

There were discussions about moving to a larger space and what that would mean to the group. It wasn't simply a matter of getting a new space; there were serious concerns about how growth would change the intimacy of the group. The lament, "Let's stay small and keep the family feeling," would be heard from then on. But when a larger storefront became available around the corner on Shattuck Avenue, the opportunity was too good to pass up.

In typical Cheese Board style, the members embraced the store's new home.

We've always had the notion of doing everything ourselves. When we moved from the old store to the new store on Shattuck all this construction had to happen. A lot of us thought, "Well, we can make the new store and do everything that's necessary, relying on our own expertise." I love that philosophy.

—MICHAEL

It wasn't long before the Cheese Board was one of many food establishments in the area. There was Peet's; Pig-by-the-Tail, a charcuterie; Lenny's meat market; North Berkeley Wine; the restaurant Chez Panisse; Cocolat, a decadent chocolate shop; the Fish Market, right next door to the Cheese Board; and the Juice Bar, another collective, which took over the original Cheese Board location. The neighborhood exchanged ideas over food, and there was a shared belief that good food was essential, honest, and important. Alice Kahn, a local writer and humorist, labeled the neighborhood the Gourmet Ghetto, a title that has stuck to this day. We didn't know it at the time, but we were in the middle of a food revolution, one that could never have happened without the support of the whole community.

When the food thing really started happening in the mid-seventies our lives changed. We had thought that we were going to be artists, but a lot of us ended up being food people. What was the support, or the economic base, for the career, ended up being the career. There was a transformation where food became an art form, and a life —a life in food.

—JOHN HARRIS

BAGUETTES

The conflict between personal vision and the "collective good" has always been a challenge to the group. The collective fosters personal freedom and at the same time suppresses it. While everyone is an owner, everyone is also a worker.

There's really no structure for personal creativity in terms of coming up with a new product or initiating a change. It requires certain personalities, people who can't resist or help themselves.

—D. W.

If anyone thinks of a new product, everyone gets cranky. It's not easy to innovate —it's the hardest thing to do.

—LISA

The new store, Shattuck Avenue, 1975.

You have to invent new products on your own time, or else you risk inflicting your desire to create something new onto the shift, which can cause stress. The process makes it really difficult to create something new, but the product in question inevitably becomes better.

—CATHY

The most fun is making the baguettes—rolling and baking them. I love the rhythm of doing the same thing over and over. And then there's the final product, a wonderfully crusty bread with a delicious sour tang and beautiful mahogany sheen.

—S. S.

Despite initial hesitations, the collective members eventually embraced the idea of offering warm, house-made baguettes to eat with cheese. The customers loved them, and the members began to delve deeper into the art and challenges of baking.

The baguettes were started by just playing around. They were really terrible at first, but in a way they were good —sour and interesting. Bob made people mad at him by experimenting with sourdough on the shift. He had no support, and people would tell him, "You will never make money with bread." Then we started doing some accounting and discovered that bread did *make money.*

—FRIEDA DILLOO

Though innovation is a source of struggle and tension at the Cheese Board, it is crucial to our creative dynamic. Each product undergoes scrutiny and experimentation until it is impossible to recall the prototype after all its incarnations. The reward of the process is universal pride of ownership as the new product makes its daily appearance on our shelves. Each of the many bakers has brought their own contributions to the recipes; our store's master recipe book, tattered and scribbled with notations and corrections, is a testament to this.

Back when we first started making baguettes, almost nobody knew what a baguette was—the word was hardly known in Berkeley. Of course, ten years later you would see as many people walking around with a baguette under their arm as you would in Paris.

—FRIEDA DILLOO

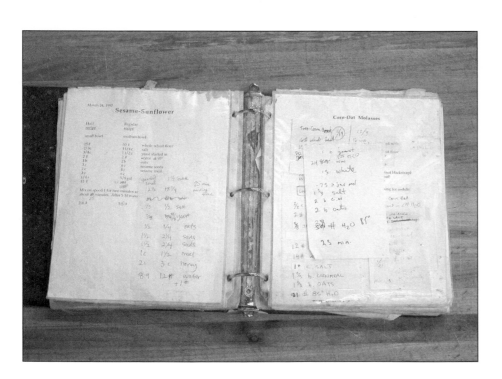

Our master recipe book.

Shattuck Avenue, 1982.

PIZZA, 1985

When the recession of the eighties hit us in California, the business suffered and we were worried about our economic stability. We brainstormed about ways to stay viable. There was talk of taking a pay cut. As business was slow, there was time to play around.

Initially, someone started making pizza once a week on Tuesdays. Then people on other shifts began experimenting, too.

—ART

Pizza became a regular staff lunch. Someone grabbed cheese from the case, someone else would run next door to the Produce Center for vegetables. A half an hour later, pizza was served. Customers noticed and wanted a piece, too. Before we knew it, we were selling slices for lunch.

We had all been talking about what to do because business was slow. At a meeting we decided to try serving pizza on Friday nights from 7:00 to 9:00 P.M. —for fun, you know, just for fun. And that's how it happened. That first Friday night, everyone stayed after work to check it out. It was a good thing because we needed their help.

—ART

What started out as a whim ended up reinvigorating our sales. It was so successful that we needed to open an entirely separate storefront and add new members to handle the volume.

By opening the pizzeria as a separate division, the pizzeria was able to expand. I was one of the first people hired for the pizza collective, just as it was in the process of splitting off from the Cheese Board. Cheese Board members were beginning to have babies and didn't have the time to put into a new product.

—PAM

The pizzeria quickly developed its own distinct character. Nowadays, friends and families listen to live jazz while sitting at café tables inside and out on the sidewalk in front. The tiny space fills up quickly and spills out into the neighborhood. In good weather, picnickers spread out on the median strip, and the sidewalk is full of people eating a slice as they walk along. The line out the door is echoed down the block by the coffee line at the French Hotel.

BAKING AND BUILDING

The opportunity to expand presented itself again when the Fish Market next door closed in 1989. The membership voted to take a pay cut to fund the remodel of the space. With no particular plans for how we would use the space, we closed our eyes and jumped in, employing our in-house talent to do the remodeling.

Fortunately, Berkeley city laws allow the owner of the business to do the work. When I went to get the permits I said, "I'm the owner. I don't have a contractor's license, and I'm not an architect, but I do know how to do the drawings, and I do know how to do the work." They moaned and groaned, but ultimately they allowed me to do the work.

—MICHAEL

The Pizzeria, 2003.

I had been coming to the store on and off since '84. It looked different then —it seemed small and exciting. Then as the store changed and spread out, that was nice. There was more of the same energy glowing in a bigger space.

—JOSÉ RUIZ, FORMER MEMBER

By the beginning of nineties, the original concept of a small cheese store had expanded greatly. The selection of cheeses from around the world was enormous, and there were many more baked goods. The marriage of bread and cheese remained strong. Nationwide there was a growing interest in rustic bread; our passion for bread making had already led us to develop many recipes, so the timing was perfect. The Cheese Board was gradually becoming as much a bakery as a specialty cheese store.

When the sixties finally ended in Berkeley, sometime around 1994, the only thing left standing from that bygone era was the Cheese Board. Odd that a time and place so thoroughly associated with outrage and rebellion should all melt down into four hundred or so tasty blobs of Camembert, Port Salut, and Bleu des Causses. Those of us old enough to remember its first tiny storefront have watched fads in politics, haircuts, nose rings, and bread dough come and go, but the Cheese Board stands alone.

—ALICE KAHN, WRITER AND CUSTOMER

With the increased space and redoubled energy, the collective members decided to push back the opening time from 10 A.M. to 7 A.M. for breakfast customers. Soon we found we were running a café—the Morning Bakery—complete with espresso drinks, homemade jam, and pastries. As the store's focus became more bakery oriented, the shifts began earlier and earlier. (Now, some shifts start as early as 2 A.M.)

I really love doing the coffee line in the morning. You get to know the customers, the regulars. You start playing a game with yourself: having the change ready in your hand.

—ERIN

2003

I have eaten my way through only about one-sixteenth of the products, but it's not just about the cheese or the sun-dried tomato focaccia. It's about the collective spirit of the place, even though like a Broadway hit, most of the original cast has come and gone. I remember when some of the new kids on the block of Shattuck near Vine cut their first slices of smoked Gouda.

—ALICE KAHN

Food is still central to our neighborhood. A former Cheese Boarder runs the Phoenix Pastificio a few blocks away; Poulet, a deli-café, is down the street; Masse's, a French bakery across Shattuck, provides us with birthday cakes; César serves Spanish-style tapas across the street; Grégoire, a tiny takeout place, is around the corner from us. And many of our old friends are still here: the Juice Bar, Saul's Deli, Chez Panisse, and Peet's.

Recently, the collective voted to close on a Saturday in October in order to march for peace in San Francisco. We met our customers and neighbors at the BART station—a familiar multigenerational group. While this new peace movement is reminiscent of the sixties, when we look back over the years, we find that the food we make has infiltrated the home more easily than our politics filtered into the American workplace. Even supermarket chains now carry artisan breads and specialty cheeses.

Much of what we have done has come about by chance, by following our passion for food with the support of our community. The belief that every voice is central has sustained us over the years. We have never wavered

from the original vision of a democratic workplace. This commitment has made it possible to constantly reinvent ourselves while remaining faithful to our political vision and our belief in good, honest food.

I think we are political in a more subtle, natural sense than in the past. We used to talk much more about politics at meetings and when we got together outside of the store. Actually, in a practical sense, we are just as political as we have ever been.

—MICHAEL

The most political thing we do is that we all own the business together. We let that be our statement.

—JULIA

To me, one of the basic principles of the Cheese Board is to create a great product at a reasonable price, with a generosity of spirit. If you can do all that, the business will thrive. If you can do all that while at the same time creating a democratic workplace, it can be an incredibly fun place to work. These components play on each other—they influence and support each other. When it's working, the sum is greater than its parts.

—S. S.

SISTER COLLECTIVES

As with many successful businesses, the impulse to expand and capitalize on a good idea occasionally infects the Cheese Board. Unlike most businesses, the motivation for the Cheese Board is not accumulating greater wealth but advancing the notion of worker cooperatives.

The first such endeavor was the Swallow Restaurant Collective. In 1972, the Cheese Board, after over a year of planning, opened a sister collective called the Swallow. The Swallow was an elegant buffet-style restaurant located on the bottom floor of the University of California Art Museum, next door to the campus film archive. Museum-goers could eat inside or outside, surrounded by sculpture. Initially, Cheese Board members joined with the new Swallow staff to launch the restaurant. After this transitional supportive phase was over, the Cheese Boarders returned to the original collective. The Swallow collective had a good run for almost two decades, but eventually succumbed to the combined difficulties of being a collective institution and trying to operate inside a university bureaucracy.

I think the Swallow was probably an example of a collective not gone wrong so much as gone wild, really not kept in check. There were incredibly high moments of great cooking at the Swallow, but it always had a wild streak in it. No one was holding it down, or together even.

—PAT DARROW

More recently, the Cheese Board has participated in an effort to launch a network of worker cooperatives modeled on the Cheese Board and using its bread and pastry recipes. The network is called the Association of Arizmendi Cooperatives, in honor of the priest José María Arizmendiarrieta, the founder of the Spanish Mondragón Cooperatives. This network has opened one Arizmendi Bakery Cooperative in Oakland and another in San Francisco. These are independent cooperatives owned and operated by their workers. The Cheese Board provided some initial seed money and training, and gave the new bakeries Cheese Board recipes. At the time of this writing, the newest Arizmendi Bakery is being established in Emeryville, just south of Berkeley. The new cooperatives, which are members of the association (and own the association), will then provide financial and technical support for starting other new cooperatives based on the same model. The Cheese Board is also a nominal part of the association.

The Cheese Board has little appetite for expanding its own enterprise beyond its borders. We want to promote worker cooperatives, but not at the risk of changing our own scale or culture. Some of our lack of ambition can be attributed to a philosophical distaste for society's dependence on and glorification of growth and expansion, and some can be because of our natural inclination to take it easy and keep things on a smaller scale.

THE CHEESE BOARD:
REMEMBRANCES AND AN ACCOLADE

My connection with the Cheese Board began in 1971, when I had the good fortune to find myself in the company of many other young enthusiasts who had a crazy notion of creating a very fine restaurant—with no previous experience. The restaurant was Chez Panisse, and I became its first chef. At the time, I was hardly a chef and Chez Panisse was hardly a restaurant. The Cheese Board, however, just around the corner, was already an established icon in what came to be a very special neighborhood in north Berkeley, California. At the time, the Cheese Board was a hole-in-the-wall with precious little interior space, so people would line up out the door to get their irresistible cheeses, always offered up with great, good vibes and free tastes by founders Elizabeth and Sahag Avedisian and their fellows. The original Peet's Coffee, Tea, and Spices store was within a few paces, as was Lenny's Famous Meats, Butcher to the Gods, and by 1973, I had opened my Pig-by-the-Tail Delicatessen across the street from Chez Panisse. Alice Medrich's original Cocolat store soon followed. The Berkeley Gourmet Ghetto was suddenly there, not by the design of one person or a firm of developers, but by the confluence of people who wished to purvey the best of what there was in artisanal foods while paying respect to the notion of sustainable goods. Though those were not bywords at the time, they were themes of our endeavors, a legacy carried on by the Cheese Board. Quickly, we became friends in that spirit and in daily community life. We celebrated together with group picnics and softball games on the Fourth of July, clapped and smiled together when babies were born, applauded when things went right, cried together when there was loss. The remarkable thing about the Cheese Board is that it began as a genuine collective and continues to be so. That means that everyone gets the same amount of money for every hour worked, and the same benefits, and no one can position him- or herself in a certain job forever until death. It's one of the most remarkable institutions/businesses in the world, and especially so because in spite of, or because of, its collective nature, it thrives and continues to grow. Well, they do have the best cheese shop in the world.

—Victoria Wise

With no boss running the show, it falls on all of us to be perceptive enough to see what needs to be done before it becomes critical. The Cheese Board is like a beautiful, functioning organic machine. The day is full of moments with all of us working together to get the job done. It's like an improvisational dance.

—JOHN

There are as many different opinions about what the collective is as there are people working here. We are a cooperative, but there are forty different interpretations of what a cooperative is. People make it what they want it to be.

—SHEHANNA

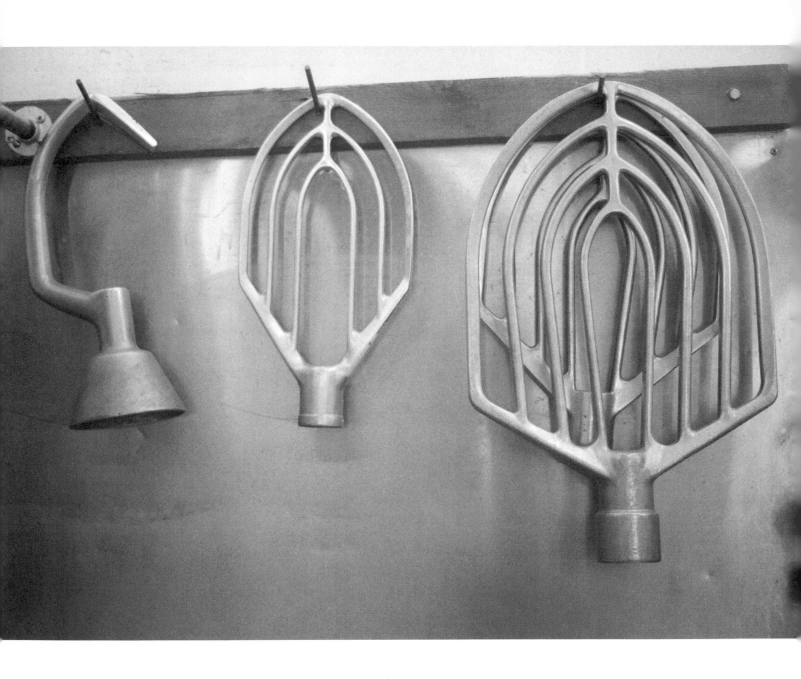

The Basics:
Equipment, Ingredients, and Methods

EQUIPMENT

At the Cheese Board, we have improvised with equipment from the start. A plastic three-pound baker's cheese bucket was the standard measure for all dry ingredients in making large and small doughs until the early 1990s, when we finally purchased a large floor scale. We didn't use baskets to proof rising sourdough loaves until a few years ago, and we still don't measure or weigh the sourdough starter; the dough maker just pours the starter into a huge spiral mixer, leaving an inch or two at the bottom of the bucket.

To bake from this book, your collection of equipment need only include the basics. The following list is simply a guide and not a set of rules. Bread has been baked for hundreds of years without any specialized tools. Oh, but you do need a metal dough scraper!

BAKING STONE

A baking stone is a slab of heat-resistant ceramic that allows you to create artisanal-style breads and pizzas in your home oven by mimicking the effect of a wood-fired brick oven. At the Cheese Board, we finish baking focaccias and pizzas by placing them directly on the stone for the final minutes of the bake, which results in a crisp bottom crust. A baking stone is also useful when baking certain sourdough breads at home, either for the entire bake or, as we prefer, for just the final minutes.

If you choose to use a baking stone, remember that you will need to preheat your oven 45 minutes in advance rather than the usual 15; the oven will not reach the desired temperature otherwise. Transfer focaccias and breads from the baking sheet to the stone 5 minutes before the end of the bake, at which point your baked good should be firm and starting to color. Using a metal spatula and an oven mitt, loosen the bread gently and lift or slide it off the sheet onto the stone to crisp the bottom crust. Pizzas are more delicate and therefore should be baked on an inverted sheet so that they can be loosened with a metal spatula and easily slid off the baking sheet directly onto the stone.

CHEESE GRATER

Of the many types of cheese graters, the most essential one is the four-sided box grater with different sizes and shapes of rasps. It is also nice to have a handheld grater that can be used at the table for grating cheese over salads, soups, and pasta.

DOUBLE BOILER

This special two-part pot is used for melting chocolate slowly over hot water. To **melt chocolate** in a double boiler, add 3 inches of water to the bottom pot and bring to a simmer over medium heat. (One can improvise a double boiler by putting a stainless steel or glass bowl on top of a saucepan. The bowl should fit into the pan snugly and not drop too far down into the pan.) Turn the heat down to low. Add the chopped chocolate to the top compartment and warm until the chocolate is just melted, stirring it occasionally and taking care not to overheat it. Do not place a lid on top of the melting chocolate or splash water into it as this will cause it to *bloom*—white splotches form on the chocolate, and although these don't mar the flavor, they affect the look of the finished product.

MEASURING CUPS AND SPOONS

Over the years we have become more conscious of the importance of consistency, and we now use a scale (see page 19) and standard measuring equipment. The home baker should have on hand both liquid and dry measuring cups, as well as a set of good-quality measuring spoons. Liquid measuring cups are spouted, graduated cups that come in 1-, 2-, and 4-cup sizes; it is useful to have more than one size. Dry measuring cups are nested in ⅛- to 1-cup sizes.

MIXER

At the Cheese Board, we make our doughs in an industrial spiral mixer with a hydraulic lift that dumps the dough into waiting twenty-gallon buckets. We also have a 140-quart Hobart mixer that is more versatile. We use this mixer, fitted with the paddle attachment, to make our scones, muffins, and cheese spreads; we use the dough hook attachment to knead smaller batches of bread. A home KitchenAid stand mixer is a miniature replica of the Hobart. Though all of our recipes can be made by hand, a KitchenAid mixer is a worthwhile investment for serious bakers.

MIXING BOWLS

Bowls of various sizes are essential. (Though, as one bachelor recipe tester found, the cavity of a wok works just fine in a pinch.) At a minimum, have small, medium, and large bowls.

PANS

Have available at least three 12 by 16 by 1-inch-high baking sheets; two heavy-gauge loaf pans (we use 8½ by 4½-inch pans, a little smaller than some loaf pans; the recipes will work fine in larger pans but the loaves will be flatter and wider); and muffin tins (enough for one dozen muffins). While all the recipes have specific pan preparation directions, note that if your pans are non-stick or well seasoned, you can often omit this step. Most of these items are easily available at a well-stocked kitchen supply store, or to mail order see page 222.

PARCHMENT PAPER AND SILICONE BAKING MATS

We like to use parchment-lined baking sheets for baking pastries. First of all, parchment paper makes cleanup so much easier because sugar often will burn on an unlined pan, which means soaking and scrubbing. Second, this molten sugar can glue the pastry to an unlined pan, making it hard to remove the pastry in one piece. Investing in a silicone baking mat—which can be used and reused forever—saves on sheets and sheets of parchment paper.

PASTRY BRUSH

It is important to use a sturdy, high-quality 2-inch-wide pastry brush. We use natural-bristle brushes because they give a smoother application onto the surface of the bread. Have two brushes on hand, one for sweets and the other for use with garlic and herb oils.

PASTRY CUTTER

This old-fashioned tool is extremely handy for cutting butter into flour. If you don't have one, use two dinner knives.

PLASTIC WRAP

Cover your bowl of rising dough with plastic wrap (or a damp kitchen towel) to create a warm, humid environment.

PROOFING BASKETS

We proof sourdough breads such as City and Suburban Breads in willow baskets. The baskets provide a comfortable form for breads that need an extended rising time; they help the loaves keep their shape; and they leave a beautiful imprint on the finished bread. Rising baskets are available at many kitchen supply stores, or you can order them (see Source List, page 222), but they can be expensive. The baskets need to be floured to prevent the rising dough from sticking. The amount of flour used should be enough so that the dough doesn't stick to the baskets, but not so much so that the finished loaves look powdery and pale instead of brown and rustic. (Maybe this is so obvious it doesn't need mentioning, but be sure to remove the loaves from the baskets before baking!)

You can use wicker baskets instead, but be sure to line them with a well-floured thin linen or cotton cloth, because the wicker tends to fray and leave fibers in the dough. You can also use a glass, plastic, or ceramic bowl lined with a floured cloth; it should be about 8 inches in diameter and 4 inches deep.

PROOFING CHAMBER

For sourdough breads, which have a long rising time, it is important to create a warm and moist environment. Professional bakeries have proofing rooms where the humidity and temperature can be controlled. We tried to mimic this effect at home by rigging up a zippered sweater bag made from heavy, clear plastic and held up by chopsticks, like a tent. A plastic bag also works well, though it needs to be large enough to loosely surround the rising bread and the pan that it is on. Place something (such as a 1-liter bottle of vegetable oil) inside the bag to function as the "tent pole," keeping the bag from touching the bread as it rises, and close the bag with a twist tie. Baking supply catalogs carry less-creative options called "proof covers" (see Source List, page 222).

RAZOR BLADE

The bakers at the Cheese Board prefer to use a new single-edged razor blade every time they begin a baking cycle, since a reused blade is too dull to make clean slashes in the dough. You won't be baking in the quantities we do in the store, but remember that razor blades do dull easily.

ROLLING PIN

A heavy rolling pin makes rolling out dough much easier. At the Cheese Board we use American-style pins, with ball bearings. For wet doughs, flouring the pin will make your job easier. Don't wash a rolling pin in water, as the bearings can rust or get clogged; simply scrape off the pin and wipe it with a dry towel.

SCALE

It's not necessary to use a baker's scale in every recipe, but some do require precise measurement. It's particularly important to use a scale when attempting our sourdough bread recipes. Before using that old kitchen scale from the back of the cupboard, make sure it is still accurate; test it by weighing a known quantity, such as a stick of butter.

SCRAPERS

Our favorite kitchen tool, hands down, is the metal dough scraper. It is the only way to remove sourdough "glue." Use one and you will never go back. Less exciting but still useful is the plastic dough scraper. These tools will get you out of lots of jams. Trust us—you will know how to use them.

SIFTER

Essential for breaking down troublesome clumps in flour and especially in baking soda. A sieve will do the same job.

SPATULAS

There are two kinds of rubber spatulas we like to use: one is the traditional flat type and the other is spoon-shaped. You will also need a metal spatula.

SPICE GRINDER

When a recipe requires freshly ground spice, use either a coffee grinder (designated for spices only) or a mortar and pestle.

SPRAYERS AND STEAMING EQUIPMENT

Water and steam help the crust development of rustic breads, especially sourdoughs. Some of our breads are misted with water before baking, and a few, like the baguettes, are misted again during the final stages of baking. You can purchase a spray bottle for this purpose at a garden supply store. (Remember, never spray near the interior oven light!)

Our ovens at the store are set up with internal steaming systems, which can be replicated on a smaller scale in the home kitchen. In recipes that require a steamy oven environment, you will need a large, high-sided metal roasting pan; 9 by 13 by 2 inches is a good size. Do not use glass or ceramic ovenware, since it will explode when used in such a manner.

THERMOMETER

If you are uncertain about the temperature of your oven, use an oven thermometer.

TIMER

Essential. Use one.

WHISK

Choose a small whisk and a large balloon whisk, both made from medium-gauge wire. For whisking yeast and water together or making an egg wash, use the small whisk. Use the larger whisk to make the filling for sticky buns, pecan rolls, or the glaze for maple pecan scones.

WIRE RACKS

All of our baked goods are cooled on cooling racks when they first come out of the oven. Have at least two wire racks on hand. A collapsible multilevel rack is a real space saver and can allow four trays to be cooled at once. They can be found at many kitchenware stores or through mail order (see Source List, page 222).

WORK SURFACE

At the Cheese Board, we work at long butcher-block tables. When we roll out sticky bun dough, it almost covers the entire surface. A large, flat surface, such as a sturdy wooden board, is essential for kneading and rolling out dough. Put a damp towel under the board to keep it from sliding.

ZESTER

This tool is designed to pare off only the top, colored layer of citrus skin and release its essential oils, leaving the bitter white pith behind.

INGREDIENTS

Your final product is only as good as your ingredients. Use the freshest dairy products, flours, in-season produce, and leavenings. Check the dates on products and shop at a reliable store that rotates its stock frequently.

BAKING SODA AND BAKING POWDER

Remember to check the expiration dates on containers of these two essential leavening ingredients, since they lose potency over time, and always sift them before using in a recipe. At the store we use aluminum-free baking powder.

BUTTER

We use only unsalted (often called "sweet") butter. Salt is used to extend the shelf life of butter; by using unsalted butter, the rich, natural flavor of the butter comes through in whatever you are baking. An additional reason for using unsalted butter is that you have more control over the saltiness in any recipe. Don't be completely put off by salted butters, though; a warm baguette with a pat of soft, lightly salted butter is the ultimate comfort food. Different brands of butter have subtle flavor differences and varying fat content. Experiment with various types to see which you like the best.

CARAMEL COLOR

This is used to impart a deep chocolate-brown color to pumpernickel rye bread (page 121). Caramel color may be hard to find at your local store, but it can be ordered (see Source List, page 222). It does not add flavor to the finished bread, so if color isn't an issue for you, go ahead and make the bread without it.

CHEESE

At the Cheese Board, any cheese we need or feel inspired to use is only a step away. For cheese breads and pizzas, have these basic cheeses on hand: sharp Cheddar, Gruyère, sheep's-milk Feta, and the Italian contingent—Mozzarella, Asiago, Provolone, Parmigiano, and Ricotta. Of course, you can substitute any cheese that works for your palate.

CHOCOLATE

The bakers at the Cheese Board always use the richest bittersweet or semisweet chocolate and unprocessed cocoa powder. In sweets where chocolate is a major flavor, it is important to use the best you can find. We use a Belgian chocolate made by Callebaut. Other good choices are Schokinag from Germany, and Berkeley's own Scharffen Berger. We order our chocolate in ten-pound bars and break it up with a hammer and chisel, using the large, uneven chunks for Chocolate Things (page 62). In our muffins, we use chips of the same high-quality chocolate. For instructions on melting chocolate in a double boiler, see page 17.

CITRUS ZEST

The white part just under the skin of citrus fruits is very bitter. When zesting the fruit, be careful to shave off only the colored layer. Try to zest directly over the rest of the ingredients to ensure that the citrus oil, loaded with flavor, makes it into your baked good as well.

COOKING SPRAY

As with parchment paper, oil spray is nothing short of miraculous in terms of its nonstick qualities. Use it to coat the wells and tops of muffin pans and the insides of small loaf pans to aid in the release of baked goods. Use only unflavored spray.

DAIRY PRODUCTS

Have you ever started a recipe and suddenly realized, "Oh no, I don't have enough sour cream"? This happened all the time to us while we were testing these recipes. Fortunately, it often works fine to fill in the missing ingredient with an equivalent milk product. For example, if the recipe calls for 1 cup of sour cream, you can substitute a mixture of sour cream and plain yogurt or simply use all yogurt. Cream, half-and-half, and milk can also be substituted for each other, but their differing fat content can affect the richness and texture of the final bread.

DRIED FRUITS

The advantages to using dried fruits is that they are available year-round and they have a long shelf life. Keep a supply of golden raisins, currants, apricots, and apples on hand. With such a variety, you will be free to experiment with endless muffin and scone combinations.

EGGS

All of our recipes are made using large eggs.

EXTRACTS

We use only pure vanilla extract in our recipes.

FLOUR

Volumes could be written about flour, but we are going to keep it simple here. The type of flour used in each recipe is important to the success of the baked good you are making. When a recipe calls for bread flour, be sure to use bread flour, not all-purpose flour, and vice versa. Made from hard wheat, bread flour is high in protein, which yields a dough with a well-developed gluten network. (Gluten is the complex protein formed when flour is mixed with water; it creates structure—and ultimately chewiness and airiness—in breads.) All-purpose flour, with its lower protein content, produces a more delicate crumb, which is what you want when making cakelike foods such as scones or muffins. Both of these flours are now widely available, but if you are having problems finding them, consult the Source List (page 222).

MOLASSES

The molasses used in most of our recipes is dark and unsulfured. Unsulfured molasses is made from the juice of sun-ripened sugarcane and has a deep, rich, sweet flavor.

Blackstrap molasses is a by-product of a third sugarcane boiling and has a bitter taste. In the recipes that specify blackstrap molasses, dark unsulfured molasses can be substituted. Both are used as an agent for fermentation, for coloring bread, and for flavoring.

NUTS AND SEEDS

Choose only fresh nuts and seeds. The most important thing to remember is that nuts are high in fat, and unless stored properly (that is, in the freezer), they can go rancid quickly.

Some of our recipes call for **toasted nuts**. To **toast nuts,** preheat the oven to 350°F. Spread the nuts evenly on a baking sheet. Bake for 5 minutes, stir, and bake for 2 to 5 minutes longer, or until lightly toasted and fragrant.

Have on hand sesame, poppy, sunflower, and fennel seeds. In recipes that call for seeds, feel free to use whatever combination you like.

OILS

Have two types of oil on hand: extra-virgin olive oil and a light vegetable oil such as safflower oil or canola oil.

OLIVES

The Cheese Board uses high-quality brine- or oil-cured olives. Make sure when using olives in bread that they have been pitted. Squeeze machine-pitted olives by hand to make sure they are free of pieces of pit.

SALT

At the Cheese Board, we almost exclusively use sea salt, both fine and coarse, because we like its pure flavor. However, since kosher salt (a coarse-grained, additive-free salt) is readily available in supermarkets across the United States, we decided to use it for the recipes in this book. Be warned that, because of the different grain sizes that salt comes in, the kind you choose makes a difference in measuring appropriate amounts for our recipes. Generally speaking, 1 teaspoon of kosher salt or coarse sea salt equals ½ teaspoon table salt or fine-grained sea salt. Thus, the finer the grind of salt, the saltier it is measure for measure.

SWEETENERS

We use honey, dark molasses, light brown sugar, granulated sugar, maple syrup, and confectioners' sugar for sweeteners.

WATER

There is nothing special about the type of water needed for our recipes. We use tap water. The temperature is given in approximate terms. When you become experienced with bread making, you will know the right temperature by feel and not worry over a degree or two. For now, use the following chart for the degree equivalent and a kitchen thermometer to measure the temperature.

Warm	Lukewarm	Cool
99°–105°F	85°–95°F	65°–75°F

YEAST

Active dry yeast is the standard for all our yeasted bread recipes. 2¼ teaspoons active dry yeast is equivalent to 1 package of active dry yeast or compressed (cake) yeast. Buy the freshest yeast you can find.

METHODS

Following is a brief overview of the basic methods and steps used to make a baked good. The section is laid out in chronological order, from the measurement of ingredients to baking and analyzing your results. Most of the technique discussion that follows pertains only to yeasted dough and sourdoughs, since quick breads like scones and muffins are easy to make and do not require many steps.

MEASURING

There are two ways we measure ingredients: by weight or by volume. While most of the recipes in this book are measured by volume, you can get a much more accurate measurement by using a scale. If you use a scale, remember that 1 cup of all-purpose or bread flour weighs approximately 5 ounces. Because accurate measures are particularly important in sourdough baking, we give both weight and volume amounts for the sourdough starter and master dough recipes.

MIXING QUICK BREADS

Scones and muffins require a gentle and swift touch. If overmixed, your scones will be flat and tough and your muffins will be cone shaped, tough, and chewy. A general guideline is to combine the dry ingredients first, then cut in the butter, either by hand with a pastry cutter or two dinner knives, or with the paddle attachment of a mixer. Next, mix the wet ingredients together. Lastly, make a well in the dry ingredients and pour in the liquid, combining the dry ingredients with the wet with a few swift strokes (see individual recipes for specific instructions).

MIXING AND KNEADING LOAF BREADS

Yeasted doughs and sourdoughs demand industrial-strength mixing and kneading to develop the gluten so they will rise properly and have good texture. Whether you hand or machine knead your dough, be sure to knead sufficiently to develop the gluten (see below).

Kneading with a stand mixer: We encourage you to use a stand mixer since it will save you effort, enable you to make wetter doughs that will result in lighter baked goods, and free you up to clean or prepare for the next step of baking. The first step of machine kneading is to mix the ingredients together on low speed until combined. Use either the paddle attachment or dough hook, as indicated in the recipe. The second step, which requires using the dough hook, is to increase the mixer speed and knead for a period of time to develop the gluten. Ideally, your dough should leave the sides of the bowl and gather around the hook, becoming smooth and elastic. (To achieve this you may need to add more flour by the tablespoonful.) The dough should become smooth and elastic. Finally, most doughs should be transferred to a lightly floured surface for hand kneading for a few minutes before being put in a bowl to rise.

Kneading by hand: In most recipes we encourage you to knead with the dough hook in a stand mixer, but kneading by hand is a blast on many levels. First, it's a wonderful way to get an upper-body workout and it's completely tactile. It is also a lesson in slowing down and staying in one place for longer than you usually do, and it can be very satisfying. A final plus is that it's next to impossible to overknead dough by hand.

Kneading by Hand

First, mix the ingredients together with a wooden spoon until they are combined. Turn the dough out onto a lightly floured work surface. Using the palm of your hand (fig. A, opposite), push the dough away from you and then bring it back toward your body (fig. B, opposite). Rotate the dough one-quarter turn and continue to push, pull, and rotate the dough, dusting with just enough extra flour to help make the dough manageable (usually 1 teaspoon at a time). The dough should lightly stick to the work surface; this resistance works like a second kneading tool. It is good to have a metal dough scraper on hand to help in the initial kneading stages, when the dough is wet and soft and not easy to manage with your hands. A light touch is a plus, since pressing down on the dough too vigorously will make it sticky.

Kneading sourdough breads: The general kneading instructions above will work for sourdoughs, but we have an additional step we find useful. This method of kneading mimics the way the dough hook on a large industrial mixer grabs the dough, pulls it to the center, and turns the mass

GLUTEN DEVELOPMENT AND THE WINDOWPANE TEST

Gluten is the substance responsible for the elastic texture of a properly kneaded dough. Gluten is formed when flour is combined with water and kneaded to the point where individual protein strands fasten together to form a sturdy network. The resulting dough is strong and springy, qualities that ultimately yield a chewy, light loaf of bread filled with air pockets.

To be sure you have kneaded the dough long enough, apply the windowpane test: Take a small piece of dough between the thumb and forefinger of each hand and stretch the dough to form a thin membrane. If it tears quickly, knead the dough for a few more minutes and test again, until it is stretchy enough to allow the windowpane to form. Rye breads are the exception to this rule; as rye flour is naturally low in gluten, the windowpane test does not apply. Instead, follow the kneading time and check the recipe's visual indicators.

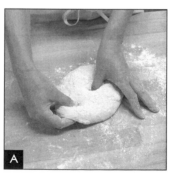
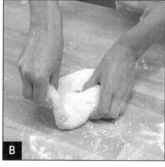

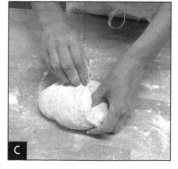

Kneading Sourdough Breads

of dough at the same time. Kneading techniques are difficult to describe, but with these directions we hope to assist you in finding your own unique and effective style.

Begin by kneading as described above. As the dough begins to feel elastic, change the motion of your hands: Plant your left thumb in the center of the dough (fig. A). With your right hand, pull the right side of the dough toward the center and push it down into the ball, rotating the dough one-quarter turn in the process (figs. B and C). Repeat this plant, pull, swivel, and press sequence; as you practice kneading this way, it will become one swift, fluid motion.

A yeasted dough or sourdough is sufficiently kneaded when it passes the *windowpane test* (see page 25) and meets other visual and textural criteria. Have you been kneading the dough for at least 10 to 15 minutes? Is the dough smooth and elastic? Is it shiny? If the answers are yes, it is time to stop kneading and let the dough rest and rise.

RISING

The rising period is the stage when the dough feeds and ferments. While chemical leaveners—baking soda and baking powder—do the job for quick breads, yeasted doughs and sourdoughs require some rising time to develop their flavor and texture. The dough is put into a bowl, covered, and placed in a warm (70°F), draft-free place. All our recipes have instructions for rising periods.

RETARDING

Some of the recipes in this book—the sourdoughs in particular—require an extended rising period in a cool place (60°F or cooler). This type of slow rise is referred to as *retarding* the dough, a technique that allows the dough to develop a deeper taste and richer texture.

There can be other reasons to retard or slow the rising of a bread. If you need to leave the house, you can cover the rising dough or proofing loaves (see page 31) with plastic wrap or a kitchen towel and place in the refrigerator. When you return home, bring out the dough or loaves and place in a warm, draft-free spot for 1 to 2 hours, until swelled and airy. Making bread takes all day, but you don't have to sit and watch it the whole time!

SHAPING

The preliminary step for shaping most breads is to form the dough into a *loose round:* Turn the dough ball out of the bowl onto a lightly floured surface. Cut the dough into the desired number of pieces. Expelling as little of the air from the dough as possible, gently shape each piece of dough into a loose round by tucking the dough underneath itself to create a smooth surface on top (figs. A and B). Don't try to seal the seam of the dough yet; that step occurs when you create the final shape. Cover the rounds with a floured kitchen towel and let them rest for 10 to 15 minutes, as specified in the recipe.

Shaping a dough into its final form is like creating an air-filled ball; by pulling the outermost layer of dough taut around the inside, you capture the airy inner mass, giving the dough something to push against as it rises in its new shape. As you shape the following bread forms, you should feel a tension between the elasticity of the dough, the bottom edges of your hands, and the surface you are working on.

Loose Round

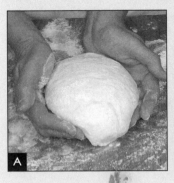 

Large Round

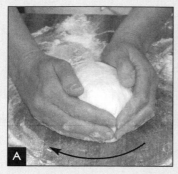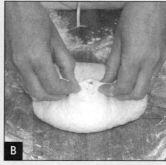

Cup your hands around the dough as if you were trying to hide the dough. Start to gently move your hands in a circular motion, keeping the bottom edges of your hands on the table (fig. A). Continue to circulate the dough ball while lightly pressing your hands down on the part of the dough that is closest to the work surface; this will draw down the outer skin of the dough, creating a seam on the bottom. You will feel a tension between the elasticity of the dough, the bottom edges of your hands, and the rolling surface.

Next, seal the seam on the bottom by pinching it closed with your fingers (fig. B). Turn the dough so that the seam is back on the work surface, and using cupped hands, roll the dough back and forth while keeping the seam on the work surface to further seal the seam. Place the round in a prepared proofing basket (fig. C) or on a baking sheet, seam side up if using a basket, seam side down if rising on a sheet.

Small Round

Cup your hand around the dough and move it in a circular motion, resting the outside of your hand on the work surface (fig. A). Use your thumb to pull the outside of the dough underneath the round. As you become accustomed to the motion, you can use both hands to roll two rounds at once.

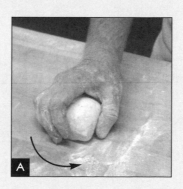

Bâtard

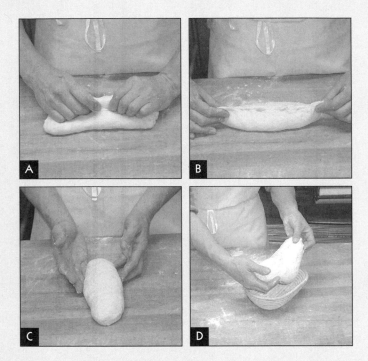

Flatten the dough into an oval. Working with the long side in front of you, tightly roll the dough into itself, creating a seam on the bottom (fig. A). Seal the seam closed (fig. B) and, with cupped hands, roll the dough into a rounded, blunt-ended oval (fig. C). Keeping the seam on the work surface, roll it back and forth, sealing the seam further. Place in a prepared proofing basket, seam side up (fig. D), or on a baking sheet, seam side down.

Oval

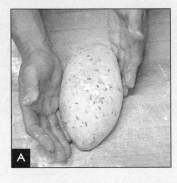

Flatten the dough into an oval. Working from the long side of the oval, tightly roll the dough into itself, creating a seam on the bottom (see *bâtard* fig. A). Seal the seam closed and, with cupped hands, roll the dough into a tapering, football-shaped oval (fig. A, above). Keeping the seam on the work surface, roll it back and forth, sealing the seam further. Place seam side down on a prepared baking sheet.

Loaf

Flatten the dough into an oval. Working from the long side of the oval, tightly roll the dough into itself, creating a seam on the bottom (see *bâtard* fig. A). Seal the seam closed and, with cupped hands, roll the dough into a slightly tapered, rounded length (fig. A, above). Keeping the seam on the work surface, roll it back and forth, sealing the seam further. Place seam side down in a prepared loaf pan.

Jelly Roll

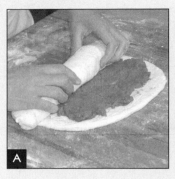
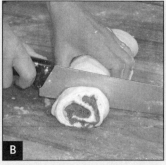

We shape cheese rolls, pecan rolls, sticky buns, marble rye, and Chocolate Things into a *jelly roll* before slicing them into individual pieces.

Working from the long side of the dough rectangle, begin to tightly roll it into a cylinder, creating as many rotations as possible (fig. A). Cut the cylinder into slices (fig. B) and place them cut side up on a baking sheet.

3-Stranded Braid

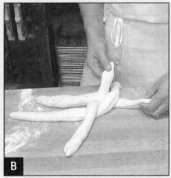
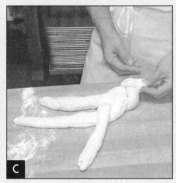
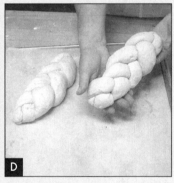

Braiding. At the store we use two different braid designs. For some people, tying, braiding, and weaving comes naturally; they can make their hands create what they visualize. For others, it takes a lot of practice.

The most traditional braid, the *3-stranded braid*, is identical in construction to the common hair braid: 3 strands woven under-over, under-over until the entire length has been used. We use this braid for some of the cheese breads and for challah. Another style of braiding is the *turban*, made by weaving together 2 strands of dough and then attaching the ends of the braid to form a circle. We use the turban shape for Sunday bread, Greek shepherd's bread, Asiago bread, and saffron bread.

To make a 3-stranded braid: Roll out 3 pieces of dough into 10-inch lengths with slightly tapering ends. Arrange 2 of the strands to form an X and lay the third lengthwise across the top (fig. A). Working from the ends closest to you, place one of the outside strands across the center strand, and do likewise with the other outside strand, laying it across the new center strand (fig. B). Continue in this fashion until you have completed one side. Pinch the ends together and tuck them under (fig. C). Rotate the dough so that the unbraided side is facing you. Complete the braid by placing the outer strands underneath the center strand. Pinch the ends together and tuck them under. Roll the loaf back and forth to tighten the braid and form the finished shape (fig. D).

2-Stranded Turban

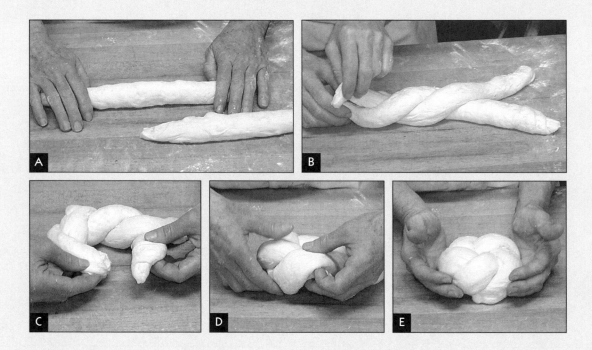

To make a 2-stranded turban: Divide the dough into 2 pieces. Roll out each piece into a 12-inch length with slightly tapering ends (fig. A). Place 1 length on top of the other, creating an X. Working from the ends, twist the strands around each other to form a coil-like rope (fig. B).

Create a loop by crossing the ends of the coiled rope so that the center of the loop is open (fig. C). Tuck the strand ends underneath the center of the loaf (fig. D). Gently rotate the loaf in a circular motion with cupped hands to tighten the braid. The finished shape should look like a turban (fig. E).

PROOFING

After the bread has been shaped and placed in a basket or on a baking sheet, it is covered and returned to a warm, draft-free place to continue rising. This step, which is called *proofing*, is critical for the development of the bread's architecture. Some breads require a quick second rise, while others like sourdoughs require a more leisurely rise. All of our recipes give a suggested proofing time and tell you what to look for in determining whether a loaf is ready to be baked. It is not always easy to tell if loaves have completed proofing. While most yeasted loaves become air-filled and rounded, rye breads and stollens move very slowly due to their heavier composition. The best test of when dough is ready to be baked is to press your finger into the top of the loaf; if an impression remains, the dough is ready. In reviewing the suggested proofing time, you should factor in the time it takes to preheat the oven since you don't want to wait an additional 15 minutes to put the bread in the oven. For example, if the recommended proofing time is 1 hour, turn the oven on after 45 minutes, or earlier if you are using a baking stone (see page 17).

EGG WASH

To create a shiny brown crust on a challah or to make a Chocolate Thing glisten, you will need to brush the outside of the proofed loaf with egg wash. Egg wash is made by whisking an egg until it is a thin and golden liquid with a uniform, velvety texture. Whisking the mixture long enough is important, as it makes the application of the egg wash much easier. Brush the tops and the sides of each roll or loaf to ensure that the whole outside will be shiny. If you don't have an egg, milk is a passable substitute.

SLASHING

Before baking, most breads require a cut into the surface to allow the bread to expand evenly during the baking period. Without the slashes, the bread will burst out wherever it chooses rather than in a controlled place. We use a single-edged razor blade for the job (see page 19).

The slashes are another opportunity for a baker's artistic expression. Experiment with designs that you like, using the gallery below as a guide. At the store, we are always studying the way various slashes work. We like

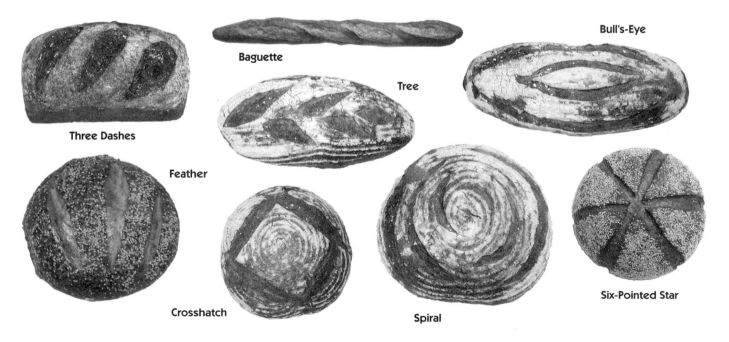

Three Dashes

Baguette

Tree

Bull's-Eye

Feather

Crosshatch

Spiral

Six-Pointed Star

THE CHEESE BOARD: COLLECTIVE WORKS

them to open generously, creating a contrast in texture and color. The quality of the slash will affect the final appearance of the bread, so take care with the execution. Visualize your design and then, with your body centered in front of the loaf and with the razor blade at a 45-degree angle to the surface of the bread, make slash marks in the bread. Don't be afraid to use a firm hand and a forceful wrist. Your motion should be swift and clean.

BAKING

At last you have arrived at the final step in bread making (besides eating). Adjust the oven racks as instructed in the recipe. Preheat the oven well before baking; in most ovens this is at least 15 minutes prior to baking. (If you are using a baking stone, the oven should be preheated for 45 minutes with the baking stone inside; see page 17.) The initial boost of heat is critical to the outcome of a light, lofty scone or muffin. Heat is also necessary for breads to develop good height, rich color, and open slashes. Some breads (like baguettes) require you to crank up your oven to 450°F, while others (like slow-baking stollens) bake at the low temperature of 325°F. Buy an oven thermometer to ensure the accuracy of your oven.

Some recipes (mostly sourdoughs) require *steaming* during the bake; this step creates a crunchy crust with an attractive color. The Cheese Board ovens have powerful internal steaming mechanisms that help produce the shiny baguettes and crusty Suburban Breads. We have developed a home-oven method using a metal roasting pan filled with ice water that reproduces pretty closely what occurs inside a Cheese Board oven. (In addition, we mist certain loaves with a spray bottle to further enhance the crust.) If the recipe calls for steaming, prior to preheating the oven place a large metal roasting pan directly on the floor of the oven and proceed with the instructions in the recipe.

At the Cheese Board, we like to bake sourdoughs until they have a dark, rusty brown finish. Challah is baked to a deep mahogany color and brioche a golden brown. The final aesthetic judgment is up to the baker (this means you).

CRUMB

After you bake a loaf of bread, let it cool and cut a slice or two to assess the crumb. *Crumb*, in the baking world, refers to the interior texture of the bread. Obviously, a different type of crumb is desirable in different baked goods. A much-prized goal at the Cheese Board is to bake a sourdough bread riddled with large holes, as this means that the bread is light, chewy, and moist. Generally speaking, a moister sourdough dough will give a better crumb. The length of the kneading time and the rising period also influence the crumb of sourdough breads.

If you are a new baker, you will find wet doughs hard to knead and shape at first. As you become more experienced in making sourdough breads, try increasing the amount of water by a small amount each time you make the recipe and lengthening the kneading and rising times, too. The holes in your bread will get larger and larger, until the only way to keep the butter and jam on your bread will be to cut it lengthwise.

In breads that employ commercial yeast, the prized end result is not chewiness and big holes, but a system of even, tiny holes that are not compacted or compressed at the bottom crust. Moisture, kneading, and an adequate rising time will help bring about the desired texture.

In the case of scones and muffins, a delicate cakelike crumb is achieved by adding enough liquid, mixing briefly and gently, and handling the dough or batter delicately.

CHAPTER ONE

THE MORNING BAKERY
Scones, Muffins, and More

WE CALL THE HOURS BETWEEN 7 AND 10 A.M. at the Cheese Board the Morning Bakery. This is when we serve coffee, tea, and many of the pastries featured in this chapter. During Morning Bakery hours, the cheese counter and refrigerated cases remain closed. The store's space is rearranged to make a counter for fast service and the preparation of hot drinks. Many of the pastries are taken out by customers to eat on the way to school or work. Regulars pause at the few tables and chairs inside, or take their chances with the weather out front on the benches under the store's awning. At ten o'clock, as if stagehands were changing sets, the coffee urn is wheeled behind the counter and covered, and the coffee-line counter is disassembled to assume its next role as a supporting member of the show by becoming the express line for breads and prepackaged cheeses.

In this chapter we have included most of our Morning Bakery goods: scones, muffins, brioche-dough breads, granola, and shortbread cookies.

What we refer to as a "scone" at the Cheese Board is actually closer to a rich buttermilk biscuit. Our scones have a fine, cakelike crumb, and we use sweet butter, cream, and buttermilk as basic ingredients. The two secrets to making them are to barely combine the liquid ingredients with the dry, and to add extra cream or buttermilk if the mixture seems too dry. Just enough liquid will produce a succulent scone, while too much liquid produces a flat scone. One other helpful piece of advice: To keep the dough from sticking to your hands when shaping scones, dip your fingers into a bowl of water first.

Our very moist, large muffins are quick and simple to make. A successful muffin is made by combining the wet ingredients and the dry ingredients in a few quick strokes. The batter should be somewhat lumpy. Overmixed muffins are tough and will fail to rise properly. The batter for most of our muffins can also be made into small loaves (see page 138).

Brioche dough is a simple, sweet egg dough. Chocolate Things, pecan rolls, and brioche are all made from this dough. At the store we refrigerate the dough overnight before we roll it out the next morning. This works well for our schedule and may work best for yours, too.

However, the dough is also sublime when made and baked the same day.

Shortbread is the only cookie we make regularly at the Cheese Board. This simple, classic cookie is prepared with sweet butter, flour, a little sugar, and a pinch of salt. The most important step in making shortbread is to cream the butter and sugar together sufficiently to make a very light, fluffy mixture (using room temperature butter makes this step much easier). The amount of flour used can vary, depending on weather conditions and the moisture content in the ingredients. Once the right amount of flour is added, mix briefly to incorporate the flour and butter into a smooth, stiff dough that can easily be rolled out to the desired thickness. Use as little flour on the rolling surface as needed to allow the dough to move outward as it is rolled. If the dough begins to stick, sprinkle flour on the top of a metal spatula and slide it under the dough to deposit the flour where needed.

There's something very bizarre about waking up in the middle of the night to go to work. Riding my bike under the stars, in the rain, or whatever weather, that's powerful. It's spectacular to have the streets to yourself early in the morning. There are no cars. Sometimes I'll weave back and forth up the middle of University Avenue—just because I can. There's no one out on the street, and the streetlights are all blinking. It's almost postapocalyptic. —ADAM

When you get up at 3 in the morning, you think, "Ughh . . . not again, not this early!" But once you get here, it's fun. You have nothing to sell, and two hours later you have all this stuff coming out of the ovens. You're taking bread off of the pans and getting it onto the shelf, and the shelves are filling up. You see a few cars going by and then a few more cars. Then it's ten to seven and there are people waiting to come in. It's that energy. And then it's a mob. And I love that mob. It just keeps you going.

—STU

THE CHEESE BOARD HOURS OF OPERATION

I can remember in the old store on Vine Street we would set up every morning, and then at quarter to ten before we opened, we'd all go out and take a break and drink coffees together. That was nice.

—A LONGTIME MEMBER

The bakery side of the store has different hours from the cheese counter (which shares the same space), so if you want a cup of coffee after 10 A.M., you're out of luck. We make and sell our pizza in a different storefront than our cheese and bakery store; and did we mention that the pizzeria has a schedule that is not the same as either the cheese counter or the bakery? In order to test our customers' patience even more, we are open only half a day on Mondays, and even then we are only halfway open, as we don't open the cheese counter on that day (unless, of course, it's near a holiday!). Why is our schedule so odd? Our business's methods and schedule may seem random, but there is a reason behind them. The operating schedule is a reflection of decisions made by the members as the store evolved and is rooted in the fundamental nature of our collective.

As with many of the other ventures that have been supported by the entire membership, the Morning Bakery began with a small group of people wanting to try something new. A few members wanted to open the doors of the store earlier to sell pastries and breads, accompanied with coffee and tea, to customers for a quick and simple breakfast. At that time, in 1991, we were open only between the hours of 10 A.M. and 6 P.M. The large demand for our bakery products was requiring us to begin our baking shifts earlier and earlier in the morning. Impatient customers, waiting on the sidewalk for our doors to open and looking through the front window, could see warm breads and pastries piling up and cooling on the shelves. We could all see that it didn't make a lot of sense. But many of us were reluctant to make a change that would require us to become a larger group and, more importantly, make us have to get up earlier in the morning!

In standard businesses, if demand grows, you simply hire more workers. We, however, try to stay a close, small group while accommodating our deep need for innovation. Our solution was to open earlier and restructure our shifts. In the end, we struck a balance between fostering creativity and honoring our group's wish to remain small. The added bonus of opening earlier was that it made space for a whole list of new products. Initially, we offered a minimal menu at the Morning Bakery, but today the shelves are completely full at 7 A.M., and we have a rotation of daily specials.

The things people think about the Cheese Board! About five years ago I was waiting in line at Andronico's and this woman said to another woman in line ahead of me, "What are you going to do now?" and she responded, "I'm going to buy a couple of baguettes at the Cheese Board." "Oh, really, you're going to go there? I heard those people sleep together, is that true?" I cracked up, I was thinking of saying, "Yep, they do, ma'am, they do. I know, I work there!" Just kidding! It's so funny.

—GUILLERMO

THE MORNING BAKERY

SCONES

Currant Scones 39

Lemon Blueberry Scones. 40

Apple Walnut Scones 41

Chocolate Chip Scones 42

Just Lemon Scones 43

Pumpkin Scones 44

Maple Pecan Scones 45

Corn Cherry Scones 46

Oat Scones 47

Cheese Scones 48

   Roasted Tomato Salsa 50

   Tomatillo Salsa 50

MUFFINS

Bran Muffins 52

Apple Apricot Muffins 53

Lemon Poppy Seed Muffins 54

Millet Pecan Muffins 54

Banana Mocha Chocolate Chip Muffins . . 56

Banana Walnut Muffins 56

Pecan Pear Muffins 58

Raspberry Orange Muffins 58

. . . AND MORE

Brioches 60

   Cranberry Brioches 61

Chocolate Things 62

Pecan Rolls 63

Sticky Buns 65

Killer Granola. 66

Killer Granola Cookies 66

Shortbread 67

Ginger Shortbread 68

Hazelnut Shortbread 69

Lemon Shortbread. 69

   Chocolate-Drizzled Stars,
   Trees, or Hearts 70

Any kid who has read *In the Night Kitchen* would want to work here when they grow up.

—ADAM

· S C O N E S ·

Currant Scones

This is the original Cheese Board breakfast scone, and for years it was the only kind of scone we baked. One of our customers dubbed it the Ur-Scone. The production of this scone has changed from its humble beginnings of about sixty scones a day to over six hundred being made on Saturdays. The pure flavor of unsalted butter is the most important component in this recipe (see page 21 for a discussion on butter). You should have on hand extra buttermilk and cream, as the amount of liquid that you will need can vary depending on weather conditions and the amount of moisture in the flour. How much cinnamon topping to use has always been a topic of discussion on the early-morning shift.

MAKES 10 TO 12 SCONES
Preparation time including baking: 45 minutes

3½ cups unbleached all-purpose flour

½ teaspoon baking soda

1 tablespoon baking powder

½ teaspoon kosher salt

¾ cup sugar

1 cup (2 sticks) cold unsalted butter, cut into
1-inch cubes

1 cup dried currants

¾ cup heavy cream

¾ cup buttermilk

Topping

¼ cup sugar

⅛ teaspoon ground cinnamon

Preheat the oven to 375°F. Line a baking sheet with parchment paper or a baking mat.

Sift the flour, baking soda, and baking powder together into the bowl of a stand mixer or a large bowl.

If using a stand mixer, add the salt and sugar to the bowl and mix with the paddle attachment on low speed until combined. Add the butter and cut it in on low speed for about 4 minutes, or until it is the size of small peas. Mix in the currants. Make a well in the center and add the cream and buttermilk. Mix briefly, just until the ingredients come together; some loose flour should remain at the bottom of the bowl.

If making by hand, add the salt and sugar to the bowl and stir with a wooden spoon until combined. Add the butter and cut it in with a pastry cutter or 2 dinner knives until it is the size of small peas. Using the spoon, mix in the currants. Make a well in the center and add the cream and buttermilk. Mix briefly, just until the ingredients come together; some loose flour should remain at the bottom of the bowl.

Gently shape the dough into balls about 2¼ inches in diameter (they should have a rough, rocky exterior) and place them on the prepared pan about 2 inches apart.

For the topping, mix the sugar and cinnamon together in a small bowl. Sprinkle the mixture on the top of the scones. Bake on the middle rack of the oven for 25 to 30 minutes, or until golden brown. Transfer the scones to a wire rack to cool.

I actually like coming in to work really early. It's kind of nice driving by the Ivy Room when people are leaving the bar and I'm going to work. I drive by there around 2:20 A.M., and the musicians are standing out there on the sidewalk. It's kind of a trip—they're getting ready to go home to go to bed and I'm going to work. And then I'm off at 10 A.M.! That's another trip.

—STU

Lemon Blueberry Scones

We love variety, but unfortunately there is a finite amount of time, shelf space, and energy. To address our desire for novelty, we make a daily-special scone. This is one of our many scone-of-the-day recipes. Although we generally prefer to use fresh ingredients, frozen fruit holds its shape better and bleeds less into the dough. In this recipe it is important not to overmix the batter. If more than a few strokes are used, you will end up with gray scones instead of light yellow ones studded with berries.

MAKES 10 TO 12 SCONES
Preparation time including baking: 45 minutes

3½ cups unbleached all-purpose flour
½ teaspoon baking soda
1 tablespoon baking powder
½ teaspoon kosher salt
¾ cup plus ¼ cup sugar
1 cup (2 sticks) cold unsalted butter, cut into
  1-inch cubes
Grated zest of 1 large lemon
1 cup fresh or frozen blueberries
½ cup heavy cream
¾ cup buttermilk

Preheat the oven to 375°F. Line a baking sheet with parchment paper or a baking mat.

Sift the flour, baking soda, and baking powder together into the bowl of a stand mixer or a large bowl.

If using a stand mixer, add the salt and the ¾ cup sugar to the bowl and mix with the paddle attachment on low speed until combined. Add the butter and cut it in on low speed for about 4 minutes, or until it is the size of small peas. Remove the bowl from the stand mixer and complete the rest of the recipe by hand.

If making by hand, add the salt and the ¾ cup sugar to the bowl and stir with a wooden spoon until combined. Add the butter and cut it in with a pastry cutter or 2 dinner knives until it is the size of small peas. Gently mix in the lemon zest

and blueberries with a few strokes of the spoon. Make a well in the center and add the cream and buttermilk. Mix briefly, just until the ingredients come together; some loose flour should remain at the bottom of the bowl.

Gently shape the dough into balls about 2¼ inches in diameter (they should have a rough, rocky exterior) and place them on the prepared pan about 2 inches apart.

Sprinkle the ¼ cup sugar on top of the scones. Bake on the middle rack of the oven for 25 to 30 minutes, or until golden brown. Transfer the scones to a wire rack to cool.

When making the scones, the butter has to be cold so that the flour gets cold at the same time when you're mixing it. I've found that when it's room temperature, especially on a warm summer day, the dough is wet and sticky. It doesn't make as fluffy and good a scone. I don't just add the two required gallons of buttermilk and cream; sometimes I add less or more. I feel the dough, I look, and I just know.

—DAVE M.

I love scones. When they are mixed just right they are cloudlike. I love eating them when they are still warm. I still have memories of coming into the Cheese Board long before I worked here. I would buy a scone and it was gone before I got home. It's stupid to sit there in your car and be in heaven over a scone. You should be someplace a little nicer than your driver's seat!

—MARTHA

Apple Walnut Scones

We tried this combination of ingredients for an autumn scone, and though the ingredients seemed ordinary, it was a very successful recipe. We use dried apples instead of fresh ones because they have a pleasing texture and an intense flavor.

MAKES 10 TO 12 SCONES

Preparation time including baking: 45 minutes

3½ cups unbleached all-purpose flour

½ teaspoon baking soda

1 tablespoon baking powder

½ teaspoon kosher salt

¾ cup sugar

1 cup (2 sticks) cold unsalted butter, cut into 1-inch cubes

1 cup coarsely chopped dried apples

¾ cup coarsely chopped walnuts

½ cup golden raisins

¾ cup heavy cream

¾ cup buttermilk

Topping

¼ cup sugar

⅛ teaspoon ground cinnamon

Preheat the oven to 375°F. Line a baking sheet with parchment paper or a baking mat.

Sift the flour, baking soda, and baking powder together into the bowl of a stand mixer or a large bowl.

If using a stand mixer, add the salt and sugar to the bowl and mix with the paddle attachment on low speed until combined. Add the butter and cut it in on low speed for about 4 minutes, or until it is the size of small peas. Mix in the apples, walnuts, and golden raisins. Make a well in the center and add the cream and buttermilk. Mix briefly, just until the ingredients come together; some loose flour should remain at the bottom of the bowl.

If making by hand, add the salt and sugar to the bowl and stir with a wooden spoon until combined. Add the butter and cut it in with a pastry cutter or 2 dinner knives until

it is the size of small peas. Using the spoon, mix in the apples, walnuts, and golden raisins. Make a well in the center and add the cream and buttermilk. Mix briefly, just until the ingredients come together; some loose flour should remain at the bottom of the bowl.

Gently shape the dough into balls about 2¼ inches in diameter (they should have a rough, rocky exterior) and place them on the prepared pan about 2 inches apart.

For the topping, mix the sugar and cinnamon together in a small bowl. Sprinkle the mixture on top of the scones. Bake on the middle rack of the oven for 25 to 30 minutes, or until golden brown. Transfer the scones to a wire rack to cool.

WHITTLING WHILE SCONES BURN . . .

I like the scones to be a medium golden brown without too much sugar on top. —CARRIE

I like sugar. Some of us don't put enough sugar on top of the scones. I don't think that the dough itself without the sugar on top is sweet enough. —DAVE M.

Chocolate Chip Scones

Adding chocolate to scones might seem extravagant, but once you eat these you will rank them with your favorite chocolate chip cookie. Buy the best-quality chocolate chips; we use a bittersweet Belgian variety.

MAKES 10 TO 12 SCONES
Preparation time including baking: 45 minutes

3½ cups unbleached all-purpose flour
½ teaspoon baking soda
1 tablespoon baking powder
½ teaspoon kosher salt
¾ cup plus ¼ cup sugar
1 cup (2 sticks) cold unsalted butter, cut into
    1-inch cubes
1 cup chocolate chips
¾ cup heavy cream
¾ cup buttermilk

Preheat the oven to 375°F. Line a baking sheet with parchment paper or a baking mat.

Sift the flour, baking soda, and baking powder together into the bowl of a stand mixer or a large bowl.

If using a stand mixer, add the salt and the ¾ cup sugar to the bowl and mix with the paddle attachment on low speed until combined. Add the butter and cut it in on low speed for about 4 minutes, or until it is the size of small peas. Mix in the chocolate chips. Make a well in the center and add the cream and buttermilk. Mix briefly, just until the ingredients come together; some loose flour should remain at the bottom of the bowl.

If making by hand, add the salt and the ¾ cup sugar to the bowl and stir with a wooden spoon until combined. Add the butter and cut it in with a pastry cutter or 2 dinner knives until it is the size of small peas. Using the spoon, mix in the chocolate chips. Make a well in the center and add the cream and buttermilk. Mix briefly, just until the ingredients come together; some loose flour should remain at the bottom of the bowl.

Gently shape the dough into balls about 2¼ inches in diameter (they should have a rough, rocky exterior) and place them on the prepared pan about 2 inches apart.

Sprinkle the ¼ cup sugar on top of the scones. Bake on the middle rack of the oven for 25 to 30 minutes, or until golden brown. Transfer the scones to a wire rack to cool.

THE CHEESE BOARD AT 4:30 A.M.

When we interview potential new Cheese Board members, we always ask the questions, "Do you mind working very early mornings? And every Saturday? And during the holidays?" Inevitably the answer is, "No, I don't mind." So, having said no myself, I find myself arriving for a 4:30 A.M. baking shift twice a week. Mostly, I love it. Some mornings I wake to the alarm, and the first thing I do is plan when I will take a nap later in the day. Walking into a darkened Cheese Board with no noise from fans, mixers, ovens, or voices, and slowly preparing the kitchen for the day's work is one of my favorite things. We start the day with a skeleton crew that gradually builds as the hours go by. The transformation from the rested store to coffee mills grinding, oven timers buzzing, traffic noises, conversations, and music is nothing short of a complete metamorphosis—and I love it.

When my shift is over it's hard to leave, hard to concentrate. I need a shower and a nap.

—Cathy

The scones are a uniquely sublime product. Ten years before I worked here, that was the only Cheese Board product that I ate. I never even knew there was a cheese counter. I just went for the scones.　　—ADAM

Just Lemon Scones

The beauty of this recipe is its simplicity. Candied lemon peel and lemon zest provide the sweet and fragrant flavor for this scone.

MAKES 10 TO 12 SCONES
Preparation time including baking: 45 minutes

  ¼ cup finely minced candied lemon peel
  Grated zest of 1 large lemon
  ¾ cup plus ¼ cup sugar
  3½ cups unbleached all-purpose flour
  ½ teaspoon baking soda
  1 tablespoon baking powder
  ½ teaspoon kosher salt
  1 cup (2 sticks) cold unsalted butter, cut into
    1-inch cubes
  ¾ cup heavy cream
  ¾ cup buttermilk

Preheat the oven to 375°F. Line a baking sheet with parchment paper or a baking mat.

Combine the lemon peel, lemon zest, and the ¾ cup sugar in a small bowl.

Sift the flour, baking soda, and baking powder together into the bowl of a stand mixer or a large bowl.

If using a stand mixer, add the salt and lemon sugar to the bowl and mix with the paddle attachment on low speed until combined. Add the butter and cut it in on low speed for about 4 minutes, or until it is the size of small peas. Make a well in the center and add the cream and buttermilk. Mix briefly, just until the ingredients come together; some loose flour should remain at the bottom of the bowl.

If making by hand, add the salt and lemon sugar to the bowl and stir with a wooden spoon until combined. Add the butter and cut it in with a pastry cutter or 2 dinner knives until it is the size of small peas. Make a well in the center and add the cream and buttermilk. Mix briefly with the spoon, just until the ingredients come together; some loose flour should remain at the bottom of the bowl.

Gently shape the dough into balls about 2¼ inches in diameter (they should have a rough, rocky exterior) and place them on the prepared pan about 2 inches apart.

Sprinkle the ¼ cup of sugar on top of the scones. Bake on the middle rack of the oven for 25 to 30 minutes, or until golden brown. Transfer the scones to a wire rack to cool.

Pumpkin Scones

We make these all year round. You would think that the pumpkin would make this scone heavy, but the reverse is true. These have a fluffy, cloudlike texture, and their light orange color is unusual.

MAKES 10 TO 12 SCONES
Preparation time including baking: 45 minutes

1/2 cup heavy cream

3/4 cup buttermilk

1 cup canned or homemade pumpkin purée

3 1/2 cups unbleached all-purpose flour

1/2 teaspoon baking soda

1 tablespoon baking powder

1/4 teaspoon ground cinnamon

1/8 teaspoon ground ginger

1/8 teaspoon ground nutmeg

1/2 teaspoon kosher salt

3/4 cup sugar

1 cup (2 sticks) cold unsalted butter, cut into
     1-inch cubes

Topping
1/4 cup sugar

1/8 teaspoon ground cinnamon

Preheat the oven to 375°F. Line a baking sheet with parchment paper or a baking mat.

In a medium bowl, whisk together the cream, buttermilk, and pumpkin.

Sift the flour, baking soda, baking powder, cinnamon, ginger, and nutmeg together into the bowl of a stand mixer or a large bowl.

If using a stand mixer, add the salt and sugar to the dry ingredients and mix with the paddle attachment on low speed until combined. Add the butter and cut it in on low speed for about 4 minutes, or until it is the size of small peas. Make a well in the center and add the pumpkin mixture. Mix briefly, just until the ingredients come together; some loose flour should remain at the bottom of the bowl.

If making by hand, add the salt and sugar to the dry ingredients and stir with a wooden spoon until combined. Add the butter and cut it in with a pastry cutter or 2 dinner knives until it is the size of small peas. Make a well in the center and add the pumpkin mixture. Mix briefly with the spoon, just until the ingredients come together; some loose flour should remain at the bottom of the bowl.

Gently shape the dough into balls about 2 1/4 inches in diameter (they should have a rough, rocky exterior) and place them on the prepared pan about 2 inches apart.

For the topping, mix the sugar and cinnamon together in a small bowl. Sprinkle the mixture on the top of the scones. Bake on the middle rack of the oven for 25 to 30 minutes, or until golden brown. Transfer the scones to a wire rack to cool.

Over the years I have actually seen some of the customers more than my dearest, closest friends, so in a way they have become dear, close friends, because they are the ones I do get to see on a daily basis.   —VICKI

ONE TOO MANY CAPPUCINOS....

Maple Pecan Scones

This scone is different from our usual scone because it has an additional step. Maple syrup and confectioners' sugar are combined to form a glaze that is spooned on top of each scone. It is important to wait 10 minutes before glazing them. If the scones are hot, the glaze becomes too thin and runs off; if the scones have completely cooled, the glaze will sit on top of them instead of spreading over them.

MAKES 10 TO 12 SCONES
Preparation time including baking: 1 hour

3¹/₂ cups unbleached all-purpose flour
¹/₂ teaspoon baking soda
1 tablespoon baking powder
¹/₂ teaspoon kosher salt
³/₄ cup sugar
1 cup (2 sticks) cold unsalted butter, cut into
    1-inch cubes
1¹/₄ cups coarsely chopped pecans
³/₄ cup heavy cream
³/₄ cup buttermilk

Glaze
²/₃ cup maple syrup
1¹/₂ cups confectioners' sugar, sifted

Preheat the oven to 375°F. Line a baking sheet with parchment paper or a baking mat.

Sift the flour, baking soda, and baking powder together into the bowl of a stand mixer or a large bowl.

If using a stand mixer, add the salt and sugar to the bowl and mix with the paddle attachment on low speed until combined. Add the butter and cut it in on low speed for about 4 minutes, or until it is the size of small peas. Mix in the pecans. Make a well in the center and add the cream and but-termilk. Mix briefly, just until the ingredients come together; some loose flour should remain at the bottom of the bowl.

If making by hand, add the salt and sugar to the bowl and stir with a wooden spoon until combined. Add the butter and cut it in with a pastry cutter or 2 dinner knives until it is

the size of small peas. Using the spoon, mix in the pecans. Make a well in the center and add the cream and buttermilk. Mix briefly, just until the ingredients come together; some loose flour should remain at the bottom of the bowl.

Gently shape the dough into balls about 2¹/₄ inches in diameter (they should have a rough, rocky exterior) and place them on the prepared pan about 2 inches apart.

Bake on the middle rack of the oven for 25 to 30 minutes, or until golden brown.

To make the glaze, 5 minutes before the scones come out of the oven, pour the maple syrup into a medium bowl. Gradually whisk in the confectioners' sugar to make a smooth mixture.

Line a work surface with newspaper and place a wire rack on top. Transfer the scones to the rack. Let cool for 10 minutes, then pour 1 tablespoonful maple glaze over the top of each scone. Let the glaze set before serving.

When I started working here, I thought that it was just like any other job and that I was an employee. Then people all around me started talking about motivation. They told me to start thinking like an owner. Suddenly, I came to realize that I was a part owner of the business. It was a dream fulfilled. I never thought I would ever own a business, and here it was, part mine.

—ARTEMIO

Ultimately, you know in a collective that if you choose to take a stand and live by it and assert yourself you can't be fired. It's not that way in the real world, where you have to do what somebody else tells you to do, and therein lies the difference.

—VICKI

Corn Cherry Scones

A few years ago, we trained a group of people starting a new bakery cooperative. In order to do this, we opened the store on Mondays, a day we had been closed on for years. A lot of experimenting was done on those Monday mornings. This is one of the creations from those hectic training days. We tried the corn cherry scone first as a muffin, then as a biscuit, until its final version emerged, a buttery, sweet scone studded with dried cherries. The cornmeal tends to make the batter heavy and slow rising, so only buttermilk is added. This acts with the leavening to create a lighter scone. The initial high oven temperature also helps give this scone a push so it doesn't flatten out while baking. It crumbles when eaten, and the crumbs are very popular with the sparrows and dogs that hang out in front of the store.

MAKES 10 TO 12 SCONES
Preparation time including baking: 45 minutes

> 2 cups unbleached all-purpose flour
> 1/2 teaspoon baking soda
> 1 tablespoon baking powder
> 1/2 teaspoon kosher salt
> 2/3 cup plus 1/4 cup sugar
> 1 1/2 cups medium-grind yellow cornmeal
> 1 cup (2 sticks) cold unsalted butter, cut into
>   1-inch cubes
> 3/4 cup dried sweet cherries
> 1 1/4 cups buttermilk

Preheat the oven to 425°F. Line a baking sheet with parchment paper or a baking mat.

Sift the flour, baking soda, and baking powder together into the bowl of a stand mixer or a large bowl.

If using a stand mixer, add the salt, the 2/3 cup sugar, and the cornmeal to the bowl and mix with the paddle attachment on low speed until combined. Add the butter and cut it in on low speed for about 4 minutes, or until it is the size of small peas. Mix in the cherries. Make a well in the center and add the buttermilk. Mix briefly, just until the ingredients come together; some loose flour should remain at the bottom of the bowl. Let the batter stand for 5 minutes.

If making by hand, add the salt, the 2/3 cup sugar, and the cornmeal to the bowl and stir with a wooden spoon until combined. Add the butter and cut it in with a pastry cutter or 2 dinner knives until it is the size of small peas. Using the spoon, mix in the cherries. Make a well in the center and add the buttermilk. Mix briefly, just until the ingredients come together; some loose flour should remain at the bottom of the bowl. Let the batter stand for 5 minutes.

Gently shape the dough into balls about 2 1/4 inches in diameter (they should have a rough, rocky exterior) and place them on the prepared pan about 2 inches apart.

Sprinkle the 1/4 cup sugar on top of the scones. Place the scones in the oven on the middle rack and immediately turn the temperature down to 375°F. Bake for 20 to 25 minutes, or until the scones are golden. Transfer the scones to a wire rack to cool.

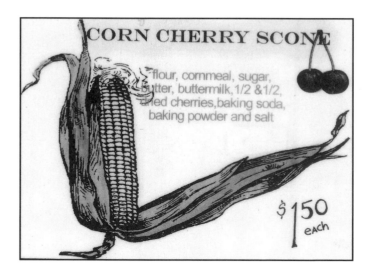

CORN CHERRY SCONE
flour, cornmeal, sugar, butter, buttermilk, 1/2 & 1/2, dried cherries, baking soda, baking powder and salt
$1 50 each

When I first worked here, seeing the overwhelmingly huge mountain of dough was exciting. I'd think, "How many thousands of scones do we have to make before seven o'clock and we open up?"

—JOSÉ

LIFE AS A WHOLE

I had gone to work right out of college for General Electric, in the jet engine department. I realized in a relatively short amount of time that I wasn't a good fit for a corporation because they really wanted to mold you into a certain type of person. I was in management, and they wanted me to wear a dark coat and dark pants and a dark tie. You were a company man there; you weren't really an individual. I wasn't drafted right off because I had a deferment as I was working on jet engines that were going to Vietnam. During the day I was working on these engines, and in the evening and on weekends I was involved in the movement protesting the Vietnam War. One of the things that I hated about that work was that duality: living two lives, not really being one person. It didn't make any sense to me.

Joining the Cheese Board allowed me to bring my life together into one circle, one whole. My political philosophies coincided more naturally with the Cheese Board and the politics of the collective movement it embodied. I was finally able to express, through my work, my philosophy about life, politics, society, and the relationship between myself, my friends, and my workmates, and it has been that way ever since.

—Michael

Oat Scones

An oat scone makes a hearty breakfast. It has a lingering caramel taste. The addition of oats makes it necessary for the dough to sit for a bit so that the oats can absorb some of the liquid. Rolling and folding the dough gives the finished scone a layered, flakier crumb. Unlike most Cheese Board scones, this scone can be treated like a biscuit and split in half for jam.

MAKES 10 TO 12 SCONES
Preparation time including baking: 1 hour

1 cup unbleached all-purpose flour
1/2 cup whole-wheat flour
1 teaspoon baking soda
1/2 teaspoon baking powder
1 teaspoon kosher salt
1/2 cup packed brown sugar
2 cups old-fashioned rolled oats
3/4 cup (1 1/2 sticks) cold unsalted butter, cut into
     1-inch cubes
3/4 cup dried currants
1/2 cup heavy cream
3/4 cup buttermilk
1 egg, beaten

Preheat the oven to 375°F. Line a baking sheet with parchment paper or a baking mat.

Sift the flours, baking soda, and baking powder together into the bowl of a stand mixer or a large bowl.

If using a stand mixer, add the salt, brown sugar, and oats to the bowl and mix with the paddle attachment on low speed until combined. Add the butter and cut it in on low speed for about 4 minutes, or until it is the size of small peas. Mix in the currants. Make a well in the center and add the cream and buttermilk. Mix briefly, just until the ingredients come together. Add a bit more buttermilk or cream if the dough seems too dry. Let the batter stand for 10 minutes.

If making by hand, add the salt, brown sugar, and oats to the bowl and stir with a wooden spoon until combined. Add the butter and cut it in with a pastry cutter or 2 dinner knives until it is the size of small peas. Using the spoon, mix in the currants. Make a well in the center and add the cream and buttermilk. Mix briefly, just until the ingredients come together. Add a bit more buttermilk or cream if the dough seems too dry. Let the batter stand for 10 minutes.

Place the dough on a generously floured surface. Pat it into a 2-inch-thick rectangle and dust the top with flour. Using a rolling pin, roll it into a 1-inch-thick rectangle. Fold the rectangle in half, short ends together, and roll it out again until it is 1 inch thick. Repeat this process a second time. Fold a third time and roll out into a rectangle with a final size of 6 by 12 by 1¼ inches thick.

Dip a 3-inch circular biscuit cutter or drinking glass into flour and cut out scones from the dough. Place the scones on the prepared pan about 2 inches apart. The scraps can be rolled out again and the process repeated until all the dough is used.

Brush the tops and sides of the scones with the beaten egg. Bake on the middle rack of the oven for 30 to 35 minutes, or until a rich, golden brown. Transfer the scones to a wire rack to cool.

Cheese Scones

Out of the twelve different kinds of Cheddar we stock, we selected a three-year-old Wisconsin Cheddar for this recipe. This cheese was the perfect choice because of its sharp flavor and beautiful orange color. The scones are spiked with a dash of cayenne, then gently patted out and cut into triangles. Many of us love this scone for lunch with a side of cottage cheese and homemade salsa (see page 50).

MAKES 10 TO 12 SCONES
Preparation time including baking: 50 minutes

3 cups unbleached all-purpose flour

½ teaspoon baking soda

1½ teaspoons baking powder

Pinch of cayenne pepper, or to taste

1 teaspoon kosher salt

2 tablespoons finely ground yellow cornmeal

½ cup (1 stick) plus 1 tablespoon cold unsalted butter, cut into 1-inch cubes

½ pound sharp orange Cheddar cheese, cut into ½-inch cubes

½ cup heavy cream

1 cup buttermilk

1 egg, beaten

Preheat the oven to 375°F. Line a baking sheet with parchment paper or a baking mat and sprinkle it lightly with cornmeal.

Sift the flour, baking soda, baking powder, and cayenne together into the bowl of a stand mixer or a large bowl.

If using a stand mixer, add the salt and cornmeal to the bowl and mix with the paddle attachment on low speed until combined. Add the butter and cut it in on low speed for about 4 minutes, or until it is the size of small peas. Gently mix in the Cheddar. Make a well in the center and add the cream and buttermilk. With a few rotations of the paddle, mix just until the ingredients come together. Do not over-mix the batter; the cheese should remain in chunks and there should be some loose flour at the bottom of the bowl.

If making by hand, add the salt and cornmeal to the bowl and stir with a wooden spoon until combined. Add the butter and cut it in with a pastry cutter or 2 dinner knives until it is the size of small peas. Very briefly mix in the Cheddar. Make a well in the center and add the cream and buttermilk. With a few strokes of a wooden spoon, mix just until the ingredients come together. Do not overmix the bat-ter; the cheese should remain in chunks and there should be some loose flour at the bottom of the bowl.

Place the dough on a generously floured surface. Pat it into a 6 by 9 by 1½-inch-thick rectangle. Divide the dough in half lengthwise and then cut each piece into 6 even tri-angles. Place the scones on the prepared pan about 2 inches apart.

Brush the tops of the scones with the beaten egg. Bake on the middle rack of the oven for 30 minutes, or until light brown. Transfer the scones to a wire rack to cool.

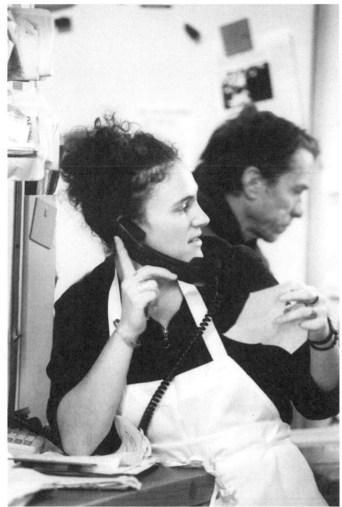

I do a lot of baking by sound. The scones have a sound they make when they have mixed the right length of time and have the right amount of liquid. It's a smacking, kissing sort of sound. You have to make the scones many times to get to know what that sound is.

—CARRIE

Roasted Tomato Salsa

This is the traditional Mexican-style tomato salsa we sell at the Cheese Board. We make it by the five-gallon bucketful. The tomatoes and chiles are roasted and then puréed, blackened skin and all. If you prefer a milder salsa, cut back on the number of chiles.

MAKES 3 CUPS
Preparation time: 20 minutes

5 Roma tomatoes
3 jalapeño chiles, stemmed
1 clove garlic, minced
$1/_2$ cup finely chopped green onions (including green parts)
$1/_2$ cup loosely packed fresh cilantro leaves, chopped
$1/_8$ teaspoon kosher salt

In a cast-iron skillet over medium heat, roast the tomatoes and chiles until the tomato skins are blackened and beginning to fall off, about 10 minutes. Put the tomatoes and chiles in a food processor with the garlic and green onions and pulse for 15 seconds, or until the salsa has a chunky consistency. Pour the mixture into a bowl and stir in the cilantro and salt. Taste and adjust the seasoning.

Never add sugar to salsa; just use great tomatoes in season. Roasting the tomatoes adds flavor and character to the salsa.   —MATEO

Tomatillo Salsa

This bright, tart salsa with a deep green color is enlivened by confetti-like pieces of red and yellow bell pepper.

MAKES 3 CUPS
Preparation time: 30 minutes

$3/_4$ pound tomatillos, husked and rinsed
6 jalapeño chiles, stemmed
1 cup finely diced red bell pepper
1 cup finely diced yellow bell pepper
2 small cloves garlic, minced
$3/_4$ cup finely chopped green onions (including green parts)
1 cup loosely packed fresh cilantro leaves, chopped
$1/_8$ teaspoon kosher salt

In a large saucepan combine the tomatillos and jalapeños. Add water to cover and bring to a low boil. Cook for 25 minutes, or until the tomatillos are soft and starting to fall apart. Drain and transfer to a food processor. Add the bell peppers and garlic and pulse for 20 seconds, or until just puréed. Pour the mixture into a bowl and stir in the green onions, cilantro, and salt. Taste and adjust the seasoning.

When you boil the jalapeños in the water, it mellows the heat, but you still get their flavor. This salsa is great with goat meat or *lengua* tacos. Any traditional Mexican barbecue has to have green salsa.

—MATEO

MEETINGS AND MAKING DECISIONS

Many people ask us, "How do you make decisions by consensus with forty people? Your meetings must be very long and tedious." On the contrary, we meet only once a month for three hours, and the meetings are productive and entertaining. There is a lot of banter mixed in with the business.

Meetings not only provide us with the opportunity to make business decisions, but provide the social glue that holds us together. Often the only time some members cross paths is at meetings.

Trust is a necessary ingredient of a collectively run business. Right now we are in a period where the level of trust is extremely high. When there is that underlying trust and respect for each other, it is easier to satisfy our primary goal of reaching an agreement that satisfies all the members of the group. When that trust is absent, this goal becomes elusive.

We have the added advantage that many of us have worked together for years and have come to recognize and appreciate each other's idiosyncrasies and foibles. At times we are like a family. Like any family, the dynamics are very complicated, and sometimes the group might seem dysfunctional. However, the underlying friendship and mutual caring make our common purpose more important than our differences.

—S. S.

The older people here are more powerful because they are more respected. They are more stuck in their ways of doing things because they have seen what has worked and what hasn't worked. Young people want to have the power to make their own mistakes. For an older person who has been here and already made that mistake, that isn't very appealing. But it is important to feel empowered. If I have more power because I have been here longer and I'm telling new members that they can't try their new idea, I'm basically telling them it's really not theirs to experiment with.   —ADAM

I think the power structure is unspoken, but there is one. There is going to be a power structure anywhere you have a group of people, even here where it's a collective and everyone is supposed to be equal. I'm comfortable with it. I've never felt held back. I don't feel like it prevents anyone from doing what they really want to do.   —OLIVIA

I like this new, younger crowd. It seems more refreshed. New life, new blood.   —LYNN

I think it's good that the older members allow the new members to take over and have a lot of influence on the direction of the business. It's good, it's a very healthy thing.   —MICHAEL

· M U F F I N S ·

Bran Muffins

For many years this was the only muffin the Cheese Board offered for sale. This recipe produces bran muffins with a crusty top and a moist interior. The molasses, whole-wheat flour, and bran all make the batter a very dark color. Because of this, it is easy to be fooled into thinking that the muffins are through baking before they actually are. Before removing them from the oven, touch the tops gently; if they spring back, they are done.

MAKES 12 MUFFINS
Preparation time including baking: 1 hour

2 eggs

1 cup buttermilk

¹/₃ cup vegetable oil (safflower or canola)

³/₄ cup dark molasses

¹/₂ cup water

³/₄ cup unbleached all-purpose flour

³/₄ cup whole-wheat flour

1 teaspoon baking soda

¹/₂ teaspoon kosher salt

¹/₂ cup wheat bran

¹/₂ cup All-Bran cereal

¹/₂ cup raw wheat germ

³/₄ cup coarsely chopped walnuts

²/₃ cup raisins

Preheat the oven to 350°F. Generously butter or spray the top and cups of a 12-cup muffin pan.

In a medium bowl, combine the eggs, buttermilk, oil, molasses, and water. Whisk until blended.

Sift the flours and baking soda together into the bowl of a stand mixer or a large bowl.

If using a stand mixer, add the salt, wheat bran, bran cereal, wheat germ, walnuts, and raisins to the dry ingredients. With the paddle attachment on low speed, mix until combined. Make a well in the center and pour in the wet ingredients. With a few rotations of the paddle, gently combine, taking care not to overmix the batter. Let the batter rest for at least 15 minutes to allow the ingredients to soak and expand fully.

If making by hand, add the salt, wheat bran, bran cereal, wheat germ, walnuts, and raisins to the dry ingredients. Stir with a wooden spoon until combined. Make a well in the center and pour in the wet ingredients. With a few strokes of the spoon, gently combine, taking care not to overmix the batter. Let the batter rest for at least 15 minutes to allow the ingredients to soak and expand fully.

Using an ice cream scoop or large soup spoon, fill the prepared muffin cups until the batter just peeks over the top of the pan. Bake on the middle rack of the oven for 30 to 35 minutes, or until the muffins are dark brown and springy. Let cool in the pan for 10 minutes. Unmold the muffins onto a wire rack to cool.

I like working at the Cheese Board because I consider us to be like a big pie—every piece is important here. Without one piece, the pie is not complete.   —JESÚS

Apple Apricot Muffins

After ten years of only bran muffins for sale at the store, along came the moist, chewy apple apricot muffins, full of fruit and nuts and spiced with cinnamon. This recipe can be baked right away, or (because the batter is full of grains that expand and hold it together) it can be mixed in advance and refrigerated, then scooped out and baked the following morning.

MAKES 12 MUFFINS
Preparation time including baking: 1 hour

2 eggs

1¹⁄₂ cups buttermilk

¹⁄₃ cup vegetable oil

1 teaspoon pure vanilla extract

1¹⁄₄ cups unbleached all-purpose flour

1 teaspoon baking soda

¹⁄₂ teaspoon ground cinnamon

¹⁄₂ teaspoon kosher salt

³⁄₄ cup old-fashioned rolled oats

¹⁄₄ cup granulated sugar

¹⁄₂ cup packed light brown sugar

¹⁄₂ cup raw wheat germ

¹⁄₂ cup chopped dried apples

¹⁄₂ cup chopped dried apricots

2 tablespoons chopped pecans

Preheat the oven to 350°F. Generously butter or spray the top and cups of a 12-cup muffin pan.

In a medium bowl, combine the eggs, buttermilk, oil, and vanilla extract. Whisk until blended.

Sift the flour, baking soda, and cinnamon together into the bowl of a stand mixer or a large bowl.

If using a stand mixer, add the salt, oats, sugars, wheat germ, apples, apricots, and pecans to the dry ingredients. With the paddle attachment on low speed, mix until combined. Make a well in the center and pour in the wet ingredients. With a few rotations of the paddle, gently combine, taking care not to overmix the batter. Let the batter rest for

at least 15 minutes to allow the ingredients to soak and expand fully.

If making by hand, add the salt, oats, sugars, wheat germ, apples, apricots, and pecans to the dry ingredients. Stir with a wooden spoon until combined. Make a well in the center and pour in the wet ingredients. With a few strokes of the spoon, gently combine, taking care not to overmix the batter. Let the batter rest for at least 15 minutes to allow the ingredients to soak and expand fully.

With an ice cream scoop or large soup spoon, fill the prepared muffins cups until the batter just peeks over the top of the pan. Bake on the middle rack of the oven for 30 to 35 minutes, or until the muffins are a deep golden brown, firm, and springy. Let cool in the pan for 10 minutes. Unmold the muffins onto a wire rack to cool.

I loved doing the early-morning baking shifts by myself. I would come in a little before five in the morning and I'd have the whole store to myself for about an hour and a half. I loved it. It was like the fantasy you have when you are a little kid and you get to run the store all by yourself. Nowadays, you hardly ever work a shift alone.   —URSULA

Lemon Poppy Seed Muffins

Lemon poppy seed is a classic muffin and one of our favorites. The poppy seeds add an interesting texture, and the tartness of the lemon keeps the muffin from being overly sweet. During the holidays we turn this recipe, and many of those that follow, into small loaves—perfect for Thanksgiving or Christmas brunch (see page 138).

MAKES 12 MUFFINS

Preparation time including baking: 45 minutes

- 1 cup plus 2 tablespoons sugar
- Grated zest and juice of 1 large lemon
- 2 eggs
- 1 cup sour cream or plain yogurt
- 1 cup heavy cream
- 3 cups unbleached all-purpose flour
- 1/2 teaspoon baking soda
- 1 tablespoon baking powder
- 1/2 teaspoon kosher salt
- 3/4 cup (1 1/2 sticks) cold unsalted butter, cut into 1-inch cubes
- 3 tablespoons poppy seeds

Preheat the oven to 375°F. Generously butter or spray the top and cups of a 12-cup muffin pan.

Combine the sugar and lemon zest in a small bowl.

In a medium bowl, combine the lemon juice, eggs, sour cream, and cream. Whisk until blended.

Sift the flour, baking soda, and baking powder together into the bowl of a stand mixer or a large bowl.

If using a stand mixer, add the salt and lemon sugar to the dry ingredients and mix with the paddle attachment on low speed until combined. Add the butter and cut it in on low speed for about 4 minutes, or until it is the size of small peas. Mix in the poppy seeds. Make a well in the center and pour in the wet ingredients. With a few rotations of the paddle, gently combine, taking care not to overmix the batter.

If making by hand, add the salt and lemon sugar to the dry ingredients and stir with a wooden spoon until combined.

Add the butter and cut it in with a pastry cutter or 2 dinner knives until it is the size of small peas. Mix in the poppy seeds. Make a well in the center and pour in the wet ingredients. With a few strokes of the spoon, gently combine, taking care not to overmix the batter.

With an ice cream scoop or large soup spoon, fill the prepared muffin cups until the batter just peeks over the top of the pan. Bake on the middle rack of the oven for 25 to 30 minutes, or until the muffins are light golden brown, firm, and springy. Let cool in the pan for 10 minutes. Unmold the muffins onto a wire rack to cool.

Millet Pecan Muffins

These are made with brown sugar and sweet, nutty millet grain. This is a great muffin to have with a cup of coffee.

MAKES 12 MUFFINS

Preparation time including baking: 45 minutes

- 2 eggs
- 1 cup sour cream or plain yogurt
- 1/2 cup milk
- 1/2 teaspoon pure vanilla extract
- 2 1/2 cups unbleached all-purpose flour
- 1 teaspoon baking soda
- 1/2 teaspoon baking powder
- 1/2 teaspoon ground cinnamon
- 1/2 teaspoon kosher salt
- 1/2 cup granulated sugar
- 1/4 cup packed light brown sugar
- 1/2 cup millet
- 1/2 cup (1 stick) cold unsalted butter, cut into 1-inch cubes
- 1/2 cup coarsely chopped pecans
- 1/4 cup golden raisins

Preheat the oven to 375°F. Generously butter or spray the top and cups of a 12-cup muffin pan.

In a medium bowl, combine the eggs, sour cream, milk, and vanilla extract. Whisk until blended.

Sift the flour, baking soda, baking powder, and cinnamon together into the bowl of a stand mixer or a large bowl.

If using a stand mixer, add the salt, sugars, and millet to the dry ingredients and mix with the paddle attachment on low speed until combined. Add the butter and cut it in on low speed for about 4 minutes, or until it is the size of small peas. Mix in the pecans and raisins. Make a well in the center and pour in the wet ingredients. With a few rotations of the paddle, gently combine, taking care not to overmix the batter.

If making by hand, add the salt, sugars, and millet to the dry ingredients and stir with a wooden spoon until combined. Add the butter and cut it in with a pastry cutter or 2 dinner knives until it is the size of small peas. Mix in the pecans and raisins. Make a well in the center and pour in the wet ingredients. With a few strokes of the spoon, gently combine, taking care not to overmix the batter.

With an ice cream scoop or large soup spoon, fill the prepared muffin cups until the batter just peeks over the top of the pan. Bake on the middle rack of the oven for 30 to 35 minutes, or until the muffins are golden brown, firm, and springy. Let cool in the pan for 10 minutes. Unmold the muffins onto a wire rack to cool.

Banana Mocha Chocolate Chip Muffins

Many Cheese Boarders are very fond of bananas, chocolate, and coffee, which is why these muffins appear so frequently in the store compared to other daily-special muffins.

MAKES 12 MUFFINS
Preparation time including baking: 45 minutes

1 egg

1 egg yolk

2 bananas, mashed

1/2 teaspoon pure vanilla extract

1/2 cup strong brewed coffee, cooled

1 cup sour cream or plain yogurt

2 1/4 cups unbleached all-purpose flour

1/4 teaspoon baking soda

2 teaspoons baking powder

1/4 teaspoon kosher salt

3/4 cup sugar

1/2 cup (1 stick) cold unsalted butter, cut into
   1-inch cubes

1 cup chocolate chips

Preheat the oven to 375°F. Generously butter or spray the top and cups of a 12-cup muffin pan.

In a medium bowl, combine the egg, egg yolk, bananas, vanilla extract, coffee, and sour cream. Whisk until blended.

Sift the flour, baking soda, and baking powder together into the bowl of a stand mixer or a large bowl.

If using a stand mixer, add the salt and sugar to the dry ingredients and mix with the paddle attachment on low speed until combined. Add the butter and cut it in on low speed for about 4 minutes, or until it is the size of small peas. Mix in the chocolate chips. Make a well in the center and pour in the wet ingredients. With a few rotations of the paddle, gently combine, taking care not to overmix the batter.

If making by hand, add the salt and sugar to the dry ingredients and stir with a wooden spoon until combined. Add the butter and cut it in with a pastry cutter or 2 dinner knives until it is the size of small peas. Mix in the chocolate chips. Make a well in the center and pour in the wet ingredients. With a few strokes of the spoon, gently combine, taking care not to overmix the batter.

With an ice cream scoop or large soup spoon, fill the prepared muffin cups until the batter just peeks over the top of the pan. Bake on the middle rack of the oven for 25 to 30 minutes, or until the muffins are golden brown, firm, and springy. Let cool in the pan for 10 minutes. Unmold the muffins onto a wire rack to cool.

Banana Walnut Muffins

This is a traditional banana walnut muffin. Warm from the oven and spread with cream cheese, they are reminiscent of banana cake from the 1950s.

MAKES 12 MUFFINS
Preparation time including baking: 45 minutes

1 egg

1 egg yolk

2 ripe bananas, mashed

1 cup sour cream or plain yogurt

1 cup buttermilk

1/2 teaspoon pure vanilla extract

2 1/2 cups unbleached all-purpose flour

1/4 teaspoon baking soda

2 teaspoons baking powder

1/4 teaspoon kosher salt

1/2 cup granulated sugar

1/4 cup packed light brown sugar

1/2 cup (1 stick) cold unsalted butter, cut into
   1-inch cubes

1 cup coarsely chopped walnuts

Preheat the oven to 375°F. Generously butter or spray the top and cups of a 12-cup muffin pan.

In a medium bowl, combine the egg, egg yolk, bananas, sour cream, buttermilk, and vanilla extract. Whisk until blended.

Sift the flour, baking soda, and baking powder together into the bowl of a stand mixer or a large bowl.

If using a stand mixer, add the salt and sugars to the dry ingredients and mix with the paddle attachment on low speed until combined. Add the butter and cut it in on low speed for about 4 minutes, or until it is the size of small peas. Mix in the walnuts. Make a well in the center and pour in the wet ingredients. With a few rotations of the paddle, gently combine, taking care not to overmix the batter.

If making by hand, add the salt and sugars to the dry ingredients and stir with a wooden spoon until combined. Add the butter and cut it in with a pastry cutter or 2 dinner knives until it is the size of small peas. Mix in the walnuts. Make a well in the center and pour in the wet ingredients. With a few strokes of the spoon, gently combine, taking care not to overmix the batter.

With an ice cream scoop or large soup spoon, fill the prepared muffin cups until the batter just peeks over the top of the pan. Bake on the middle rack of the oven for 25 to 30 minutes, or until the muffins are a deep golden brown, firm, and springy. Let cool in the pan for 10 minutes. Unmold the muffins onto a wire rack to cool.

I tend to be someone who wants to make everyone happy. When

I started working here, instead of one boss to make happy, I felt

like I had thirty bosses to make happy. It kind of drove me crazy

at first.   —TINA

Pecan Pear Muffins

If you want a quick, rich muffin for breakfast, this is a good choice. The pears impart a luscious sweetness that is balanced by the buttery flavor of the pecans.

MAKES 12 MUFFINS
Preparation time including baking: 45 minutes

1 egg

1 egg yolk

½ cup buttermilk

1 cup sour cream or plain yogurt

½ teaspoon pure vanilla extract

2¼ cups unbleached all-purpose flour

¼ teaspoon baking soda

2 teaspoons baking powder

¼ teaspoon kosher salt

½ cup granulated sugar

¼ cup packed light brown sugar

½ cup (1 stick) cold unsalted butter, cut into
   1-inch cubes

1 cup diced dried pears

⅓ cup coarsely chopped pecans

Preheat the oven to 375°F. Generously butter or spray the top and cups of a 12-cup muffin pan.

In a medium bowl, combine the egg, egg yolk, buttermilk, sour cream, and vanilla extract. Whisk until blended.

Sift the flour, baking soda, and baking powder together into the bowl of a stand mixer or a large bowl.

If using a stand mixer, add the salt and sugars to the dry ingredients and mix with the paddle attachment on low speed until combined. Add the butter and cut it in on low speed for about 4 minutes, or until it is the size of small peas. Mix in the pears and pecans. Make a well in the center and pour in the wet ingredients. With a few rotations of the paddle, gently combine, taking care not to overmix the batter.

If making by hand, add the salt and sugars to the dry ingredients and stir with a wooden spoon until combined. Add the butter and cut it in with a pastry cutter or 2 dinner knives until it is the size of small peas. Mix in the pears and pecans. Make a well in the center and pour in the wet ingredients. With a few strokes of the spoon, gently combine, taking care not to overmix the batter.

With an ice cream scoop or large soup spoon, fill the prepared muffin cups until the batter just peeks over the top of the pan. Bake on the middle rack of the oven for 25 to 30 minutes, or until the muffins are golden brown, firm, and springy. Let cool in the pan for 10 minutes. Unmold the muffins onto a wire rack to cool.

Raspberry Orange Muffins

Oranges and raspberries are both sweet and tart, and the sour cream in this recipe marries these flavors gracefully. Sneak a spoonful of the batter—it tastes like ice cream.

MAKES 12 MUFFINS
Preparation time including baking: 45 minutes

½ cup finely chopped candied orange peel

1 cup sugar

Grated zest and juice of 1 orange

2 eggs

1 cup sour cream or plain yogurt

1 cup buttermilk

2 cups unbleached all-purpose flour

¼ teaspoon baking soda

2 teaspoons baking powder

½ teaspoon kosher salt

½ cup (1 stick) cold unsalted butter, cut into
   1-inch cubes

1½ cups fresh or frozen raspberries

Preheat the oven to 375°F. Generously butter or spray the top and cups of a 12-cup muffin pan.

In a small bowl, combine the candied orange peel, sugar, and zest.

In a medium bowl, combine the orange juice, eggs, sour cream, and buttermilk. Whisk until blended.

Sift the flour, baking soda, and baking powder together into the bowl of a stand mixer or a large bowl.

If using a stand mixer, add the salt and orange sugar to the dry ingredients and mix with the paddle attachment on low speed until combined. Add the butter and cut it in on low speed for about 4 minutes, or until it is the size of small peas. Make a well in the center and pour in the wet ingredients. With a few rotations of the paddle, gently combine, taking care not to overmix the batter. Using a rubber spatula, gently fold in the berries.

If making by hand, add the salt and orange sugar to the dry ingredients and stir with a wooden spoon until combined. Add the butter and cut it in with a pastry cutter or 2 dinner knives until it is the size of small peas. Make a well in the center and pour in the wet ingredients. With a few strokes of the spoon, gently combine, taking care not to overmix the batter. Gently fold in the berries.

With an ice cream scoop or large soup spoon, fill the prepared muffin cups until the batter just peeks over the top of the pan. Bake on the middle rack of the oven for 25 to 30 minutes, or until the muffins are golden brown, firm, and springy. Let cool in the pan for 10 minutes. Unmold the muffins onto a wire rack to cool.

THE FIRST CHEESE BOARD TEENAGE INTERN

Being a teenage intern here was hard because of the cultural differences. I was in a different world, getting kicked out of a lot of classes at Berkeley High. I didn't consider myself racist, but I had a lot of anger toward America. For me, the Cheese Board was the perfect place because there was every kind of "white person" here. Everyone was so nice and worried about my well-being. They offered me whatever I needed. And I thought, "Why are all these white people wanting to help me? They just want to put their name out there that they are helping some little kid out of the 'hood." That's what I said to myself and I thought, "Well, let it be, as long as I get paid, that's all I care about." The checks started coming in, and it was good money for a teenager; I could buy clothes and give my mom money for food. Then I started noticing how this place works, how people have meetings and they talk over things with everybody else before they decide to do something. I'd say, "Why don't you just go out and buy it? Why do you have to ask ten people? Just go out and buy it!"

Working here molded me into the kind of person I am now. I was so wrong about this place! It was a cultural shock for me—it was so open. Honestly, at the time I didn't have any white friends. I certainly didn't have any grown-up white friends. The only ones I knew were the people we stole bikes from in Albany Village. That was the closest we got to them. When I came to work here, everybody cared about each other. It did a 180 on me. It was cool.

This place changes people, but it takes time. I tell you, when I came here and they gave me the keys to this place—I was fifteen, sixteen years old! They gave me all the combinations to all the locks. I thought, "Wow, these people trust this little hoodlum!" Everyone knew where all the money was, and you could have stolen it if you wanted to. That just blew me away. Not even my own mom trusted me that well. Honest to God, maybe in some other place I would have stolen something, but everyone trusted me so much and let me be myself. That made me think, "I am not going to blow this! I am not going to blow this—this is too good to be true." Two years ago when I came in I didn't know what trust was. But now I feel that it's been running through my body all this time.

—Guillermo

• . . . AND MORE •

Brioches

We never know quite how to explain why this pastry is called a brioche. It isn't related to a French brioche at all; in fact, it is more like your grandmother's yeasted cinnamon knot. Tying hundreds of these pastries is mesmerizing work in the dark hours of a morning shift. You can make the dough the evening before and refrigerate it overnight to make the brioches for brunch. The aroma of cinnamon is your first indication that the brioches are almost done and it's time to brew your coffee.

MAKES 12 BRIOCHES
Preparation time including rising and baking: 3¹/₄ hours;
active time: 50 minutes

> ¹/₂ cup heavy cream
> ¹/₂ cup buttermilk
> 2¹/₄ teaspoons active dry yeast
> 2¹/₂ cups unbleached all-purpose flour
> 6 tablespoons unsalted butter at room temperature
> ¹/₃ cup sugar
> 2 eggs
> 1¹/₂ teaspoons kosher salt
> ²/₃ cup golden raisins

Topping
> ¹/₂ cup sugar
> ¹/₄ teaspoon ground cinnamon

In a small saucepan, heat the cream and buttermilk over low heat until small bubbles form around the edges of the pan. Pour into the bowl of a stand mixer or a large bowl. Let cool until just warm, then whisk in the yeast until dissolved. Let stand for 5 minutes.

If using a stand mixer, add the flour, butter, sugar, 1 of the eggs, and the salt to the bowl. With the paddle attachment on medium speed, mix until the ingredients are combined, about 2 minutes. If the dough is too soupy, add extra flour by the tablespoonful until the dough forms a loose ball around the paddle. Switch to the dough hook and knead on medium speed for 7 minutes, or until the dough is smooth, silky, and elastic. Add the raisins and knead just long enough to incorporate them.

If making by hand, add the flour, butter, sugar, 1 of the eggs, and the salt to the bowl. Mix with a wooden spoon until the ingredients are combined. If the dough is too soupy, add extra flour by the tablespoonful. Transfer to a lightly floured surface and knead the dough for 10 minutes, or until it is smooth, silky, and elastic. Gently flatten the dough and sprinkle the raisins over the surface. Fold the dough over and continue kneading just long enough to incorporate the raisins.

Form the dough into a ball and place it in a large oiled bowl. Turn the dough over to coat it with oil. Cover the bowl with plastic wrap or a damp kitchen towel and let it rise in a warm, draft-free place for 1 hour, or until doubled in size. Or, refrigerate the dough to rise slowly overnight. The next morning, remove the dough from the refrigerator and let stand in a warm place for at least 1 hour.

In a wide, shallow bowl, mix the cinnamon and sugar together.

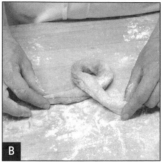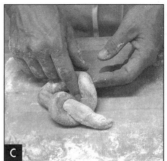

Line a baking sheet with parchment paper or a baking mat. Turn the dough out onto a lightly floured surface. Divide the dough into 12 pieces. Let rest for 5 minutes. Using your palms, roll each piece into a 10-inch-long length with slightly tapered ends (fig. A). Toss the lengths in the cinnamon-sugar mixture. Place one end of the length over the other, creating a loop with 2 tails (fig. B). Grasp the bottom tail and thread it through the loop from top to bottom (fig. C). Fold both tails underneath the knot and push them gently up into the center while using your thumbs to pull down on the outside edge of the roll (fig. D).

Place the brioches on the prepared pan about 2 inches apart. Cover them with a floured kitchen towel and let rise in a warm place for at least 1 hour, or until increased in size by one-third.

Fifteen minutes prior to baking, preheat the oven to 350°F. In a small bowl, whisk the remaining egg. Using a pastry brush, brush the tops and sides of each brioche with the beaten egg. Bake on the middle rack of the oven for 30 to 35 minutes, or until golden brown. Transfer the brioches to a wire rack to cool.

Cranberry Brioches

We make these brioches for two weeks during the winter holidays. The substitution of tart cranberries for raisins dramatically transforms the everyday brioche into an entirely different product. Some customers wait all year for these; others wait for the New Year and the return of their favorite golden raisin brioche.

²/₃ cup coarsely chopped cranberries, substituted for the raisins

Add the cranberries in place of the raisins, taking care not to overmix the dough since the cranberries will turn it pink.

The thing that I like about working here is the fact that I have more than a little bit of control over my work environment. I get a say in how things are done. That feels good. I don't get my way all the time; that's fine. I get outvoted a lot! But at least I feel that I have input. I feel that people know where I'm coming from.

—ARTHUR

Chocolate Things

A Chocolate Thing is a puffy, rounded bun created solely as a vehicle for chocolate. The surrounding dough is luxuriously buttery. It can be difficult to keep all the pieces of chocolate incorporated into the dough, but the chocolate must be added last so that it remains in large, discrete pieces. You can eat these while the chocolate is warm and meltingly smooth, or wait until later for it to become firm.

MAKES 12 THINGS

Preparation time including rising and baking: 3¼ hours; active time: 50 minutes

---

½ cup heavy cream

½ cup buttermilk

2¼ teaspoons active dry yeast

2½ cups unbleached all-purpose flour

6 tablespoons unsalted butter at room temperature

⅓ cup sugar

2 eggs

1½ teaspoons kosher salt

6 ounces dark chocolate, chopped into 1-inch pieces

In a small saucepan, heat the cream and buttermilk over low heat until small bubbles form around the edges of the pan. Pour into the bowl of a stand mixer or a large bowl. Let cool until just warm, then whisk in the yeast until dissolved. Let stand for 5 minutes.

If using a stand mixer, add the flour, butter, sugar, 1 of the eggs, and the salt to the bowl. With the paddle attachment on medium speed, mix until the ingredients are combined, about 2 minutes. If the dough is too soupy, add extra flour by the tablespoonful until the dough forms a loose ball around the paddle. Switch to the dough hook and knead on medium speed for 7 minutes, or until the dough is smooth, silky, and elastic. Add the chocolate and knead just long enough to incorporate it (do this step as quickly as possible, as overmixing will result in broken pieces of chocolate and a discolored dough).

If making by hand, add the flour, butter, sugar, 1 of the eggs, and the salt to the bowl. Mix with a wooden spoon until

combined. If the dough is too soupy, add extra flour by the tablespoonful. Transfer to a lightly floured surface and knead the dough for 10 minutes, or until it is smooth, silky, and elastic. Flatten the dough into a 1-inch-thick round and place the chocolate in the center. Gather the dough around the chocolate and knead just long enough to incorporate it.

Form the dough into a ball and place it in a large oiled bowl. Turn the dough over to coat it with oil. Cover the bowl with plastic wrap or a damp kitchen towel and let it rise in a warm, draft-free place for 1 hour, or until doubled in size. Or, refrigerate the dough to rise slowly overnight. The next morning, remove the dough from the refrigerator and let stand in a warm place for at least 1 hour.

Line a baking sheet with parchment paper or a baking mat. Transfer the dough to a lightly floured surface and roll it out into a 10 by 12-inch rectangle. In a small bowl, beat the remaining egg with a whisk. Using a pastry brush, brush a stripe down one of the long edges. Working from the other long edge, roll the dough up like a jelly roll (see page 29); the egg wash will glue it together. Using a sharp knife, cut the roll into twelve 1-inch-thick slices and place on the prepared pan, cut side up, about 2 inches apart. Cover them with a floured kitchen towel and let rise in a warm place for 1 hour, or until the rolls are increased in size by one-third.

Fifteen minutes prior to baking, preheat the oven to 350°F. Using a pastry brush, brush the tops and sides of each roll with the beaten egg. Bake on the middle rack of the oven for 30 to 35 minutes, or until golden brown. Transfer to a wire rack to cool.

Pecan Rolls

This recipe makes the quintessential gooey cinnamon roll. The rolls are hard to eat when warm, as the syrupy filling drips out along with chewy pieces of pecan. When we make them at the Cheese Board, the dough takes up the entire worktable. We can never make enough for the demand—customers have to show up at the store by 10 A.M. to be sure to get one.

MAKES 20 ROLLS

Preparation time including rising and baking: 2³/₄ hours; active time: 1 hour

- ¹/₂ cup heavy cream
- ¹/₂ cup buttermilk
- 2¹/₄ teaspoons active dry yeast
- 2¹/₂ cups unbleached all-purpose flour
- 6 tablespoons unsalted butter at room temperature
- ¹/₃ cup sugar
- 1 egg
- 1¹/₂ teaspoons kosher salt

Filling
- ³/₄ cup (1¹/₂ sticks) unsalted butter
- 1 cup packed light brown sugar
- ¹/₄ teaspoon ground cinnamon
- 2 cups pecan halves or pieces

In a small saucepan, heat the cream and buttermilk over low heat until small bubbles form around the edges of the pan. Pour into the bowl of a stand mixer or a large bowl. Let cool until just warm, then whisk in the yeast until dissolved. Let stand for 5 minutes.

If using a stand mixer, add the flour, butter, sugar, egg, and salt to the bowl. With the paddle attachment on medium speed, mix until the ingredients are combined, about 2 minutes. If the dough is too soupy, add extra flour by the tablespoonful until it forms a loose ball around the paddle. Switch to the dough hook and knead on medium speed for 7 minutes, or until the dough is smooth, silky, and elastic.

If making by hand, add the flour, butter, sugar, egg, and salt to the bowl. Mix with a wooden spoon until the ingredi-

ents are combined. If the dough is too soupy, add extra flour by the tablespoonful. Transfer to a lightly floured surface and knead the dough for 10 minutes, or until it is smooth, silky, and elastic.

Form the dough into a ball and place it in a large oiled bowl. Turn the dough over to coat it with oil. Cover the bowl with plastic wrap or a damp kitchen towel and let it rise in a warm, draft-free place for 1 hour, or until doubled in size. Or, refrigerate the dough to rise slowly overnight. The next morning, remove the dough from the refrigerator and let stand in a warm place for at least 1 hour.

Ten minutes before the end of the rising period, make the filling. In a medium saucepan, melt the butter over low heat. Remove from the heat and whisk in the brown sugar to make a satiny syrup. Spread one-third of the filling onto a 12 by 16 by 1-inch-deep baking sheet, leaving a 2-inch border free of filling.

Transfer the dough to a lightly floured surface and roll it out into a 20 by 8-inch rectangle. Evenly spread the remaining syrup over the dough and sprinkle it with the cinnamon. Distribute the pecans over the gooey dough. Starting with the long edge closest to you, roll the dough up like a jelly roll (see page 29). Using a sharp knife, cut into twenty 1-inch-thick slices and place, cut side up, touching each other on the prepared pan. Let rest in a warm place for 15 minutes. Meanwhile, preheat the oven to 350°F.

Bake on the middle rack of the oven for 25 minutes, or until brown and bubbly. Being very careful not to get burned, use a metal spatula to invert the rolls, syrup side up, onto a serving dish. Let cool for at least 10 minutes before eating.

Maybe the Cheese Board keeps going because there is a wisdom in the collective, a wisdom in the group that is not readily apparent to its members. When the group gets together, I think there is a metaknowledge. I think that this group knowledge functions as a safety guard that gives us a higher kind of intuition.

—D. W.

The music we are playing together here in the store is great fun. We do it not just because we might record it, but to spend time together after the shift. When I was young, music was my life. This group is made up of so many different cultures. My idea is that someone from each culture could teach us a song in their own language.　　　　—MATEO

Dan was talking to people and found out about all the different instruments they played. He had the idea that we should just get together and see what happens. I play the mandolin, and I love it. I'm learning as we go. We play music that I've never even heard before, let alone would have thought of playing: Fellini movie music, mariachi music, some Tex-Mex stuff, and a lot of strange accordion and violin music. It's pushing me to get better at my instrument. People are accepting of all the different levels of expertise. That's the great thing about this place.

—PAUL

What I have noticed recently is that there are some incredible groups within the collective that get together and have fun. They play music together or go places, and when they come in they greet each other with hugs. There has been a rebirth of the familial feeling, which was a very big part of the Cheese Board at the beginning that we lost for a while. It's a whole new generation; they're young and this is their family.

—ART

Sticky Buns

The dough for our sticky buns is similar to the challah dough. It is the perfect light, buttery base for the filling of melted butter, brown sugar, and walnuts. We call this filling "goo," and any goo that is left over on the pans after the buns are done baking is hoarded like gold. It is then used in muffins and granola as our secret ingredient.

MAKES 24 BUNS

Preparation time including rising and baking: 2³/₄ hours; active time: 1 hour

2 tablespoons active dry yeast

1 cup warm water

4¹/₂ cups unbleached all-purpose flour

¹/₂ cup sugar

2 teaspoons kosher salt

¹/₂ cup (1 stick) unsalted butter, cut into 1-inch cubes, at room temperature

3 eggs

Filling

1 cup (2 sticks) unsalted butter

2¹/₂ cups packed light brown sugar

2¹/₂ cups walnut halves or pieces

In a small bowl, whisk the yeast into the warm water until dissolved. Let stand for 5 minutes.

In the bowl of a stand mixer or a large bowl, combine the flour, sugar, and salt.

If using a stand mixer, add the butter to the dry ingredients and cut it in with the paddle attachment on low speed for about 4 minutes, or until it is the size of small peas. Add yeast mixture and eggs, and mix until the ingredients are combined, about 2 minutes. Switch to the dough hook, increase the mixer speed to medium, and knead for 10 minutes, or until the dough begins to acquire a satiny sheen. Transfer to a lightly floured surface and knead by hand for a few minutes, until the dough is smooth, silky, and elastic.

If making by hand, add the butter to the dry ingredients and cut it in with a pastry cutter or 2 dinner knives until it is the size of small peas. Add the yeast mixture and eggs, and mix with a wooden spoon until the ingredients are combined. Transfer to a lightly floured surface and knead for 12 minutes, or until the dough is smooth, silky, and elastic.

Form the dough into a ball and place it in a large oiled bowl. Turn the dough over to coat it with oil. Cover the bowl with plastic wrap or a damp kitchen towel and let rise in a warm, draft-free place for 1 hour, or until doubled in size.

Ten minutes before the end of the rising period, make the filling. In a medium saucepan, melt the butter over low heat. Remove from the heat and whisk in the brown sugar to make a satiny syrup. Spread one-third of the filling onto two 12 by 16 by 1-inch-deep baking sheets, leaving a 2-inch border free of filling.

Transfer the dough to a lightly floured surface and roll it out into a 12 by 16-inch rectangle. Evenly spread the remaining syrup over the dough. Distribute the walnuts over the gooey dough. Cut the rectangle in half crosswise to make two 8 by 12-inch rectangles. Starting with the long edge closest to you, roll each of the rectangles up like a jelly roll (see page 29). Using a sharp knife, cut each roll into twelve 1-inch-thick slices and place, cut side up, touching each other on the prepared pans. Let rest in a warm place for 15 minutes. Meanwhile, preheat the oven to 350°F.

Bake on the 2 middle racks of the oven for 25 minutes, or until brown and bubbly. Being very careful not to get burned, use a metal spatula to invert the rolls, syrup side up, onto a serving dish. Let cool for at least 10 minutes before eating.

When you make pecan rolls or sticky buns, the dough covers the entire four by eight-foot table. Then you pour at least a gallon of sticky goo made from brown sugar and melted butter on top of that. Next, you race around the table rolling and cutting as quickly as possible before it pours over the edge. It's utterly impossible to keep from getting covered in the stuff. I always have to change my apron afterward. **—URSULA**

toasted. Add the honey and brown sugar, reduce the heat to low, and stir until melted and combined. Remove from the heat and stir in the vanilla extract.

In a large bowl, combine the oats, coconut, sunflower seeds, and sesame seeds. Add the sugar mixture and toss until the oats are evenly coated.

Spread the granola evenly on the prepared pan. Place in the oven on the middle rack and bake for 15 minutes. Remove from the oven and stir to redistribute the granola. Bake for an additional 10 minutes, or until golden brown.

Let cool completely on the baking sheet. Store the granola in an airtight container.

Killer Granola

Our granola is made with coconut, nuts, and butter, which give it a cookielike flavor. The membership opted to call it Killer Granola after a concerned collectivist explained that most people think of granola as a low-fat healthful food. The name says it all.

MAKES 3 CUPS GRANOLA
Preparation time: 40 minutes

> 2 tablespoons unsalted butter
> Pinch of salt
> 1 cup chopped pecans or other nuts
> 2 teaspoons honey
> 1/4 cup packed light brown sugar
> 1/8 teaspoon pure vanilla extract
> 1 1/4 cups old-fashioned rolled oats
> 1/2 cup unsweetened coconut flakes
> 1/2 cup sunflower seeds
> 1/4 cup sesame seeds

Preheat the oven to 325°F. Line a baking sheet with parchment paper or a baking mat.

In a small saucepan, melt the butter with the salt over low heat. Add the chopped nuts, increase the heat to medium, and cook, stirring frequently, for 5 minutes, or until lightly

Killer Granola Cookies

Beverly, a sales representative for a cheese distributor we do business with, developed these cookies. She had been enjoying our granola as a breakfast cereal and decided to try it in a cookie recipe.

MAKES ABOUT 36 COOKIES
Preparation time including baking: 45 minutes

> 1 cup (2 sticks) unsalted butter at room temperature
> 3/4 cup firmly packed light brown sugar
> 1 1/2 cups Killer Granola (see opposite)
> 1 teaspoon pure vanilla extract
> 1/2 teaspoon kosher salt
> 2 scant cups all-purpose flour
> 1/3 cup chopped pecans

If using a stand mixer, cream the butter and brown sugar together in the bowl with the paddle attachment on medium speed for about 4 minutes, until light and fluffy. Add the granola, vanilla extract, salt, flour, and pecans. Mix just until the ingredients are incorporated.

If making by hand, cream the butter and sugar together in a large bowl with a wooden spoon until light and fluffy. Add the granola, vanilla extract, salt, flour, and pecans. Mix just until incorporated.

Transfer the dough to a lightly floured surface and divide it into 2 pieces. Using your palms, roll each piece into a log about 4½ inches long and 2 inches wide. Wrap in plastic and refrigerate for at least 2 hours or up to 24 hours..

Preheat the oven to 350°F. Line 2 baking sheets with parchment paper or baking mats.

Cut each log into ¼-inch-thick pieces and place the cookies 1 inch apart on the prepared pans. Bake on the 2 middle racks of the oven for about 20 minutes, or until the cookies are golden brown. Transfer the cookies to a wire rack to cool.

The market is very important in many cultures because that is where people meet and see each other. We're a community here. We know the customers and they know us and know that we will treat them well. For me that part is important—I couldn't work anywhere where I can't have this relationship with the customer.

—JESÚS

Shortbread

This is one of the first sweets that appeared for sale at the Cheese Board. These cookies are less salty and sugary than most versions of shortbread—the butter provides most of the flavor. If you leave the butter out at room temperature for an hour before mixing the dough, the task of creaming it with the sugar is considerably easier. The shortbread recipes that follow this one are variations on the master recipe. Shortbread keeps well for up to 1 month in an airtight container.

MAKES 24 COOKIES
Preparation time including baking: 45 minutes

⅔ cup (1 stick plus 3 tablespoons) unsalted butter at room temperature

½ cup sugar

¼ teaspoon kosher salt

2¼ cups unbleached all-purpose flour

Preheat the oven to 350°F. Line 2 baking sheets with parchment paper or baking mats.

If using a stand mixer, add the butter, sugar, and salt to the bowl. With the paddle attachment on medium speed, cream the mixture together for about 4 minutes, until light and fluffy. Add 2 cups of the flour and mix on low speed for 2 minutes, or until blended. Gradually add the remaining ¼ cup flour by the tablespoonful as needed to make a smooth dough.

If making by hand, add the butter, sugar, and salt to a large bowl. Cream the mixture together with a wooden spoon until light and fluffy. Add 2 cups of the flour and mix until blended. Gradually add the remaining ¼ cup flour by the tablespoonful as needed to make a smooth dough.

Transfer the dough to a lightly floured surface. Pat it into an oblong shape, then roll it out with a floured rolling pin to a thickness of ½ inch. Using a knife, cut the dough into 2½-inch squares. Using a lightly floured metal spatula, lift the cookies and slide them off onto the prepared pans, placing them at least 1 inch apart.

Bake on the 2 middle racks of the oven for 15 minutes. Rotate the pans and bake for another 10 minutes, or until the cookies are light golden brown. Let cool completely on the baking sheets, set on wire racks. Store in an airtight container.

The bottom line at our meetings is compromise. If you say ten and I say five, we argue, and then we settle on six or seven, and we're happy about it.

—YESHI

This is more than a job, this is a second home.

—STU

Ginger Shortbread

These cookies are spicy and crisp, with a distinct bite. We roll them very thinly and cut them out with a ravioli cutter to give them a decorative look. The wavy edge also helps to distinguish them from the other types of shortbread we sell. Ginger shortbread is best baked until a deep golden brown.

MAKES 48 COOKIES

Preparation time including baking: 50 minutes

1½ inches by 3 inches of fresh ginger, peeled (about 1½ ounces)
⅔ cup candied ginger
Dash of finely ground white pepper
1 cup (2 sticks) unsalted butter at room temperature
½ cup sugar
½ teaspoon kosher salt
2¼ cups unbleached all-purpose flour

Preheat the oven to 350°F. Line 3 baking sheets with parchment paper or baking mats.

In a food processor, combine the fresh ginger, candied ginger, and pepper. Process for 1 minute, or until both gingers are finely ground. Or, chop finely by hand using a sharp chef's knife. Don't be concerned about the ginger hairs; the fibers don't present a problem later on.

If using a stand mixer, add the butter, sugar, and salt to the bowl. With the paddle attachment on medium speed, cream the mixture together for about 4 minutes, until light and fluffy. Add the ginger purée and mix for 2 minutes, or until blended. Add 2 cups of the flour and mix on low speed for 2 minutes, or until blended. Gradually add the remaining ¼ cup flour by the tablespoonful as needed to make a smooth dough.

If making by hand, add the butter, sugar, and salt to a large bowl. Cream the mixture together with a wooden spoon until light and fluffy. Stir in the ginger purée until blended. Add 2 cups of the flour and mix until blended. Gradually add the remaining ¼ cup flour by the tablespoonful as needed to make a smooth dough.

Transfer the dough to a lightly floured surface and divide it into 2 pieces. Pat each piece into an oblong shape, then roll it out with a floured rolling pin to a thickness of ⅛ inch. Using a ravioli cutter or a knife, cut the dough into 2 by 3-inch rectangles. Using a lightly floured metal spatula, lift the cookies and slide them off onto the prepared pans, placing them at least 1 inch apart. Repeat with the second piece of dough.

Bake on the 2 middle racks of the oven for 10 minutes. Rotate the pans and bake for another 10 minutes, or until the cookies are deep golden brown. Remember: Thin cookies bake quickly; these will change from being almost done to totally done in a flash! Let cool completely on the baking sheets, set on wire racks. Repeat the process for the third sheet of cookies. Store in an airtight container.

I try to avoid buying stringy ginger. Ideally it should be smooth (not wrinkly) and firm, and not have too many little knobs because they make peeling more labor-intensive. If there are a lot of little knobs, I cut them off. To peel ginger, I use the European-style potato peeler—it's sharper and a lot easier on your wrists.

—OLIVIA

Hazelnut Shortbread

Hazelnuts add richness and a crunchy texture to basic shortbread. Toast the hazelnuts to make a cookie with a strong hazelnut flavor.

MAKES 30 COOKIES

Preparation time including baking: 45 minutes

> $^2/_3$ cup (1 stick plus 3 tablespoons) unsalted butter at room temperature
> $^1/_2$ cup sugar
> $^1/_2$ teaspoon kosher salt
> $2^1/_2$ cups all-purpose flour
> 1 cup coarsely chopped toasted hazelnuts (see page 23)

Preheat the oven to 350°F. Line 2 baking sheets with parchment paper or baking mats.

If using a stand mixer, add the butter, sugar, and salt to the bowl. With the paddle attachment on medium speed, cream the mixture together for about 4 minutes, until light and fluffy. Add $2^1/_4$ cups of the flour and mix on low speed for 2 minutes, or until blended. Gradually add the remaining $^1/_4$ cup flour by the tablespoonful as needed to make a smooth dough. Add the hazelnuts and mix until incorporated.

If making by hand, combine the butter, sugar, and salt in a large bowl. Cream the mixture together with a wooden spoon until light and fluffy. Add $2^1/_4$ cups of the flour and mix until blended. Gradually add the remaining $^1/_4$ cup flour by the tablespoonful as needed to make a smooth dough. Stir in the hazelnuts until incorporated.

Transfer the dough to a lightly floured surface. Pat it into an oblong shape, then roll it out with a floured rolling pin to a thickness of $^1/_2$ inch. Using a knife, cut the dough into $2^1/_2$-inch squares. Using a lightly floured metal spatula, lift the cookies and slide them off onto the prepared pans, placing them at least 1 inch apart.

Bake on the 2 middle racks of the oven for 15 minutes. Rotate the pans and bake for another 10 minutes, or until the cookies are light golden brown. Let cool completely on the baking sheets, set on wire racks. Store in an airtight container.

Lemon Shortbread

One of the challenges in developing a new bread or pastry is finding the time to make it and the oven space in a crowded baking schedule to bake it. This cookie appears now and again, when the Monday morning crew can swing it. Using a food processor to pulverize the candied lemon peel into the sugar works best; if you don't have a food processor you can mince the lemon peel into the sugar with a sharp chef's knife to achieve a similar effect.

MAKES 36 COOKIES

Preparation time including baking: 45 minutes

> 1 cup plus 2 tablespoons sugar
> $^3/_4$ cup candied lemon peel
> 1 cup (2 sticks) unsalted butter at room temperature
> $^3/_4$ teaspoon kosher salt
> $1^2/_3$ cups unbleached all-purpose flour

Preheat the oven to 350°F. Line 3 baking sheets with parchment paper or baking mats.

In a blender or a food processor, combine the sugar and lemon peel. Process for 1 minute, or until the peel is finely ground. Or, combine the sugar and peel on a cutting board and mince the peel into the sugar using a sharp chef's knife.

If using a stand mixer, add the butter, salt, and lemon sugar to the bowl. With the paddle attachment on medium speed, cream the mixture together for about 4 minutes, until light and fluffy. Add $1^1/_3$ cups of the flour and mix on low speed for 2 minutes, or until blended. Gradually add the remaining $^1/_3$ cup flour by the tablespoonful as needed to make a smooth dough.

If making by hand, add the butter, salt, and lemon sugar to a large bowl. Cream the mixture together with a wooden spoon until light and fluffy. Add 1⅓ cups of the flour and mix until blended. Gradually add the remaining ⅓ cup flour by the tablespoonful as needed to make a smooth dough.

Transfer the dough to a lightly floured surface. Pat it into an oblong shape, then roll it out with a floured rolling pin to a thickness of ⅜ inch. Using a ravioli cutter or a knife, cut the dough into 2½-inch squares. Using a lightly floured metal spatula, lift the cookies and slide them off onto the prepared pans, placing them at least 1 inch apart.

Bake on the 2 middle racks of the oven for 15 minutes. Rotate the pans and bake for another 10 minutes, or until the cookies are light golden brown. Let cool on the baking sheets, set on wire racks. Repeat the process for the third sheet of cookies. Store in an airtight container.

In the beginning, it was hard making decisions in meetings. I didn't feel like I really knew what was going on. Some new people get right into voting, but it took me awhile to understand the place and feel confident voting.

—WILLA

I think the way we make decisions is fair. People are heard. Some people have more ideas than others do, but that's no problem for me because I feel they have a lot more experience than I do. I am becoming more and more comfortable at meetings. At first I was embarrassed to talk. Now I speak more because I know people better. —FRANCISCO

Chocolate-Drizzled Stars, Trees, or Hearts

Here's an easy holiday cookie. While it looks fancy, there is nothing to it. We make these in star and tree shapes during the winter holidays and in the shape of hearts for Valentine's Day.

Preparation time including baking: 55 minutes

8 ounces bittersweet chocolate, coarsely chopped
Shortbread cookies in shapes of stars, trees, or hearts (your choice, pages 67–69)

In a double boiler, melt the chocolate over barely simmering water (see page 17).

Use a rubber spatula to drizzle lines of chocolate over the tops of the cookies, crisscrossing to create interesting patterns. Let the chocolate set for at least 2 hours prior to handling the cookies.

Our product is the result of our collective process. Everybody's input is valued. Every bread you see on the shelf is the culmination of many minute decisions made by a series of bakers.

—CATHY

I had never baked or been in a bakery setting when I started working at the Cheese Board. People encouraged me to learn dough-making even though I had only been here three months. The trust that people had in me was pretty incredible. That trust adds to the feeling that we are really a part of our business. Both the product we sell and the process by which we run our business are important to me. While I very much care about what our product looks like, I love that so many of us get to make the doughs and bake. Sometimes the person who is making the doughs or baking isn't always the best person for the job. But I am committed to, and love, the idea that we don't just say, "Oh, these people get to do this because they are naturally good at it and these people don't get to." That, to me, goes totally against who and what we are. Everyone working here knows that opportunity is there for them if they want it.

—SHEHANNA

CHAPTER TWO

YEASTED BREADS

AT THE CHEESE BOARD, we separate our breads into two categories: sourdough breads and yeasted breads. Since a sourdough starter is made from captured wild yeast, breads made with a sourdough starter technically belong within the yeasted bread group; however, what we mean by "yeasted" dough is a dough that is made with commercial yeast. The rising times are short compared to sourdough breads—you can easily make a yeasted bread in three to four hours, a fun way to spend a small part of your day.

The same principles apply when making a yeasted dough as when making a sourdough. It is important to use fresh ingredients, knead the dough long enough to pass the windowpane test, let it rise the appropriate time, and bake the loaves at the correct temperature. Some yeasted doughs, like the challah and the Sunday Bread, are very forgiving, with a lot of room for trial and error. The whole-wheat breads are a little trickier. Because of the

dense quality of the grains in these doughs, they can become very heavy loaves of bread if not handled properly. Whole-wheat doughs tend to be stickier in the kneading stages than other doughs. Don't be tempted to skimp on the water in order to make the dough more manageable—it is ample amounts of water and kneading that make these breads successful.

Many of the doughs in this chapter are shaped and then placed into traditional loaf pans. In the early years at the Cheese Board, all of the breads were shaped into rounds and baked on baking sheets, which made for an old-world rustic look. Then some of us began to complain that the only way to make a respectable sandwich was to use the two center slices. These loaf breads were developed to address the need of many Cheese Boarders (and their family members) for a proletariat sandwich bread: a hearty whole-wheat bread to smear peanut butter and jelly on.

YEASTED BREADS

Challah 75

   Holiday Challah. 76

Sunday Bread. 76

Potato Bread 78

Corn Oat Molasses Bread 80

Sesame Sunflower Bread. 81

Plain and Simple Bread 82

Coriander Wheat Bread. 83

Multigrain Bread. 84

The beauty of this place is the fact that we are owners and that we are so proud of this place. We really care about what we make. We feel like it has to be perfect; if it isn't, we discuss it among ourselves and decide whether to pull it off the shelves or mark it down. I love that. That's what the whole place is about. Everyone has a voice because it is *our* business.

—ERIN

Challah

We make this braided egg bread every Friday morning, and more people reserve it on a regular basis than any other bread we make. Our challah is light and airy and faintly sweet. The tops of the loaves can be left plain and shiny, or sprinkled with sesame or poppy seeds, as you like.

MAKES 3 LOAVES
Preparation time including rising and baking: 3½ hours;
active time: 50 minutes

2 tablespoons active dry yeast

1 cup warm water

4½ cups bread flour

½ cup sugar

2 teaspoons kosher salt

½ cup (1 stick) unsalted butter, cut into 1-inch cubes, at room temperature

5 eggs

2 tablespoons poppy or sesame seeds (optional)

In a small bowl, whisk the yeast into the warm water until dissolved. Let stand for 5 minutes.

In the bowl of a stand mixer or a large bowl, combine the flour, sugar, and salt.

If using a stand mixer, add the butter to the dry ingredients and cut it in with the paddle attachment on low speed for about 4 minutes, or until it is the size of small peas. Add the yeast mixture and 3 of the eggs, and mix until the ingredients are combined, about 2 minutes. Switch to the dough hook, increase the mixer speed to medium, and knead for about 10 minutes, or until the dough loses its rough texture. Transfer to a lightly floured surface and knead by hand for a few minutes, until the dough is smooth and elastic.

If making by hand, add the butter to the dry ingredients and cut it in with a pastry cutter or 2 dinner knives until it is the size of small peas. Add the yeast mixture and 3 of the eggs, and mix with a wooden spoon until the ingredients are combined. Transfer to a lightly floured surface and knead for 12 minutes, or until the dough is smooth and elastic.

Form the dough into a ball and place it in a large oiled bowl. Turn the dough over to coat it with oil. Cover the bowl with plastic wrap or a damp kitchen towel and let rise in a warm, draft-free place for 1 hour, or until doubled in size.

Transfer the dough to a lightly floured surface and divide it into 3 pieces. Gently form each piece into a loose round (see page 26) and cover with a floured kitchen towel. Let rest for 10 minutes. Shape each piece into a 3-stranded braid (see page 29).

Line 2 baking sheets with parchment paper or baking mats. Place 2 loaves on a prepared pan and 1 loaf on the second pan, leaving plenty of room between the 2 loaves so they do not touch each other as they rise and bake. Cover the loaves with a floured kitchen towel and let them rise in a warm place for about 45 minutes, or until increased in size by one-third and a finger pressed into the dough leaves an impression.

Fifteen minutes before the loaves have finished rising, arrange the oven racks in the upper and lower thirds of the oven. Preheat the oven to 375°F.

In a small bowl, whisk the remaining 2 eggs. Using a pastry brush, brush the top and sides of each loaf with the beaten eggs. Repeat this step and sprinkle the breads with poppy seeds or sesame seeds.

Bake for 15 minutes, then rotate the pans front to back and trade their rack positions. Bake for another 20 minutes, for a total baking time of 35 minutes, or until the loaves are golden brown and sound hollow when tapped on the bottom. Transfer the loaves to wire racks to cool.

Note: This recipe can be made into 1 large challah for special occasions. Remove all but the middle rack from the oven, preheat the oven to 350°F, and bake the large challah for 45 to 50 minutes. This large challah is also beautiful shaped as a 2-stranded turban (see page 30).

Holiday Challah

In early September, our customers call to remind us to make this variation on our usual Friday challah for Rosh Hashanah and Yom Kippur. This celebratory bread is filled with dried fruit and shaped like an ornate turban.

½ cup golden raisins
½ cup diced dried apricots
½ cup dried currants

Add the golden raisins, diced dried apricots, and dried currants to the challah dough when the kneading is almost finished. Proceed with the regular challah recipe, shaping the dough into three 2-stranded turbans (see page 30).

Every Friday I make the challah, joining the long tradition of challah makers at the Cheese Board. Although I make several other breads on Fridays, my whole day (which starts at 4:30 A.M.) leads up to the rolling and baking of this bread. Our recipe is rich in eggs and butter, and sweetened with white sugar. We make four hundred pounds of challah dough, which is proofed in six twenty-gallon plastic bins. Four members gather around the rolling table, and for one hour we braid the straw-colored dough into 160 loaves. The sun shines into the store from the front window, and while some of the customers watch the bread-making process, we talk, laugh, and roll bread. Sometimes it seems like we will never be finished, and when we finally are, I want to roll just one more loaf.

—CATHY

Sunday Bread

Although this cinnamon-egg bread is named Sunday Bread, we make it on Saturday. Studded with nuts and raisins, it is meant to be a festive addition to a Sunday brunch. It resembles a braided turban when baked and is a shiny mahogany in color.

MAKES 2 LOAVES
Preparation time including rising and baking: 6 hours; active time: 50 minutes

1 tablespoon plus 1 teaspoon active dry yeast
¼ cup warm water
3 cups bread flour
⅔ cup unbleached all-purpose flour
2 teaspoons kosher salt
2 teaspoons ground cinnamon
⅔ cup buttermilk
3 eggs
½ cup honey
⅓ cup unsalted butter, melted and cooled
½ cup raisins
½ cup whole almonds
½ cup walnuts

In a small bowl, whisk the yeast into the warm water until dissolved. Let stand for 5 minutes.

In the bowl of a stand mixer or a large bowl, combine the flours, salt, and cinnamon.

If using a stand mixer, add the yeast mixture, buttermilk, 2 of the eggs, the honey, and melted butter to the bowl. Using the paddle attachment on low speed, mix until the ingredients are combined, about 2 minutes. Switch to the dough hook, increase the mixer speed to medium, and knead for about 10 minutes, or until the dough loses its rough texture. Add the raisins and the nuts and continue to knead just until incorporated. Transfer to a lightly floured surface and knead by hand for a few minutes, until the dough is smooth and elastic.

If making by hand, add the yeast mixture, buttermilk, 2 of the eggs, the honey, and melted butter to the bowl and

mix with a wooden spoon until the ingredients are combined. Transfer to a lightly floured surface and knead for 12 minutes, or until the dough is tacky and soft. Flatten the dough into a 1-inch-thick round. Add the raisins and the nuts, fold the dough over, and continue to knead for a few minutes, until the dough is smooth and elastic.

Form the dough into a ball and place it in a large oiled bowl. Turn the dough over to coat it with oil. Cover the bowl with plastic wrap or a damp kitchen towel and let rise in a warm, draft-free place for 3 hours, or until doubled in size.

Transfer the dough to a lightly floured surface and divide it into 2 pieces. Gently form each piece into a loose round (see page 26) and cover with a floured kitchen towel. Let rest for 10 minutes. Shape each piece into a 2-stranded turban (see page 30).

Line a baking sheet with parchment paper or a baking mat. Place the loaves on the prepared pan, leaving at least 4 inches between the loaves. Cover them with a floured kitchen towel and let rise in a warm place for 1 to 1¼ hours, or until increased in size by one-third and a finger pressed into the dough leaves an impression.

Fifteen minutes before the loaves have finished rising, preheat the oven to 375°F.

In a small bowl, whisk the remaining egg. Using a pastry brush, brush the top and sides of each loaf with the beaten egg. Repeat this step.

Bake on the middle rack of the oven for 20 minutes, then turn the baking sheet front to back. Bake 20 minutes longer, for a total baking time of 40 minutes, or until the loaves are shiny, deep brown, and sound hollow when tapped on the bottom. Transfer the loaves to a wire rack to cool.

Initially, I wasn't interested in the fact that the Cheese Board is a collective. It was attractive because it was a job that paid much better than what I was making. Now I feel I'm lucky to have worked at the Cheese Board, partly because of the collectiveness and because of the opportunity it has given me to pursue my goals, whether they are work related or not. I actually enjoy coming to work. I've worked in a regular work place, a nine-to-five office, and I know what it feels like to not want to go to work. I feel that I have a luxury of time that somebody earning six figures doesn't have. It's very precious to me. Only in a place like this could I have that.

—OLIVIA

Potato Bread

A simple white bread, potato bread is a vigorous riser with a particularly light, springy texture because potatoes facilitate yeast growth. In order to give the loaves a chewy, slightly crisp crust, we steam them during baking (see page 33). A dash of black pepper gives this bread a bite that balances the sweetness of the potatoes and makes it the perfect base for a croque-monsieur.

MAKES 2 LOAVES
Preparation time including rising and baking: 3³/₄ hours; active time: 45 minutes

1 tablespoon plus ¹/₂ teaspoon active dry yeast

¹/₄ cup warm water

4 cups bread flour

1 tablespoon plus ¹/₂ teaspoon kosher salt

1 teaspoon coarsely ground black pepper

1 tablespoon olive oil

1¹/₄ cups lukewarm water

2 russet potatoes, baked, cooled, and shredded

In a small bowl, whisk the yeast into the warm water until dissolved. Let stand for 5 minutes.

In the bowl of a stand mixer or a large bowl, combine the flour, salt, and pepper.

If using a stand mixer, add the yeast mixture, olive oil, and lukewarm water to the bowl. Using the paddle attachment on low speed, mix until the ingredients are combined, about 2 minutes. Switch to the dough hook, increase the mixer speed to medium, and knead for 7 minutes. Add the shredded potatoes and continue to knead for 1 minute, or until the potatoes are incorporated. (Do not knead the dough too long at this point, or the potatoes will cause it to become gummy.) Transfer to a lightly floured surface and knead by hand for a few minutes, until the dough is soft but still holds its shape.

If making by hand, add the yeast mixture, olive oil, and lukewarm water to the bowl and mix with a wooden spoon until the ingredients are combined. Transfer to a lightly floured surface and knead for 10 minutes. Flatten the dough out, put the shredded potatoes on top, and roll the dough into a ball. Continue to knead for 2 minutes, or until the potatoes are incorporated and the dough is soft but still holds its shape. (Do not knead the dough too long at this point, or the potatoes will cause it to become gummy.)

Form the dough into a ball and place it in a large oiled bowl. Turn the dough over to coat it with oil. Cover the bowl with plastic wrap or a damp kitchen towel and let rise in a warm, draft-free place for 1 hour, or until doubled in size.

Lightly spray 2 loaf pans with cooking spray. Transfer the dough to a lightly floured surface and divide it into 2 pieces. Gently form each piece into a loose round (see page 26) and cover with a floured kitchen towel. Let rest for 10 minutes. Shape each piece into a loaf (see page 28) and place in the prepared pans. Sprinkle flour over the tops of the loaves and spread it out evenly. Cover with a floured kitchen towel and let rise in a warm place for 45 minutes, or until the dough has risen 1½ inches above the rim of the pan and a finger pressed into the dough leaves an impression.

Fifteen minutes before the loaves have finished rising, remove all but the middle rack from the oven. Place a metal roasting pan on the floor of the oven. Preheat the oven to 450°F.

Slash the top of each of the loaves (see page 31). Let them rest for 5 minutes to allow the slashes to open.

Pour ½ cup cold water into a measuring cup and add enough ice cubes to bring the volume to 1 cup. Working

quickly so that you don't lose too much heat, place the loaf pans in the oven and pour the ice water into the roasting pan. Immediately close the oven door to maintain a steamy environment.

Bake for 5 minutes, then prepare another round of ice water and repeat the procedure. Bake 10 minutes longer, then rotate the pans front to back and switch sides from left to right. Bake 25 to 30 minutes longer, for a total baking time of 40 to 45 minutes, or until the loaves are golden and sound hollow when tapped on the bottom. Unmold the loaves onto a wire rack to cool.

"SO, HOW DOES THE CHEESE BOARD WORK?"

I love telling people all about the Cheese Board. I probably love doing it too much. Sometimes I find people's eyes glazing over after they have asked me, "So how *does* the Cheese Board work?" and I launch into my collective-work explanation. For me, the most fun is trying to explain how we function to people who have spent their lives working with regular businesses. The whole idea that important business decisions can be made by group consensus seems impossible to these people. They usually exclaim, "You can't run a business that way! It just won't work!" But at the same time they are fascinated by the idea of shared power, responsibility, and control. I always tell them that with no boss breathing down my neck, if business decisions are made that I disagree with, at least I had input into the decision-making process.

One of my favorite of such conversations occurred over a dinner with a good friend who is a successful developer and owns a great deal of retail space. He asked me how much we grossed a year, and then before I could respond, he said, "No, wait, I can tell you. What is the square footage of your store?" We estimated the footage, he worked out a standard formula for gross income per square foot, and he proudly announced the result. When I told him that we make twice that amount, he was astounded. I felt surprised myself. It felt good to learn that we were successful by anybody's standards.

—Charlie

Corn Oat Molasses Bread

A relative of anadama bread, this bread has a high, rounded shape. The cornmeal adds crunchiness, and toasting this bread makes it even more nutty and crisp.

MAKES 2 LOAVES

Preparation time including rising and baking: 3½ hours; active time: 40 minutes

1 tablespoon active dry yeast
1 cup warm water
3 cups bread flour
2¾ cups whole-wheat flour
¾ cup plus ¼ cup medium-grind yellow cornmeal
¾ cup old-fashioned rolled oats
1 tablespoon plus 1 teaspoon kosher salt
1¾ cups lukewarm water
⅔ cup dark unsulfured molasses

In a small bowl, whisk the yeast into the warm water until dissolved. Let stand for 5 minutes.

In the bowl of a stand mixer or a large bowl, combine the flours, the ¾ cup cornmeal, the oats, and salt.

If using a stand mixer, add the yeast mixture, lukewarm water, and molasses to the bowl. Using the paddle attachment on low speed, mix until the ingredients are combined, about 2 minutes. Switch to the dough hook, increase the mixer speed to medium, and knead for 10 minutes, or until the dough pulls away from the sides of the bowl. Transfer to a lightly floured surface and knead by hand for a few minutes, until the dough is soft but still holds its shape.

If making by hand, add the yeast mixture, lukewarm water, and molasses to the bowl and mix with a wooden spoon until the ingredients are combined. Transfer to a lightly floured surface and knead for at least 12 minutes, or until the dough is soft but still holds its shape.

Form the dough into a ball and place it in a large oiled bowl. Turn the dough over to coat it with oil. Cover the bowl with plastic wrap or a damp kitchen towel and let rise in a warm, draft-free place for 1 hour, or until doubled in size.

Lightly spray 2 loaf pans with cooking spray. Transfer the dough to a lightly floured surface and divide it into 2 pieces. Gently form each piece into a loose round (see page 26) and cover with a floured kitchen towel. Let rest for 10 minutes. Shape each piece into a loaf (see page 28) and place in the prepared pans. Using a spray bottle, mist the tops of the loaves with water and sprinkle with the ¼ cup cornmeal. Cover with a floured kitchen towel and let rise in a warm place for 45 minutes to 1 hour, or until the dough has risen 1½ inches above the rim of the pan and a finger pressed into the dough leaves an impression.

Fifteen minutes before the loaves have finished rising, slash the tops (see page 31). Remove all but the middle rack from the oven. Preheat the oven to 450°F.

Place the loaves in the oven and bake for 5 minutes. Reduce the oven temperature to 400°F and bake 20 minutes longer. Turn the loaf pans around front to back and switch sides left to right. Bake 15 to 20 minutes longer, for a total baking time of 40 to 45 minutes, or until the loaves are a deep brown and sound hollow when tapped on the bottom. Unmold the loaves onto a wire rack to cool.

Lots of people have come and gone; each person has left a bit of themselves in how the shifts work and how we work together. I feel that I've been changed. I feel like I do put myself into the job and the process of working here. I know I could do more, and the fact of that knowing means I am not done.

—JOHN

Sesame Sunflower Bread

This bread was born out of desperation. The morning baker came into the store to find that the ingredients for multigrain bread were not in stock, so she improvised this recipe. Like all our bread recipes, this one has been refined over the years by succeeding generations of bakers. It makes a lightly sweetened and moist loaf.

MAKES 2 LOAVES
Preparation time including rising and baking: 3½ hours;
active time: 40 minutes

1 tablespoon active dry yeast
1 cup warm water
7 cups whole-wheat bread flour
½ cup old-fashioned rolled oats
⅓ cup sunflower seeds
⅓ cup plus ¼ cup sesame seeds
1 tablespoon plus 1 teaspoon kosher salt
2 cups lukewarm water
½ cup honey

In a small bowl, whisk the yeast into the warm water until dissolved. Let stand for 5 minutes.

In the bowl of a stand mixer or a large bowl, combine the flour, oats, sunflower seeds, the ⅓ cup sesame seeds, and the salt.

If using a stand mixer, add the yeast mixture, lukewarm water, and honey to the bowl. Using the paddle attachment on low speed, mix until the ingredients are combined, about 2 minutes. Switch to the dough hook, increase the mixer speed to medium, and knead for 10 minutes, or until the dough pulls away from the sides of the bowl. Transfer to a lightly floured surface and knead by hand for a few minutes, until the dough is soft but still holds its shape.

If making by hand, add the yeast mixture, lukewarm water, and honey to the bowl and mix with a wooden spoon until the ingredients are combined. Transfer to a lightly floured surface and knead for at least 12 minutes, or until the dough is soft but still holds its shape.

Form the dough into a ball and place it in a large oiled bowl. Turn the dough over to coat it with oil. Cover the bowl with plastic wrap or a damp kitchen towel and let rise in a warm, draft-free place for 1 hour, or until doubled in size.

Lightly spray 2 loaf pans with cooking spray. Transfer the dough to a lightly floured surface and divide it into 2 pieces. Gently form each piece into a loose round (see page 26) and cover with a floured kitchen towel. Let rest for 10 minutes. Shape each piece into a loaf (see page 28) and place in the prepared pans. Using a spray bottle, mist the tops of the loaves with water and sprinkle them with the ¼ cup sesame seeds. Cover with a floured kitchen towel and let rise in warm place for 45 minutes to 1 hour, or until the dough has risen 1 inch above the rim of the pan and a finger pressed into the dough leaves an impression.

Fifteen minutes before the loaves have finished rising, slash the tops (see page 31). Remove all but the middle rack from the oven. Preheat the oven to 450°F.

Place the loaves in the oven and bake for 5 minutes. Reduce the oven temperature to 400°F and bake 20 minutes longer. Turn the loaf pans around front to back and switch sides left to right. Bake 15 to 20 minutes longer, for a total baking time of 40 to 45 minutes, or until the loaves are a deep brown and sound hollow when tapped on the bottom. Unmold the loaves onto a wire rack to cool.

Plain and Simple Bread

We make this loaf on Thursday mornings. It is just what it's called: a plain whole-wheat bread, simple to make and satisfying to eat—the quintessential peanut butter and jelly sandwich bread. As with all whole-wheat bread, the longer you knead the dough, the greater the gluten development and the lighter your final product will be.

MAKES 2 LOAVES
Preparation time including rising and baking: 3½ hours; active time: 40 minutes

- 1 tablespoon active dry yeast
- 1 cup warm water
- 6½ cups whole-wheat flour
- 1 tablespoon kosher salt
- 1½ cups lukewarm water
- ½ cup honey

In a small bowl, whisk the yeast into the warm water until dissolved. Let stand for 5 minutes.

In the bowl of a stand mixer or a large bowl, combine the flour and salt.

If using a stand mixer, add the yeast mixture, lukewarm water, and honey to the bowl. Using the paddle attachment on low speed, mix until the ingredients are combined, about 2 minutes. Switch to the dough hook, increase the mixer speed to medium, and knead for 10 minutes, or until the dough pulls away from the sides of the bowl. Transfer to a lightly floured surface and knead by hand for a few minutes, until the dough is soft but still holds its shape.

If making by hand, add the yeast mixture, lukewarm water, and honey to the bowl and mix with a wooden spoon until the ingredients are combined. Transfer to a lightly floured surface and knead for at least 12 minutes, or until the dough is soft but still holds its shape.

Form the dough into a ball and place it in a large oiled bowl. Turn the dough over to coat it with oil. Cover the bowl with plastic wrap or a damp kitchen towel and let rise in a warm, draft-free place for 1 hour, or until doubled in size.

Lightly spray 2 loaf pans with cooking spray. Transfer the dough to a lightly floured surface and divide it into 2 pieces. Gently form each piece into a loose round (see page 26) and cover with a floured kitchen towel. Let rest for 10 minutes. Shape each piece into a loaf (see page 28) and place in the prepared pans. Sprinkle flour over the tops of the loaves and spread it out evenly. Cover with a floured kitchen towel and let rise in a warm place for 45 minutes to 1 hour, or until the dough has risen 1 inch above the rim of the pan and a finger pressed into the dough leaves an impression.

Fifteen minutes before the loaves have finished rising, slash the tops (see page 31). Remove all but the middle rack from the oven. Preheat the oven to 450°F.

Place the loaves in the oven and bake for 5 minutes. Reduce the oven temperature to 400°F and bake 20 minutes longer. Turn the loaf pans around front to back and switch sides left to right. Bake 15 to 20 minutes longer, for a total baking time of 40 to 45 minutes, or until the loaves are a deep brown and sound hollow when tapped on the bottom. Unmold the loaves onto a wire rack to cool.

I like to laugh, and I never take anything seriously. My wife came into the store and she watched us working and said, "Now I know why you like to work here—it's because all you guys are so crazy!" We're not crazy, we're just fun.

—DWIGHT

Coriander Wheat Bread

This slightly sweet and aromatic whole-wheat bread is quick to rise and easy to make at home. Grind the coriander seeds just before using them for a more intense flavor. We recommend using a stand mixer for two reasons: the dough should be kneaded for a long time to develop the springy texture that is its hallmark, and it is a terrifically sticky, wet dough that is messy to handle.

MAKES 2 LOAVES
Preparation time including rising and baking: 3¹/₂ hours; active time: 45 minutes

1 tablespoon active dry yeast
1 cup warm water
5 cups whole-wheat bread flour
1¹/₄ cups old-fashioned rolled oats
²/₃ cup sunflower seeds
1 tablespoon plus 1 teaspoon kosher salt
2 tablespoons ground coriander
2 cups lukewarm water
¹/₂ cup dark unsulfured molasses

In a small bowl, whisk the yeast into the warm water until dissolved. Let stand for 5 minutes.

In the bowl of a stand mixer or a large bowl, combine the flour, oats, sunflower seeds, salt, and coriander.

If using a stand mixer, add the yeast mixture, lukewarm water, and molasses to the bowl. Using the paddle attachment on low speed, mix until the ingredients are combined, about 2 minutes. Switch to the dough hook, increase the mixer speed to medium, and knead for at least 12 minutes, or until the dough pulls away from the sides of the bowl. Transfer to a lightly floured surface and knead by hand for a few minutes, until the dough is sticky and soft but still holds its shape.

If making by hand, add the yeast mixture, lukewarm water, and molasses to the bowl and mix with a wooden spoon until the ingredients are combined. Transfer to a lightly floured surface and knead for at least 15 minutes, or until the dough is sticky and soft but still holds its shape.

Form the dough into a ball and place it in a large oiled bowl. Turn the dough over to coat it with oil. Cover the bowl with plastic wrap or a damp kitchen towel and let rise in a warm, draft-free place for 1 hour, or until doubled in size.

Lightly spray 2 loaf pans with cooking spray. Transfer the dough to a lightly floured surface and divide it into 2 pieces. Gently form each piece into a loose round (see page 26) and cover with a floured kitchen towel. Let rest for 10 minutes. Shape each piece into a loaf (see page 28) and place in the prepared pans. Sprinkle flour over the tops of the loaves and spread it out evenly. Cover with a floured kitchen towel and let rise in a warm place for 45 minutes to 1 hour, or until the dough has risen 1 inch above the rim of the pan and a finger pressed into the dough leaves an impression.

Fifteen minutes before the bread has finished rising, slash the loaves (see page 31). Remove all but the middle rack from the oven. Preheat the oven to 450°F.

Place the loaves in the oven and bake for 5 minutes. Reduce the oven temperature to 400°F and bake 20 minutes longer. Turn the loaf pans around front to back and switch sides left to right. Bake 15 to 20 minutes longer, for a total baking time of 40 to 45 minutes, or until the loaves are a deep brown and sound hollow when tapped on the bottom. Unmold the loaves onto a wire rack to cool.

If you screw up often enough, you will hear about it. But it's clear that not all of us feel the same way about the products we produce and what's acceptable for sale. It's always been an area of contention. What is overrisen, too dark, overbaked, or burnt? We need a little color chart, a paint chip: if it's not this color, we can't sell it.   —D. W.

Multigrain Bread

This dense multigrain bread made from wheat flour and whole grains is our Saturday-special wheat loaf. The whole millet seeds add crunch; steel-cut oats and cracked wheat add heft. If you like a smoother crumb, soak the steel-cut oats, cracked wheat, and millet overnight to soften them and help integrate them into the dough.

MAKES 2 LOAVES
Preparation time including rising and baking: 4³/₄ hours; active time: 40 minutes

- 1 tablespoon active dry yeast
- 1 cup warm water
- 5 cups whole-wheat bread flour
- ¹/₄ cup steel-cut oats
- ¹/₄ cup cracked wheat
- ¹/₂ cup sesame seeds
- ¹/₄ cup millet
- ¹/₃ cup old-fashioned rolled oats
- ¹/₃ cup wheat bran
- 1 tablespoon plus 1 teaspoon kosher salt
- 1¹/₄ cups lukewarm water
- ²/₃ cup dark unsulfured molasses

In a small bowl, whisk the yeast into the warm water until dissolved. Let stand for 5 minutes.

In the bowl of a stand mixer or a large bowl, combine the flour, steel-cut oats, cracked wheat, sesame seeds, millet, rolled oats, bran, and salt.

If using a stand mixer, add the yeast mixture, lukewarm water, and molasses to the bowl. Using the paddle attachment on low speed, mix until the ingredients are combined, about 2 minutes. Switch to the dough hook, increase the mixer speed to medium, and knead for 10 minutes, or until the dough pulls away from the sides of the bowl. Transfer to a lightly floured surface and knead by hand for a few minutes, until the dough is soft but still holds its shape.

If making by hand, add the yeast mixture, lukewarm water, and molasses to the bowl and mix with a wooden spoon until the ingredients are combined. Transfer to a lightly floured surface and knead for at least 12 minutes, or until the dough is soft but still holds its shape.

Form the dough into a ball and place in a large oiled bowl. Turn the dough over to coat it with oil. Cover the bowl with plastic wrap or a damp kitchen towel and let rise in a warm, draft-free place for 1 to 1½ hours, or until doubled in size.

Lightly spray 2 loaf pans with cooking spray. Transfer the dough to a lightly floured surface and divide it into 2 pieces. Gently form each piece into a loose round (see page 26) and cover with a floured kitchen towel. Let rest for 10 minutes. Shape each piece into a loaf (see page 28) and place in the prepared pans. Sprinkle flour over the tops of the loaves and spread it out evenly. Cover with a floured kitchen towel and let rise in a warm place for 1½ to 1¾ hours, or until the dough has risen ¾ inch above the rim of the pan and a finger pressed into the dough leaves an impression.

Fifteen minutes before the loaves have finished rising, slash the tops (see page 31). Remove all but the middle rack from the oven. Preheat the oven to 450°F.

Place the loaves in the oven and bake for 5 minutes. Reduce the oven temperature to 400°F and bake 20 minutes longer. Turn the loaf pans around front to back and switch sides left to right. Bake 15 to 20 minutes longer, for a total baking time of 40 to 45 minutes, or until the loaves are a deep brown and sound hollow when tapped on the bottom. Unmold the loaves onto a wire rack to cool.

I love moving bread in and out of the oven all morning long.

—ARAYAH

I like production, making lots of things, and I like feeding people. I think that a person should be fed regardless of who they are or what they do or don't do.

—CARRIE

Making food is both an art and a craft. To me, it's life. My mom was a good cook. She had a wok in the fifties, a nice Jewish lady with a wok. I love shopping. I love to watch food grow. I love playing with it. I love eating.

—PAM

Times are so different now from when I joined the collective twenty years ago. Most of the members didn't have kids back then, and our social life centered around the store. Then everyone started having kids. At one time we had twelve infants and toddlers in the collective. With this change we needed so much more from the store—income, benefits, flexibility. While the loss of intimacy was difficult, we managed to transform the collective into an incredibly supportive workplace for families.

—S. S.

CHAPTER THREE

SOURDOUGH BREADS

THE CHEESE BOARD'S sourdough-starter culture is twenty-five years old. Begun simply, with soured milk, flour, and water in a yeast-filled atmosphere, it has been fed and refed all these years. Nearly indestructible, the starter has been passed on to customers, fledgling collectives, friends, and family. It is not our store secret, but it has secrets of its own.

When we began working on the sourdough section for this book, it was tempting just to scoop up two cups of starter from the five-gallon buckets that sit in the dough room at the Cheese Board. But we had vowed to make a homemade product that we could pass on to you, so we forged ahead. The living starters created in our home kitchens launched us into a journey of sourdough bread discovery.

We were surprised that, even with our combined experience of dough making, we could still become so excited with each successful step and be baffled by the simplest failures.

For months we tinkered with starter amounts, rising times, oven temperatures, and steaming techniques, only to be constantly disappointed with gray matte finishes, unsatisfying crumbs, and incomplete flavors. Without professional ovens with powerful internal sprayers and convection fans, it seemed impossible to re-create a baguette like the ones we bake at the Cheese Board. We were disheartened but not discouraged, and kept returning to the drawing board. Since the Cheese Board baguette is one of our specialties, it didn't seem right to offer an inferior product for this book.

After two years of experimenting—and inflicting many homely loaves of bread on friends and family—we finally perfected the recipe for making a beautiful, shiny, crusty baguette in the home kitchen.

This chapter includes the two basic doughs from which we make all our sourdough breads: the master sourdough and the Suburban dough. Although you will not need two years to learn how to make a delightful sourdough loaf, it will likely take you a few attempts to produce a truly great bread. A wild-yeast starter is a less predictable leavener than commercial yeast, but if home-baked sourdoughs are your quest, the journey is worth it.

The methods we developed for baking sourdough at home are based on our experiences using professional baking equipment. At the Cheese Board we bake sourdough loaves at high temperatures (500° to 560°F) and steam them several times. Similar results can be achieved at home with lower oven temperatures by using a baking stone and by steaming certain breads in a two-step process using a metal roasting pan filled with ice water, sometimes in tandem with a spray bottle. With the steaming technique, timing is of the utmost importance to achieve a deep, rich color on the crust; the second steaming is particularly important in producing a crunchy crust on the loaves and a beautiful glossy finish on the baguettes. Baking stones, when thoroughly preheated for at least 45 minutes prior to baking, retain enough heat to keep the oven temperature high during a bake (especially important during a bake that requires the oven door to be opened often). A stone also mimics a wood-fired oven by providing a surface on which to bake breads directly, a wonderful way to make the bottom crust of a bread crunchy.

THE SOURDOUGH EXPERIENCE

When I joined the Cheese Board, I conveniently stepped into a well-developed routine of rotating, feeding, refeeding, and refreshing the twenty-five-year-old starter. Initially, my biggest concern as a novice dough maker was not the condition of the starters, but rather how long to mix each dough, how much water I should use, and what the final temperature should be when the kneading was done. The frothy, bubbly, ammonia-smelling starters were the least of my concerns.

When I finally turned my attention to this ancient method of leavening bread, I began to notice that weather conditions, water temperature, and flour-to-water ratio could all contribute to the condition of the starters. I have read about the science of sourdough—gas emissions and chemical reactions—but for me it still feels like a mystery every time I make sourdough bread. You have to have that leap of faith that the starter will do what it should do.

On a less romantic note, one of the messiest jobs at the Cheese Board is mixing the starters. We make them in five-gallon buckets and have at least fifteen of them on hand. I measure out eight pounds of flour and six pounds of water into the saved starter. Next, I stick my hand—up to my elbow—into the glop and stir it up. What remains on my arm is glue that only a Tuffy scrub brush and three showers can remove.

—Cathy

SOURDOUGH BREADS

Sourdough Starter 90

Master Sourdough 92

Sourdough Baguettes 93

   Bastille Day Baguettes 94

City Bread 97

English Muffins 98

Cheesy Muffins 98

Zampanos 99

Bialys 100

FOCACCIA

Small Olive Focaccia Rounds 101

Tomato, Caper, and Olive Focaccia . . 102

Rosemary Focaccia 104

Sun-Dried Tomato Focaccia 105

Pesto Focaccia 106

Ricotta Salata, Lemon Zest, and
   Cilantro Focaccia 107

Suburban Bread 109

Cheese Rolls 111

Wolverines 114

Sourdough Starter

Thousands of years before commercial yeast was invented, people all over the world used sourdough starter to leaven bread. Water, flour, and wild yeasts from the air combine to create a living culture, the most basic, ancient form of bread leavening. The tradition of passing sourdough starter on to neighbors, family, and friends links us to past and future generations of bread makers.

At any given time at the Cheese Board, we have at least fifteen buckets of sourdough starter in differing stages of fermentation. The buckets are lined up in rows and labeled with the date and the time of day they were mixed. While all the ingredients in the sourdough breads are important, the starter is crucial because it is what enables the bread to rise.

Starting your own homegrown sour culture is a simple process that takes about 12 days to complete. If it is replenished on a regular basis, your starter will last indefinitely. Starter can be left unattended in the refrigerator for up to 1 month. If you wish to bake with a starter that has been refrigerated, you will need to start feeding it (to revive it to full strength) 36 hours before you wish to make bread with it. Rye is a great host for wild yeasts, making it a good addition to a new starter recipe. We use an organic rye flour (see Source List), as we have found that the yeasts grow particularly well when feeding on it.

This starter is the foundation of all the sourdough recipes in this book.

MAKES ABOUT 2 CUPS

> 3 1/2 cups lukewarm water, plus additional depending on baking schedule
>
> 3/4 cup medium organic rye flour
>
> 4 2/3 cups bread flour, plus additional depending on baking schedule

Day 1

In a medium nonreactive (stainless steel, glass, plastic, or ceramic) bowl, using a wooden spoon, stir 1/2 cup of the lukewarm water and the rye flour together until smooth. Cover the bowl loosely with plastic wrap and let stand at room temperature (65° to 70°F) for 48 hours, when small bubbles should begin to appear on the surface.

Day 3

Now you are ready to feed your starter: Stir 2/3 cup of the bread flour into the rye mixture until smooth; it will be the consistency of a thick pancake batter. Put the starter into a nonreactive container with high sides and cover it loosely with plastic wrap. Let stand at room temperature for 48 hours. The starter will have some large bubbles on top and begin to smell like sourdough bread.

Day 5

Remove 1/4 cup of the starter and discard the rest. Return the reserved starter to the container. Add 1/2 cup lukewarm water, scrape down the sides of the container, and mix with a spatula or wooden spoon. Then add 2/3 cup of the bread flour. Mix until the starter is smooth and thick. Cover the container with plastic wrap and let stand at room temperature for 48 hours.

Day 7

Replenish the starter by repeating the instructions for Day 5. Cover the container and allow it to ferment for 48 hours.

Day 9

Replenish the starter again, repeating the instructions for Day 5. Cover the container and allow it to ferment for 24 hours. By Day 9, your starter should have risen 1 1/2 times its original size and fallen back within a 24-hour period.

Day 10

Replenish the starter again, repeating the instructions for Day 5. Cover the container and allow it to ferment for 24 hours.

Day 11

You now have a sourdough starter. You have the following options:

If you plan to bake in the next day or two: You will need to increase the amount of starter so there is enough for the sourdough recipes. Remove 1/4 cup of the starter and discard the rest. Return the reserved starter to the container. Add 1 cup lukewarm water, scrape down the sides of the container, and mix with a spatula or wooden spoon. Add 1⅓ cups bread flour and mix until the starter is smooth. Cover and let stand at room temperature for at least 12 hours, or until bubbly. The starter is now ready to use for baking. Plan to use this starter within the next 12 hours. (Be sure to reserve ¼ cup of the starter to reestablish your starter supply. To do so, follow the recipe for Day 5. Refrigerate the starter directly after feeding it and follow the instructions below about maintaining your starter and reinvigorating it prior to baking.)

If you do not plan to make bread in the next day or two: Replenish the starter again, repeating the instructions for Day 5. Refrigerate the starter directly after feeding it and follow the instructions below about maintaining your starter and reinvigorating it prior to baking.

If you plan to bake regularly: Keep your starter at room temperature, feeding it every 24 hours using the amounts for the first Day 11 option above. The starter should rise easily and become bubbly. Allow a minimum of 12 hours of fermentation before making bread and a maximum of 24 hours.

MAINTAINING YOUR STARTER

With monthly feedings, sourdough starter will last indefinitely in the refrigerator. To feed it, remove it from the refrigerator, discard all but ¼ cup, and stir in ½ cup lukewarm water and ⅔ cup bread flour. Cover and let stand at room temperature for 48 hours. Repeat the process, but return the starter directly to the refrigerator after the second feeding.

REINVIGORATING YOUR STARTER FOR BAKING

To prepare your starter for baking, remove it from the refrigerator, discard all but ¼ cup, and stir in ½ cup lukewarm water and ⅔ cup bread flour. Cover and let stand at room temperature for 24 hours. (The starter should look bubbly and rise and fall back during this time.) Discard all but ¼ cup of starter and stir in 1 cup lukewarm water and 1⅓ cups bread flour. Let stand for an additional 12 hours, or up to 24 hours, before making bread.

Note: You will know that your starter is vigorous if it has grown in size, has bubbles in its interior, and has a sour odor. Your starter may need more or less time to become reinvigorated; generally, the more frequently a starter is used, the less time is needed to bring it up to full potency for dough making.

Starter that has been refrigerated and forgotten for a long time separates into a dark liquid and a firmer mass. Discard the liquid and use the firmer portion for reinvigorating the starter—it will often be fine after a few feedings.

If your starter has developed any kind of mold on the surface or it smells bad (as opposed to just sour), throw it away and start over.

Sometimes customers just don't notice that we make bread here. It's so strange—they see the ovens, they're right there, and they see the bread coming out. Once I was waiting on a guy at the bread counter, a well-dressed guy in his thirties. He grabbed a hot baguette and he was so amazed that it was hot. I said, "Well, it just came out of the oven." And he said, "Came out of the *oven* . . . ?" At first I thought he was pulling my leg because it seemed like he was amazed by the fact that a bread that comes out of the oven is hot. Then I realized he wasn't pulling my leg. I had to bite my tongue to stop myself from being sarcastic! It was the way he said it "Oh . . . oven . . . hot!" and I thought, "Yeah . . . freezer . . . cold!"

—OLIVIA

Master Sourdough

From this master recipe you can make baguettes, City Breads, focaccia, English muffins, Zampanos, and bialys. All of the latter recipes were developed over the years from the sourdough we had on hand in abundance for making baguettes. (We used to joke that if we could have figured out a way to make sticky buns from this recipe we would have.) What gives each bread its own identity is the way it is handled after the dough has completed its first long rising period. Adding different ingredients later and baking the breads at different temperatures yields completely different breads.

Before you begin, be sure to read through the master recipe, the "Methods" discussion in the Basics section, as well as the recipe for the bread you are planning to make. Both volume and weight measurements are given in the sourdough recipes. Use the weight measures if you are a beginning baker, as a greater degree of accuracy will help you succeed. As you become more experienced, you will know what to look for in a dough.

Preparation time through the first rise: 5 hours
(unless rising overnight); active time: 45 minutes

- 4 cups (20 ounces) bread flour
- 1¼ cups cool water
- 1 tablespoon plus 1 teaspoon kosher salt
- 1½ cups (8 ounces) Sourdough Starter (page 90)

Put the flour in the bowl of a stand mixer or a large bowl.

If using a stand mixer, add the water to the bowl and mix on low speed with the paddle attachment until the ingredients are thoroughly combined, about 2 minutes. Let rest for 10 minutes. Add the salt and sourdough starter. Switch to the dough hook, increase the mixer speed to medium, and knead for 12 minutes, or until the dough is slightly tacky and soft. (After a couple of minutes, the dough should gather around the hook; you can add extra flour by the tablespoonful if the dough does not pull away from the sides of the bowl.) Transfer to a lightly floured surface and knead by hand for about 5 minutes (see page 25), or until the dough is smooth, shiny, and passes the windowpane test.

If making by hand, add the water to the bowl and mix with a wooden spoon until the ingredients are thoroughly combined. Let rest for 10 minutes. Add the salt and sourdough starter and mix until all the ingredients are combined. Transfer to a lightly floured surface and knead for 15 minutes (see page 25), adding flour by the tablespoonful as necessary to keep the dough from sticking. The kneading is complete when the dough is smooth, shiny, and passes the windowpane test.

Form the dough into a ball and place it in a large oiled bowl. Turn the dough over to coat it with oil. Cover the bowl with plastic wrap or a damp kitchen towel and let rise in a warm, draft-free place for at least 4 hours, or until doubled in size, at which point the dough is ready to be used in the recipes that follow. Alternatively, either put the dough in a cool place (60°F) and let it rise overnight, or refrigerate the dough overnight and let it stand at room temperature for 2 hours the next day before proceeding with the recipe.

People are more invested in the product if they get to play with it. When I came here as the new guy, I asked, "Where did these recipes come from, how did they get to this point?" Most people said, "The recipes just kind of evolved as we went along."

—PAUL

I think it takes somebody with strong initiative to take an idea, test it out, and present it to the group. I think even as a new member, if I really had a product that I wanted to try out, I could bring it to the group and give it a go.

—DAN

Sourdough Baguettes

At the Cheese Board, we make hundreds of pounds of sourdough baguettes a day, and it doesn't take long for a new "baguette roller" to learn the rolling style. Technique is everything: it is crucial to create adequate surface tension when shaping the dough in order to make a rounded baguette with slashes that open generously. You can achieve this result by rolling the dough in such a way as to simultaneously create tension on the outside of the loaf while maintaining an inner airiness, as shown in the illustrations below. Just remember that even if your first tries are not beautiful, they will still taste delicious and tempt you into trying again and again until you've made a perfect baguette.

MAKES 4 BAGUETTES
Preparation time including rising and baking: 9 hours (unless rising overnight); active time: 1 hour

1 recipe Master Sourdough (page 92)

Optional Topping
¹/₂ cup sesame seeds
2 tablespoons poppy seeds
2 tablespoons fennel seeds

Transfer the dough to a lightly floured surface. Gently pat the dough with your open palms into a 7 by 11-inch rectangle (with the shorter side facing you). Cover with a floured kitchen towel and let rest for 10 minutes.

Lightly dust 2 baking sheets with flour. Cut the dough horizontally into 4 equal portions. Lightly flour your hands and the work surface just enough to keep the dough from sticking.

To shape the baguettes, roll a piece of dough into itself (fig. A) and turn the cut side down. Working from one end of the length, cup your hands and use your thumbs and lower palms to roll the baguette gently but firmly, rocking back and forth and making sure that the bottom of the dough stays on the bottom (fig. B). Do not smash or flatten the dough; your aim is to keep the baguette as rounded as possible while increasing the tension on the surface. When one end is rolled out into a tight, cylindrical length, repeat this technique with the other end until you have a 14-inch length (fig. C). Now you should have 2 nicely shaped ends, a slightly bulging center, and ideally no visible seam. Beginning at the center, roll the baguette outward to one end and then to the other end, creating an even baguette that is about 16 inches long. Gently pick up the baguette and place it, seam side down, butted up against the inside edge of one of the prepared pans (the edge of the pan gives the rising baguette support; fig. D). Repeat these steps with the remaining dough.

Put the baguettes in a proofing chamber (see page 19) and let rise in a warm place for 2 to 3 hours, or until an impression remains when the dough is pressed with a finger. The baguettes may not look higher but should have increased in width by one-third.

To make the topping, mix the sesame seeds, poppy seeds, and fennel seeds together in a small bowl. Set aside.

Fifteen minutes before the baguettes have finished rising, place a metal roasting pan on the floor of the oven.

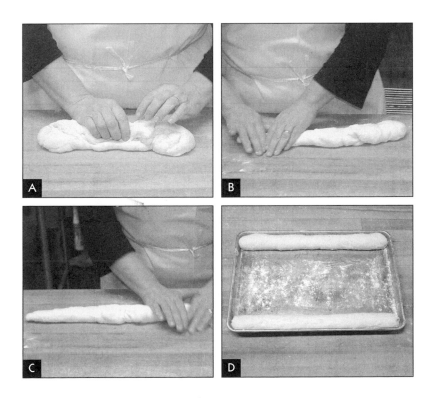

Arrange the oven racks in the upper and lower thirds of the oven. Preheat the oven to 450°F.

Pour ½ cup cold water into a measuring cup and add enough ice cubes to bring the volume to 1 cup. Using a spray bottle, generously mist the baguettes with water and sprinkle with the topping. Slash the top of the baguettes (see page 31) and mist them again. Working quickly so that you don't lose too much heat, place the baking sheets in the oven and pour the ice water into the roasting pan. Immediately close the oven door to maintain a steamy environment.

Bake for 5 minutes, then prepare another round of ice water and repeat the process. Bake for 15 minutes longer, then rotate the baking sheets front to back and trade their rack positions. Bake 15 to 20 minutes longer, for a total baking time of 35 to 40 minutes, or until the baguettes are golden brown. Using the spray bottle, mist the loaves, immediately close the oven door, and bake for 1 more minute. Transfer the loaves to a wire rack to cool.

Bastille Day Baguettes

This simple and fun variation on the baguette recipe is for serious garlic lovers.

1 head (about 18 cloves) garlic, peeled
¼ cup extra-virgin olive oil

Mince 2 of the garlic cloves and combine with the olive oil in a small bowl. Set aside.

Place 4 cloves along each cut length of dough and roll them into the dough as you shape the baguette.

Follow the recipe above for rising and baking instructions. Upon removing the baguettes from the oven, brush each with the garlic oil.

We are always talking about the slash: the depth, the angle of it, what it looks like. The true beauty of the slash is not the slash itself but the space between the slashes . . . the negative space.

—LAURA

I used to bake on Thursday afternoons. I loved how I could make the baguettes look beautiful, especially at a certain time of year when the sunlight comes in and washes across the table where we decant the baguettes from the trays. I always wanted my four-by-five camera: the baguettes looked just beautiful, like they were varnished.　　　　　—CHARLIE

One of the funniest days at the Cheese Board was the millennium New Year's Eve. We had made a huge amount of baguette dough, 1,300 pounds, but by 2 P.M. all the baguettes were gone, not only from our store but from all the other bakeries and supermarkets. All of Berkeley was in a panic. Berkeley people may be progressive with their politics, but they must have their baguettes!

—CATHY

FLOUR, WATER, AND SALT

A couple of hundred pounds of flour, approximately 60 percent of that in water and ice, some salt, and about twelve gallons of sourdough starter with a gazillion or so little critters working away in it, and I'm ready to start mixing a big batch of baguette dough. Everything is dumped altogether into a big 250-pound-capacity spiral mixer. The timer is set, and ten to twelve minutes later, I stick my fingers in the dough to test how it feels. Then I take its temperature, pick up a bit and stretch it, and if all seems right, I have a large batch of dough ready to start rising. Hydraulics lift and tilt the mixer up and over on its side, and the dough slowly begins to flow out to be separated into seven twenty-gallon barrels, where it will rise overnight. Sometimes it seems like alchemy, other times like the most basic, wonderful organic thing I could possibly do.

Even after ten years of making doughs, the process remains fascinating, and it still makes me very anxious. I prepare an overnight dough that will be ready for the early shift, which starts rolling bread around 4:30 A.M. If I have done my job right, the dough will be smooth and silky, with just enough muscle to roll out properly and then rise a second time into a proper loaf. I want those sleepy early-morning people to have an easy and enjoyable time creating all the products that come from this one dough, and there are many: baguettes; baguette pieces; City Breads, plain and seeded; City Bâtards; oniony bialys; spicy Zampanos; small round olive focaccias; large sheets of sun-dried tomato foccacia; and English muffins. If I haven't done my "organic alchemy" right, I'm going to have some very upset coworkers, let alone lots of disappointed customers. I must admit I sometimes still call the store early and ask, "Was my dough okay?"

—Charlie

City Bread

Though made from the same dough as the sourdough baguettes, these breads have a greater crumb-to-crust ratio and therefore stay moist longer. Shaped and left to rise in proofing baskets, City Bread takes on a rustic appearance. Misting and steaming these loaves produces a crunchy, golden brown crust. If you own a baking stone, the bread crust will be enhanced by using it. For loaves risen on sheets, try topping them with seeds after misting them.

MAKES 2 LOAVES
Preparation time including rising and baking: 11 hours
(unless rising overnight); active time: 1 hour

1 recipe Master Sourdough (page 92)

Transfer the dough to a lightly floured surface and divide it into 2 pieces. Gently form each piece into a loose round (see page 26) and cover with a floured kitchen towel. Let rest for 10 minutes.

Shape the dough into large rounds (see page 27). Flour the insides of 2 proofing baskets or lightly flour a baking sheet. Place the loaves in the baskets, seam side up, or seam-side down on the prepared pan. Or, shape the dough into *bâtards* (see page 28) and let rise in oblong proofing baskets or directly on a prepared baking sheet.

Put the loaves in a proofing chamber (see page 19) and let rise in a warm place for 4 to 5 hours, or until increased in size by one-half and a finger pressed into the dough leaves an impression.

If using a baking stone, 45 minutes before the loaves have finished rising, arrange the oven racks in the upper and lower thirds of the oven. Place the baking stone on the lower rack and place a metal roasting pan on the floor of the oven. Preheat the oven to 450°F.

If using a baking sheet only, 15 minutes before the loaves have finished rising, remove all but the middle rack from the oven and place a metal roasting pan on the floor of the oven. Preheat the oven to 450°F.

If rising the dough in baskets, lightly dust a baking sheet with flour and turn the baskets upside-down to gently release the loaves onto the sheet 4 inches apart. Slash the top of the loaves (see page 31). If rising on a sheet, slash the top of the loaves and, using a spray bottle, generously mist them with water.

Pour ½ cup cold water into a measuring cup and add enough ice cubes to bring the volume to 1 cup. Working quickly so that you don't lose too much heat, place the baking sheet in the oven and pour the ice water into the roasting pan. Immediately close the oven door to maintain a steamy environment.

Bake for 5 minutes, then prepare another round of ice water and repeat the process. Bake for 15 minutes longer, then rotate the baking sheet front to back. Bake for at least 25 more minutes, for a total baking time of 45 minutes, or until the bread is deep brown and sounds hollow when tapped on the bottom. Or, if using a baking stone, 5 minutes before the end of the bake, transfer the breads from the pan directly onto the stone and finish the bake. Transfer the loaves to a wire rack to cool.

I love making the dough on Thursday afternoon and then tasting

it on Friday morning. It is a thrill for me.

—JOHN

English Muffins

The crumb of these English muffins is filled with wide, uneven holes. Split in two, toasted, and eaten with butter and jam, they make a perfect simple breakfast. The dough scraps can be recycled and used in other ways (for bialys, Zampanos, or even a single pizza), but don't reuse them for English muffins since the crumb will be dense and tough.

MAKES 12 ENGLISH MUFFINS
Preparation time including rising and baking: 8 hours
(unless rising overnight); active time: 1 hour

> 1 recipe Master Sourdough (page 92)
> 6 tablespoons medium-grind yellow cornmeal

Transfer the dough to a lightly floured surface and divide it into 2 pieces. Gently pat and stretch each piece into a 10 by 8 by ¾-inch-thick rectangle. Cover the dough with a floured kitchen towel and let rest for 15 minutes.

Sprinkle a baking sheet with 2 tablespoons cornmeal. Using a 3-inch floured round cookie cutter or a floured drinking glass, cut out 6 rounds from 1 piece of dough. Place the rounds on the prepared pan and cover with a floured kitchen towel. Repeat this process with the remaining piece of dough. (To reserve the leftover scraps for another use, shape them into a loose round, cover them with a floured kitchen towel, and let rest for at least 30 minutes before proceeding.) Let the muffins rise in a warm, draft-free place for 2 hours, or until increased in size by one-fourth and a finger pressed into the dough leaves an impression.

When the muffins have almost finished rising, preheat a large cast-iron skillet or griddle over medium-low heat for at least 5 minutes. Sprinkle 2 tablespoons cornmeal on the heated pan; if the cornmeal pops and burns, the pan is too hot and should be cooled for a minute. Place a batch of muffins in the pan and cook for 8 to 10 minutes on each side, or until lightly browned. Gently squeeze the muffins; if they are soft and tacky on the sides, let them cook a little longer. Transfer to a wire rack to cool. Repeat the process, first coating the griddle with the remaining 2 tablespoons cornmeal, until all the muffins are cooked.

Cheesy Muffins

It's hard to resist eating these hot off the griddle. If you can hold off, serve them with Indian-spiced chickpeas or curried lentils to elevate them beyond a simple snack to inspiration for an entire meal.

MAKES 12 MUFFINS
Preparation time including rising and baking: 8 hours
(unless rising overnight); active time: 1 hour

> 1 recipe Master Sourdough (page 92), prepared
>   through kneading
> 1 pound sharp orange Cheddar cheese, cut into
>   ½-inch cubes
> 6 tablespoons medium-grind yellow cornmeal

Flatten the dough into a 1-inch-thick round. Add the cheese and knead just long enough to evenly distribute it.

Form the dough into a ball and place it in a large oiled bowl. Turn the dough over to coat it with oil. Cover the bowl with plastic wrap or a damp kitchen towel and let rise in a warm, draft-free place for at least 4 hours, or until doubled in size.

Transfer the dough to a lightly floured surface and divide it into 2 pieces. Gently pat and stretch each piece into a 10 by 8 by ¾-inch rectangle. Cover the dough with a floured kitchen towel and let rest for 15 minutes.

Sprinkle a baking sheet with 2 tablespoons cornmeal. Using a 3-inch floured round cookie cutter or a floured drinking glass, cut out 6 rounds from 1 piece of dough. Place the rounds on the prepared pan and cover with a floured kitchen towel. Repeat this process with the remaining piece of dough. Discard the scraps. Let the muffins rise in a warm place for 2 hours, or until increased in size by one-fourth and a finger pressed into the dough leaves an impression.

When the muffins have almost finished rising, preheat a large cast-iron skillet or griddle over medium-low heat for at least 5 minutes. Sprinkle 2 tablespoons cornmeal on the heated pan; if the cornmeal pops and burns the pan is too hot and should be cooled for a minute. Place a batch of muffins in the pan and cook for 8 to 10 minutes on each side, or until lightly browned. Gently squeeze the muffins; if they are soft, tacky, or opaque on the sides, let them cook a little longer. Transfer to a wire rack to cool. Repeat the process, first coating the griddle with the remaining 2 tablespoons cornmeal, until all the muffins are cooked.

When the collective asked me for a five-year commitment, it was a total problem. I told everybody I couldn't give that time commitment. I was twenty-six, and I just couldn't guarantee that I would stay the five years. But they decided to hire me anyway. That was over ten years ago. It's a community, mostly because people do stay so long. It's very hard to imagine my life without it now. —TINA

Zampanos

Named after the strongman from Fellini's La Strada, *the Zampano is a spicy-hot sourdough bun. Zampanos are baked at a moderate temperature so that no crust develops, then brushed with garlic olive oil and sprinkled with red pepper flakes and Parmesan cheese. They are great on their own, but they also make perfect hamburger or sandwich rolls.*

MAKES 12 TO 14 ZAMPANOS
Preparation time including rising and baking: 9 hours (unless rising overnight); active time: 1 hour

> 2 tablespoons coarse yellow cornmeal or polenta
> 1 recipe Master Sourdough (page 92)
> ¼ cup extra-virgin olive oil
> 2 cloves garlic, crushed
> 2 tablespoons coarse sea salt or kosher salt
> ½ teaspoon red pepper flakes
> ¼ cup finely grated Parmesan cheese

Sprinkle each of 2 baking sheets with 1 tablespooon cornmeal. Transfer the dough to a lightly floured surface and divide it into 12 pieces. Gently form each piece into a loose round (see page 26) and divide the rounds between the prepared pans. Cover with a floured kitchen towel and let rise in a warm, draft-free place for 1 hour, or until soft enough to flatten easily without springing back.

Combine the olive oil and crushed garlic in a small bowl. Set aside.

Flatten each round with the palm of your hand, making a 4-inch disk. Brush with half of the olive oil mixture. Cover the rounds with a floured kitchen towel and let rise in a warm place for at least 2 hours, or until increased in size by one-fourth and a finger pressed into the dough leaves an impression.

Fifteen minutes before the rounds have finished rising, arrange the oven racks in the upper and lower thirds of the oven. Preheat the oven to 375°F.

Using the tips of your fingers, dimple the Zampanos over the entire surface. Sprinkle with the sea salt. Place the baking sheets in the oven. Bake for 15 minutes, then rotate the pans front to back and trade their rack positions. Bake 5 to 10 minutes longer, for a total baking time of 20 to 25 minutes, or until little golden bubbles just begin to form on the crust. Remove from the oven and brush with the remaining garlic olive oil. Sprinkle with the red pepper flakes and Parmesan cheese. Transfer to a wire rack to cool for 5 minutes. Serve warm.

Bialys

Bialys are small, flat rounds with chopped sweet onion and poppy seeds pressed into the center. They are lightly baked so that they remain soft and just barely show the beginnings of a light golden brown hue. We sell bialys at the store for break-fast, lunch, and snacks.

MAKES 12 BIALYS
Preparation time including rising and baking: 9 hours
(unless rising overnight); active time: 1 hour

> 1 recipe Master Sourdough (page 92)
> 1 yellow onion, finely diced
> 1 teaspoon poppy seeds
> Pinch of kosher salt
> ¹/₂ teaspoon extra-virgin olive oil

Lightly dust 2 baking sheets with flour. Transfer the dough to a lightly floured surface and divide it into 12 pieces. Gently form each piece into a loose round (see page 26) and divide the rounds between the prepared pans. Cover with a floured kitchen towel and let rise in a warm, draft-free place for 1 hour, or until soft enough to flatten easily without springing back.

Sprinkle each of 2 baking sheets with 1 tablespoon corn-meal. In a small bowl, combine the onion, poppy seeds, salt, and olive oil. Set aside.

Flatten each round with the palm of your hand, making a 4-inch disk. Using the tips of your fingers, make a shallow well in the center of each round. Place 1 tablespoon of the onion mixture in each well. Cover the rounds with a floured kitchen towel and let rise in a warm place for at least 2 hours, or until increased in size by one-fourth and a finger pressed into the dough leaves an impression.

Fifteen minutes before the rounds have finished rising, arrange the oven racks in the upper and lower thirds of the oven. Preheat the oven to 375°F

Place the baking sheets in the oven. Bake for 15 minutes, then rotate the pans front to back and trade their rack positions. Bake 10 to 15 minutes longer, for a total baking time of 25 to 30 minutes, or until the rounds are a light sandy color. Transfer to a wire rack to cool for 5 minutes. Serve warm.

Working with bread is one of those things that is constantly changing and evolving. You think that you've mastered it, and the next time it is totally different.

—SHEHANNA

In the beginning it was hard because everybody told me to bake breads in different ways. It was difficult: Who was right, and who wasn't?   —FRANCISCO

Bread sometimes has a life of its own, and no matter what you do, you're not going to get a great bake.

—LAURA

• FOCACCIA •

Depending on the baker's whim, focaccia can be thick or thin, elaborately topped or coated simply with olive oil, coarse salt, and rosemary. At the Cheese Board we finish baking the large focaccias by placing them on a heated baking stone to crisp the bottom crust, giving the bread a crunchy-chewy texture.

Small Olive Focaccia Rounds

Rolled into small, flat rounds and studded with pitted Kalamata olives, these little breads appear on the Cheese Board shelves at lunchtime and again in the late afternoon.

MAKES 12 ROUNDS
Preparation time including rising and baking: 9 hours (unless rising overnight); active time: 1 hour

2 tablespoons coarse yellow cornmeal or polenta
1 recipe Master Sourdough (page 92)
3 sprigs fresh rosemary, each 2 inches long
1/4 cup extra-virgin olive oil
48 Kalamata olives, pitted (about 1 1/2 cups)

Sprinkle each of 2 baking sheets with 1 tablespoon cornmeal. Transfer the dough to a lightly floured surface and divide it into 12 pieces. Gently form each piece into a loose round (see page 26) and place them on the prepared pans. Cover with a floured kitchen towel and let rise in a warm, draft-free place for 1 hour, or until soft enough to flatten easily without springing back.

In a small bowl, combine the rosemary sprigs and olive oil. Set aside.

Flatten each round with the palm of your hand, making a 4-inch disk. Brush with the rosemary olive oil. Firmly press 4 olives into each disk an equal distance from each other. Cover the rounds with a floured kitchen towel and let rise in a warm place for at least 2 hours, or until the rounds are puffy and a finger pressed into the dough leaves an impression.

Fifteen minutes before the rounds have finished rising, arrange the oven racks in the upper and lower thirds of the oven. Preheat the oven to 375°F.

Just before baking, firmly press the olives into the rounds to secure them. Place the baking sheets in the oven. Bake for 15 minutes, then rotate the pans front to back and trade their rack positions. Bake 10 minutes longer, for a total baking time of 25 minutes, or until light brown. Transfer the focaccias to a wire rack and brush with the rosemary olive oil. Let cool for a few minutes. Serve warm.

Tomato, Caper, and Olive Focaccia

These large, round focaccias are almost like pizzas. They make a nice light lunch or dinner with a side of salad.

MAKES THREE 10- TO 11-INCH FOCACCIAS
Preparation time including risings and baking: 9 hours (unless rising overnight); active time: 1 hour

3 tablespoons coarse yellow cornmeal or polenta
1 recipe Master Sourdough (page 92)
2 sprigs fresh rosemary, each 2 inches long
¼ cup extra-virgin olive oil
8 Roma tomatoes, sliced ⅛ inch thick
30 Kalamata olives, pitted (about 1 cup)

Topping
2 teaspoons balsamic vinegar
3 tablespoons extra-virgin olive oil
Kosher salt and freshly ground pepper
3 tablespoons capers

Sprinkle each of 3 baking sheets with 1 tablespoon cornmeal. Transfer the dough to a lightly floured surface and divide it into 3 pieces. Gently form each piece into a loose round (see page 26) and place each in the center of a prepared pan. Cover with a floured kitchen towel and let rise in a warm, draft-free place for 1 hour, or until soft enough to stretch easily without springing back.

In a small bowl, combine the rosemary sprigs and olive oil. Set aside.

Gently pull, pat, and stretch the dough to make three 9- to 10-inch circles with an even thickness throughout. Brush with the rosemary olive oil. Divide the tomato slices evenly among the 3 rounds. Starting 1½ inches from the outer rim of each round, firmly press the tomato slices into the dough, leaving a little space between the slices for the olives. Firmly press the olives into the dough. Cover the rounds with a floured kitchen towel. Let rise in a warm place for at least 2 hours, or until increased in size by one-fourth.

Arrange the oven racks in the upper and lower third of the oven. If using a baking stone, 45 minutes before the focaccias have finished rising, place the stone on the floor of the oven and preheat the oven to 375°F. If using baking sheets only, preheat the oven to 375° 15 minutes before the rounds have finished rising. Just before baking, firmly press the olives into the rounds to secure them.

If using a baking stone, place a baking sheet with a focaccia on the lower oven rack and bake for 13 minutes. Rotate the focaccia to the upper rack and put the second focaccia on the lower rack. Bake each for 13 minutes, then slide the first focaccia from the pan directly onto the baking stone. Move the second focaccia to the upper rack and put the third focaccia on the lower rack. Bake the focaccia on the stone for 4 to 8 minutes, for a total baking time of 30 to 34 minutes, or until lightly browned. Finish baking the second and third focaccias in the same manner.

If using baking sheets only, place two of the pans in the oven. Bake for 15 minutes, then rotate the pans front to back and trade their rack positions. Bake 15 to 20 minutes longer, for a total baking time of 30 to 35 minutes, or until lightly browned. Repeat the process with the third baking sheet.

Transfer the focaccias to a wire rack and brush with the rosemary olive oil. Whisk the vinegar and oil together in a small bowl and season to taste with salt and pepper. Brush the tomato slices with the vinaigrette and spoon a few capers on top of each tomato slice. Let cool for a few minutes. Serve warm.

I feel like there is a healthy irreverence in the store. There is an atmosphere in the group where people feel free to just say whatever comes into their mind. That I like.

—TINA

Rosemary Focaccia

This bread is an example of delicious simplicity: a golden brown, crisp focaccia, brushed with extra-virgin olive oil and garnished with fresh rosemary leaves and coarse sea salt. The flavor of each individual ingredient comes through, yet the focaccia has a unified flavor. The crust is so lightly garnished that it has a totally different texture from other focaccias. A great accompaniment for a bowl of soup.

MAKES ONE 9 BY 12-INCH FOCACCIA
Preparation time including rising and baking: 9 hours;
(unless rising overnight); active time: 1 hour

2 tablespoons coarse yellow cornmeal or polenta
1 recipe Master Sourdough (page 92)
Leaves from 4 sprigs fresh rosemary, each 2 inches long
¼ cup extra-virgin olive oil
1 tablespoon coarse sea salt or kosher salt

Sprinkle a baking sheet with the cornmeal. Place the dough on the baking sheet and cover with a floured kitchen towel. Let rise in a warm, draft-free place for 1 hour, or until soft enough to stretch easily without springing back.

In a small bowl, combine the rosemary leaves and olive oil. Set aside.

Gently pull, pat, and stretch the dough to make a 7 by 11-inch rectangle with an even thickness throughout. Brush with the rosemary olive oil and cover with a floured kitchen towel. Let rise in a warm place for at least 2 hours, or until increased in size by one-fourth.

Remove all but the middle rack from the oven. If using a baking stone, 45 minutes before the dough has finished rising, place the stone on the floor of the oven and preheat the oven to 400°F. If using a baking sheet only, preheat the oven to 400°F 15 minutes before the dough has finished rising.

Using the tips of your fingers, dimple the dough over the entire surface. Sprinkle the sea salt evenly over the dough.

If using a baking stone, place the baking sheet on the middle rack of the oven. Bake for 15 minutes, then rotate the sheet front to back. Bake 10 minutes longer. Slide the focaccia from the pan directly onto the baking stone and bake 5 more minutes, for a total baking time of 30 minutes, or until crisp on the bottom and lightly browned on top.

If using a baking sheet only, place the focaccia in the oven. Bake for 15 minutes, then rotate the baking sheet front to back. Bake 15 minutes longer, for a total baking time of 30 minutes, or until crisp on the bottom and lightly browned on top.

Transfer the focaccia to a wire rack and brush with the rosemary olive oil. Strip the rosemary leaves from the stems and sprinkle them over the focaccia. Let cool for a few minutes. Serve warm.

Sun-Dried Tomato Focaccia

The rich flavor of the sun-dried tomato pesto on this focaccia is well matched to the sourdough crust. Use moist sun-dried tomatoes with a rich, deep red color. While it is tempting to ladle a thick layer of the pesto on the top of the focaccia, restrain yourself, since too much will make the bread soggy.

MAKES ONE 9 BY 12-INCH FOCACCIA
Preparation time including rising and baking: 9 hours
(unless rising overnight); active time: 1 hour

2 tablespoons coarse yellow cornmeal or polenta
1 recipe Master Sourdough (page 92)
2 cloves garlic, crushed
1/4 cup extra-virgin olive oil

Sun-Dried Tomato Pesto
1/2 cup sun-dried tomatoes
2 cloves garlic, peeled
1 cup warm water
2 tablespoons extra-virgin olive oil

Topping
2 green onions, thinly sliced (including green parts)
1/4 cup finely grated Parmesan cheese

Sprinkle a baking sheet with the cornmeal. Place the dough on the baking sheet and cover with a floured kitchen towel. Let rise in a warm, draft-free place for 1 hour, or until soft enough to stretch easily without springing back.

In a small bowl, combine the crushed garlic and olive oil. Set aside.

Gently pull, pat, and stretch the dough to make a 7 by 11-inch rectangle with an even thickness throughout. Brush with the garlic oil and cover with a floured kitchen towel. Let rise in a warm place for at least 2 hours, or until increased in size by one-fourth.

While the dough is rising, make the sun-dried tomato pesto. In a medium bowl, soak the sun-dried tomatoes in the warm water until softened, about 30 minutes. Drain the sun-dried tomatoes, reserving the liquid. Put the tomatoes and garlic in a food processor and process to a smooth purée. With the machine running, gradually add the olive oil. If the pesto is too thick, add a small amount of the reserved liquid. Transfer the mixture to a small bowl and set aside.

Remove all but the middle rack from the oven. If using a baking stone, 45 minutes before the dough has finished rising, place the stone on the floor of the oven and preheat the oven to 400°F. If using a baking sheet only, preheat the oven to 400°F 15 minutes before the dough has finished rising.

Using the tips of your fingers, dimple the dough over the entire surface.

If using a baking stone, place the baking sheet on the middle rack of the oven. Bake for 15 minutes, then rotate the sheet front to back. Bake 10 minutes longer. Slide the focaccia from the pan directly onto the baking stone and bake 5 more minutes, for a total baking time of 30 minutes, or until crisp on the bottom and lightly browned on top.

If using a baking sheet only, place the focaccia in the oven. Bake for 15 minutes, then rotate the baking sheet front to back. Bake 15 minutes longer, for a total baking time of 30 minutes, or until crisp on the bottom and lightly browned on top.

Transfer the focaccia to a wire rack and brush with the garlic oil. With a rubber spatula, apply a thin layer of tomato pesto. Sprinkle with the green onions and Parmesan cheese. Let cool for a few minutes. Serve warm.

Pesto Focaccia

*We use pesto in a variety of ways at the Cheese Board: to gar-
nish pizzas and focaccia, and to make pesto Brie (not to
mention the occasional staff lunch of pasta al pesto). Our
focaccia bakers know that there is a lot of competition for
available pesto, so they often hide their batch in the nooks and
crannies of the big walk-in refrigerator, to make sure they have
it when they need it. The addition of lemon juice helps keep the
color of the pesto bright.*

MAKES ONE 9 BY 12-INCH FOCACCIA
Preparation time including rising and baking: 9 hours
(unless rising overnight); active time: 1 hour

2 tablespoons coarse yellow cornmeal or polenta
1 recipe Master Sourdough (page 92)
2 cloves garlic, crushed
1/4 cup extra-virgin olive oil

Pesto
1 large bunch basil, stemmed
1 to 2 cloves garlic, crushed
1/2 cup pine nuts, lightly toasted (see page 23)
1/2 cup finely grated Parmesan cheese
1/2 cup extra-virgin olive oil
Juice of 1/2 lemon
Kosher salt

Topping
2 green onions, thinly sliced (including green parts)
1/4 cup finely grated Parmesan cheese

Sprinkle a baking sheet with the cornmeal. Place the
dough on the baking sheet and cover with a floured kitchen
towel. Let rise in a warm, draft-free place for 1 hour, or until
soft enough to stretch easily without springing back.

In a small bowl, combine the crushed garlic and olive oil.
Set aside.

Gently pull, pat, and stretch the dough to make a 7 by
11-inch rectangle with an even thickness throughout. Brush
with the garlic oil and cover with a floured kitchen towel. Let

rise in a warm place for at least 2 hours, or until increased in
size by one-fourth.

While the dough is rising, make the pesto. In a food
processor, combine the basil, garlic, and pine nuts, and process
until almost smooth. Add the Parmesan cheese and pulse to
combine. With the machine running, gradually add the olive
oil to make a smooth purée. Add the lemon juice and season
to taste with salt. Transfer the mixture to a small bowl and
set aside.

Remove all but the middle rack from the oven. If using a
baking stone, 45 minutes before the dough has finished rising, place the stone on the floor of the oven and preheat the
oven to 400°F. If using a baking sheet only, preheat the oven
to 400°F 15 minutes before the dough has finished rising.

Using the tips of your fingers, dimple the dough over the
entire surface.

If using a baking stone, place the baking sheet on the
middle rack of the oven. Bake for 15 minutes, then rotate the
sheet front to back. Bake 10 minutes longer. Slide the focaccia from the pan directly onto the baking stone and bake 5
more minutes, for a total baking time of 30 minutes, or until
crisp on the bottom and lightly browned on top.

If using a baking sheet only, place the focaccia in the
oven. Bake for 15 minutes, then rotate the baking sheet
front to back. Bake 15 minutes longer, for a total baking
time of 30 minutes, or until crisp on the bottom and lightly
browned on top.

Transfer the focaccia to a wire rack and brush with the
garlic oil. Using a rubber spatula, apply a thin layer of pesto.
Sprinkle with the green onions and Parmesan cheese. Let
cool for a few minutes. Serve warm.

We had a shift that totally forgot to make a pizza dough! I always

tell new people that no matter what you do wrong, somebody

has already done it, probably more than once.

—PAM

Ricotta Salata, Lemon Zest, and Cilantro Focaccia

Ricotta Salata is a dry, firm, salty sheep's-milk cheese traditionally used to garnish pasta. We love its saltiness. The addition of lemon and cilantro gives this Italian bread a Mexican twist. The flavors are bright, fresh, and clean, perfect for a summer day.

MAKES ONE 9 BY 12-INCH FOCACCIA

Preparation time including rising and baking: 9 hours (unless rising overnight); active time: 1 hour

2 tablespoons coarse yellow cornmeal or polenta

1 recipe Master Sourdough (page 92)

2 cloves garlic, crushed

¼ cup extra-virgin olive oil

Topping

1 scant cup (⅓ pound) grated Ricotta Salata cheese

Grated zest of 1 large lemon

2 tablespoons coarsely chopped fresh cilantro

Sprinkle a baking sheet with the cornmeal. Place the dough on the baking sheet and cover with a floured kitchen towel. Let rise in a warm, draft-free place for 1 hour, or until soft enough to stretch easily without springing back.

In a small bowl, combine the crushed garlic and olive oil. Set aside.

Gently pull, pat, and stretch the dough to make a 7 by 11-inch rectangle with an even thickness throughout. Brush with the garlic oil and cover with a floured kitchen towel. Let rise in a warm, draft-free place for at least 2 hours, or until increased in size by one-fourth.

Remove all but the middle rack from the oven. If using a baking stone, 45 minutes before the dough has finished rising, place the stone on the floor of the oven and preheat the oven to 400°F. If using a baking sheet only, preheat the oven to 400°F 15 minutes before the dough has finished rising.

Using the tips of your fingers, dimple the dough over the entire surface.

If **using a baking stone,** place the baking sheet on the middle rack of the oven. Bake for 15 minutes, then rotate the sheet front to back. Bake 10 minutes longer. Slide the focaccia off the pan directly onto the baking stone and bake 5 more minutes, for a total baking time of 30 minutes, or until crisp on the bottom and lightly browned on top.

If **using a baking sheet only,** place the focaccia in the oven. Bake for 15 minutes, then rotate the baking sheet front to back. Bake 15 minutes longer, for a total baking time of 30 minutes, or until crisp on the bottom and lightly browned on top.

Transfer the foccacia to a wire rack and brush with the garlic oil. Sprinkle with the Ricotta Salata, then the lemon zest and cilantro. Let cool for a few minutes. Serve warm.

Suburban Bread

This bread got its name because, unlike the City Bread (made with all white flour) and the now retired Country Bread (made with all whole-wheat flour), it is made with a combination of white and whole-wheat flours. Our Suburban Bread dough, like our master sourdough, can be used to make a number of other breads. A long, slow rise gives this bread its pronounced sour flavor and chewy, holey texture. Undermixing or overmixing the dough will affect the final architecture of the bread, so observe the kneading time with the knowledge that it may be necessary to knead the dough a little more or a little less to achieve a smooth, shiny dough that passes the windowpane test (see page 25). Using a baking stone will enhance the crust of this bread.

MAKES 2 LOAVES

Preparation time including rising and baking: 12 hours (unless rising overnight); active time: 1 hour

4¹/₂ cups (22.5 ounces) bread flour

²/₃ cup (3¹/₄ ounces) whole-wheat flour

1¹/₂ tablespoons wheat bran

2 cups cool water

1 tablespoon plus ¹/₂ teaspoon kosher salt

1 cup (5 ounces) Sourdough Starter (page 90)

In the bowl of a stand mixer or a large bowl, combine the flours and wheat bran.

If using a stand mixer, add the water to the bowl and mix on low speed with the paddle attachment until the ingredients are thoroughly combined, about 2 minutes. Let rest for 10 minutes. Add the salt and sourdough starter. Switch to the dough hook, increase the mixer speed to medium, and knead for 12 minutes, or until the dough is slightly tacky and soft. (After a couple of minutes, the dough should gather around the hook; you can add extra flour by the tablespoonful if the dough does not pull away from the sides of the bowl.) Transfer to a lightly floured surface and knead by hand for about 5 minutes (see page 25), or until the dough is smooth, shiny, and passes the windowpane test.

If making by hand, add the water to the bowl and mix with a wooden spoon until the ingredients are thoroughly combined. Let rest for 10 minutes. Add the salt and sourdough starter, and mix until all the ingredients are combined. Transfer to a lightly floured surface and knead for 15 minutes (see page 25), adding flour by the tablespoonful as necessary to keep the dough from sticking. The kneading is complete when the dough is smooth, shiny, and passes the windowpane test.

Form the dough into a ball and place it in a large oiled bowl. Turn the dough over to coat it with oil. Cover the bowl with plastic wrap or a damp kitchen towel and let rise in a warm, draft-free place for at least 5 hours, or until doubled in size. Alternatively, either put the dough in a cool place (60°F) and let it rise overnight, or refrigerate the dough overnight and let it stand at room temperature for 2 hours the next day before proceeding with the recipe.

Transfer the dough to a lightly floured surface and divide it into 2 pieces. Gently form each piece into a loose round (see page 26) and cover with a floured kitchen towel. Let rest for 10 minutes.

Shape the dough into large rounds (see page 27). Flour the insides of 2 proofing baskets or lightly flour a baking sheet. Place the loaves in the baskets, seam side up, or seam side down on the prepared pan. Or, shape the dough into *bâtards* (see page 28) and let rise in oblong proofing baskets or directly on a prepared baking sheet.

Put the loaves in a proofing chamber (see page 19) and let rise in a warm place for 5 hours, until increased in size by one-half and a finger pressed into the dough leaves an impression.

If using a baking stone, 45 minutes before the bread is finished rising, arrange the oven racks in the upper and lower thirds of the oven. Place the baking stone on the lower rack and place a metal roasting pan on the floor of the oven. Preheat the oven to 450°F.

If using a baking sheet only, 15 minutes before the loaves have finished rising, remove all but the middle rack from the oven and place a metal roasting pan on the oven floor. Preheat the oven to 450°F.

If rising the dough in baskets, lightly dust a baking sheet with flour and turn the baskets upside-down to gently release the loaves onto the sheet 4 inches apart. Slash the top of the loaves (see page 31). If rising on a sheet, slash the top of the loaves and, using a spray bottle, lightly mist them with water and dust with flour.

Pour ½ cup cold water into a measuring cup and add enough ice cubes to bring the volume to 1 cup. Working quickly so that you don't lose too much heat, place the baking sheet in the oven and pour the ice water into the roasting pan. Immediately close the oven door to maintain a steamy environment.

Bake for 5 minutes, then prepare another round of ice water and repeat the process. Bake for 15 minutes longer, then rotate the baking sheet front to back. Bake at least 25 more minutes, for a total baking time of 45 minutes, or until the bread is deep brown and sounds hollow when tapped on the bottom. Or, if using a baking stone, 5 minutes before the end of the bake, transfer the breads from the pan directly onto the stone and finish the bake. Transfer the loaves to a wire rack to cool.

We used to make the Suburban Bread in a little tin pie plate. I think that then everyone wanted to be an artisan baker. There was no science. Then it was touch, feel, and pray: "Maybe magic will be in the air tonight."

—D. W.

The perfect Suburban dough is not too wet, not too dry. It gets a good, long rise, so it's light. If the dough is too wet, the breads slump and the slashes aren't as definite. If it's too dry, the slashes are beautiful but it's not that nice to eat. It should be baked dark enough so that the crust holds its crunchiness for a while. When you take the bread out of the oven, it should have a mahogany look and be upright in shape.

—MARTHA

For Suburban Bread, I like to make a two-circle slash, like a bull's-eye. I make a small circle and then a larger one around the outside. It can take two movements for each circle. I always use a fresh razor blade. The drier the dough, the more beautiful the slash. You can flour the razor if it's a wet dough.

—ERIN

Cheese Rolls

The optimal time to eat a cheese roll is hot from the oven. There are customers so determined to get the hottest cheese roll that they time their shopping to coincide with the baking schedule. The rolls are a favorite of neighborhood kids and anyone else who loves a rich, flavorful snack.

MAKES 12 TO 14 ROLLS

Preparation time including rising and baking: 9 hours (unless rising overnight); active time: 45 minutes

2 cups (8 ounces) shredded Gruyère cheese
2 cups (8 ounces) shredded Asiago cheese
1 recipe Suburban Bread dough (page 109), prepared through the first rise

Combine the cheeses in a medium bowl.

Lightly dust a baking sheet with flour. Transfer the dough to a lightly floured surface and let rest for 10 minutes. Begin to gently flatten and pull the dough into a rectangular shape. Using a rolling pin, roll the dough into a 10 by 18-inch rectangle. Evenly distribute the cheese over the entire surface of the dough. Roll the rectangle up jelly roll–style (see page 29). (If cheese slips out from the roll, simply stuff it back in.) With a knife, cut into 1½-inch-thick slices. Place the rolls onto the prepared pan; it's fine if they touch each other. Cover with a floured kitchen towel and let rise in a warm, draft-free place for at least 3 hours, or until increased in size by one-half and a finger pressed into the dough leaves an impression.

Fifteen minutes before the cheese rolls are finished rising, remove all but the middle rack from the oven. Place a metal roasting pan on the floor of the oven. Preheat the oven to 450°F.

Pour ½ cup cold water into a measuring cup and add enough ice cubes to bring the volume to 1 cup. Using a spray bottle, heavily mist the rolls with water. Working quickly so that you don't lose too much heat, place the baking sheet in the oven and pour the ice water into the roasting pan. Immediately close the oven door to maintain a steamy environment.

Bake for 5 minutes, then prepare another round of ice water and repeat the process. Bake for 15 minutes longer, then rotate the baking sheet front to back. Bake for 15 to 20 more minutes, for a total baking time of 35 to 40 minutes, or until the bread is a rich brown and the cheese is hot and bubbly. Using the spray bottle, mist the rolls. Close the oven door and bake for 1 more minute. Transfer the pan to a wire rack and let the rolls cool for at least 10 minutes before eating.

HOT CHEESE ROLLS!

The best thing about working at the Cheese Board was a sense of family, a connected community. I liked how people came together in a crisis and to celebrate happy events.

—GIORGIA NEIDORF

Even people who don't know we are a cooperative say, "Something seems different here."

—LYNN

MONDRAGÓN, SPAIN

I was on the NOBAWC (pronounced "no boss") Committee (a group made up of representatives from most of the collectively run businesses in the Bay Area), and a woman came to a meeting and passed out flyers. She wanted us to go to Mondragón, in Spain, to check out the cooperatives there. I said that I'd pass the flyers out at the Cheese Board and see if anyone wanted to go. Then Julia pushed *me* to go. I didn't think that I could get away with going. It cost two thousand bucks or something, and I would need to take a week off of work. So, on the off chance, I posted it up, and people voted yes, and off I went!

It was great. We went to Mondragón, which is a little community in the Basque country filled with cooperatives, where Arizmendi started his cooperative thing. I met a lot of great people through the seminars and workshops.

I just couldn't believe life was that good there—too good to be true. So I started walking around on the streets, asking people what they thought about the cooperatives. I went in the bars and asked people, and they said, "Well, if you work for a cooperative here, you've got it made for life. Everyone is trying to get into a cooperative." It was a great experience. The people were beautiful.

I'm used to walking down the street in the United States and having old ladies grabbing onto their purse or crossing to the other side of the street to try to avoid me. In Mondragón, I was walking down the street at 3 A.M. one morning on the way back to my hotel. There was an old woman walking on the street coming toward me in the rain. There was no one on the streets, just her and me. I thought, "Ooh, here we go . . . she's going to grab her purse or cross the street." But she walked *right* up to me and asked me did I need help, was I lost? Because I didn't look like I was from around there! Wow, I just could not believe it.

—Guillermo

Wolverines

We are always asked about how this crusty little bread got its name. The fact is, it's not always easy to think up a new name for a bread as it comes out of the oven (but this is usually when the name sticks). A forward-thinking Cheese Boarder had been hoarding a name for the next new product, and as the first tray of these rolls was pulled out of the oven, she blurted out, "Now, these are Wolverines!" As no one else had an idea of what to call them, they were duly labeled and put out on the shelf.

Wolverines were first created when we were training the Arizmendi cooperative members in our bakery many years ago. Inspired by the many Bay Area sourdoughs that include nuts and dried fruits, we chose sweet cherries, golden raisins, and tangy apricots, mellowed by the buttery crunch of pecans, to contrast with the sourness of the dough. Spread with fresh Ricotta cheese and jam, these small rolls are great for breakfast.

MAKES 12 ROLLS
Preparation time including rising and baking: 9 hours (unless rising overnight); active time: 45 minutes

---

1 recipe Suburban Bread dough (page 109), prepared
    through the kneading stage
1/4 cup diced dried apricots
1/4 cup chopped pecans
1/2 cup dried sweet cherries
1/2 cup golden raisins

Flatten the dough into a 1-inch-thick round. Add the apricots, pecans, cherries, and raisins and knead for 2 minutes, or until the fruits and nuts are evenly distributed.

Form the dough into a ball and place it in a large oiled bowl. Turn the dough over to coat it with oil. Cover the bowl with plastic wrap or a damp kitchen towel and let rise in a warm, draft-free place for at least 5 hours, or until increased in size by one-half.

Lightly dust a baking sheet with flour. Transfer the dough to a lightly floured surface and divide it into 12 pieces. Cover with a floured kitchen towel and let rest for 15 minutes. Shape the pieces into small rounds (see page 27), creating a taut skin on the surface. Place the rolls on the prepared pan and cover with a floured kitchen towel. Let rise in a warm place for at least 3 hours, or until increased in size by one-third and a finger pressed into the dough leaves an impression.

At least 15 minutes before the rolls have finished rising, remove all but the middle rack from the oven and place a metal roasting pan on the oven floor. Preheat the oven to 450°F.

Pour 1/2 cup cold water into a measuring cup and add enough ice cubes to bring the volume to 1 cup. Using a spray bottle, heavily mist the rolls with water. Working quickly so that you don't lose too much heat, place the baking sheet in the oven and pour the ice water into the roasting pan. Immediately close the oven door to maintain a steamy environment.

Bake for 5 minutes, then prepare another round of ice water and repeat the process. Bake for 15 minutes longer, then rotate the baking sheet front to back. Bake 15 to 20 more minutes, for a total baking time of 35 to 40 minutes, or until the rolls are deep brown and sound hollow when tapped on the bottom. Using the spray bottle, mist the rolls. Close the oven door and bake for 1 more minute. Transfer the rolls to a wire rack and let cool for at least 10 minutes before eating.

Once I forgot to put salt in the dough. That's called a "dough-saster." —Arthur

DID I ADD THE SALT?

You would think that making bread is simple. In its most basic form, the only ingredients are flour, water, salt, and starter or yeast. It is the way these ingredients are combined, how long they are kneaded, and how long they rise that produce a great bread. But the most important thing is to remember to add *all* of the ingredients. There have been awful moments when the mixer is filled with 200 pounds of flour, 120 pounds of water, and 6 buckets of starter. I've set the mixer to knead and everything looks fine for about eight minutes. Then the fear creeps over me: Did I add the salt? I look at the dough. It is a sticky mess: no salt. Can I save the dough? If I realize the problem soon enough, dissolving the salt in some water and adding it to the dough and praying may work. Otherwise, I will have to throw the whole thing out (not an easy task) and start all over again.

On Friday mornings when I'm the dough maker, I try to be very methodical about my procedures. I like to proof the yeast in the same see-through container, and I combine the ingredients in the same order. I check the progress of the dough midway through the kneading time, and finally I taste the dough to make sure all the ingredients have been included.

I offer this as advice from someone who learned the hard way. And still the salt mocks me.

—Cathy

CHAPTER FOUR

RYE BREADS

DENSE, CHEWY, AND FLAVORFUL, rye breads are an essential part of eastern European fare. Customers come into the Cheese Board searching for the bread of their homeland, and while we have yet to make a Russian rye, we have journeyed as far east as Poland with our recipes.

When making rye bread, we prefer to use a medium or dark rye flour—both of which have some of the whole grain ground into the flour—and sometimes add pumpernickel flour or cracked rye for texture and flavor. A well-stocked natural foods store will carry a range of rye flours, or they can be mail-ordered (see page 222). We use both yeast and sourdough starter as leavening agents for all of our rye breads except the dark rye, which gives them a tangy flavor. Our rye recipes include wheat flour to augment the low gluten content of rye flour.

Rye breads present more of a challenge to the baker than do yeasted wheat breads. Because of the nature of rye flour, it is important not to overmix rye bread dough because it will become progressively stickier the longer you mix it. It is therefore crucial to add the correct amount of liquid initially and observe the stated times in the recipes, mixing the dough just enough for it to acquire a modest sheen and pull away from the sides of the bowl.

The shaping of rye loaves is less forgiving than that of other breads. Unlike most of the bread doughs in this book, rye doughs are shaped directly into their final form without the intermediate step of forming them into loose rounds. The final shape and surface of the loaf will remain almost identical to the one you initially formed, so as you knead and form the loaves, try to shape a loaf with a smooth surface and well-sealed seams. Repetition and practice are the key to success with rye breads, and a great loaf of rye is well worth the effort.

RYE BREADS

Dark Rye 119

Light Rye 120

Pumpernickel. 121

Marble Rye. 122

Sourdough Beer Rye 124

THE CHEESE BOARD: COLLECTIVE WORKS

Dark Rye

In 1968, a dense European rye loaf was given to the store by a young hippie couple with a baby. It was the perfect accompaniment to the cheese selection, and the clerks all loved it, so the couple was invited to bake this bread for sale in the shop. Thus, dark rye bread became the first bread to be sold at the store. These days we make it in-house. It is a dense, dark loaf with a graceful oval shape.

MAKES 2 LOAVES

Preparation time including rising and baking: 4¼ hours; active time: 45 minutes

1 tablespoon active dry yeast

¼ cup warm water

2½ cups whole-wheat flour

¾ cup medium or dark rye flour

2½ teaspoons kosher salt

1½ tablespoons caraway seeds (optional)

1 cup plus 2 tablespoons lukewarm water

1 tablespoon blackstrap or dark unsulfured molasses

In a small bowl, whisk the yeast into the warm water until dissolved. Let stand for 5 minutes.

In the bowl of a stand mixer or a large bowl, combine the flours, salt, and caraway seeds.

If using a stand mixer, add the yeast mixture, lukewarm water, and molasses to the bowl. Mix on low speed with the dough hook for 5 minutes, or until the ingredients are combined. Increase the speed to medium and knead the dough for 5 to 7 minutes, or until it pulls away from the sides of the bowl and begins to lose its rough texture. Transfer to a lightly floured surface and knead by hand for a few minutes, until the dough is smooth and a bit shiny.

If making by hand, add the yeast mixture, lukewarm water, and molasses to the bowl. Mix with a wooden spoon until the ingredients are combined. Transfer to a lightly floured surface and knead by hand for 10 to 15 minutes, or until the dough is smooth and a bit shiny.

Form the dough into a ball and place it in a large oiled bowl. Turn the dough over to coat it with oil. Cover the bowl with plastic wrap or a damp kitchen towel and let rise in a warm, draft-free place for 1¾ hours, or until doubled in size.

Lightly flour a baking sheet. Transfer the dough to a lightly floured surface and divide it into 2 pieces. Shape each piece into an oval (see page 28) and place on the prepared pan. Using a spray bottle, mist the loaves with water and sprinkle them with flour. Spread the flour smoothly over the tops. Cover with a floured kitchen towel and let rise in a warm place for 1 to 1½ hours, or until a finger pressed into the dough leaves an impression.

Fifteen minutes before the bread has finished rising, remove all but the middle rack from the oven. Preheat the oven to 375°F. Slash the top of each loaf (see page 27) and wait at least 10 minutes for the slashes to begin to open.

Place the loaves in the oven and bake for 20 minutes. Turn the baking sheet front to back to ensure even baking. Bake 20 to 25 minutes longer, for a total baking time of 40 to 45 minutes, or until the bread is deep brown and sounds hollow when tapped on the bottom. Transfer the loaves to a wire rack to cool.

I don't think that individuality is especially encouraged here, but that doesn't stop members from being themselves.

—DAN

I think the biggest difference between the Cheese Board and other workplaces is that because there's no boss at the Cheese Board, everyone feels free to act as eccentric as they normally would in real life.

—ERIC WONG, FORMER MEMBER

Light Rye

This bread was developed to reproduce childhood memories of eating deli sandwiches in New York City. It is moist, with a chewy crust, and it is easy to replicate at home. This is the dough we mix with pumpernickel to make marble rye (see page 122).

MAKES 2 LOAVES
Preparation time including rising and baking: 5 hours;
active time: 45 minutes

1 teaspoon active dry yeast
¼ cup warm water
2¾ cups bread flour
¾ cup medium or dark rye flour
¼ cup semolina
¼ cup cracked rye
¼ cup plus 1 tablespoon medium-grind yellow
    cornmeal
1 tablespoon kosher salt
2 tablespoons caraway seeds
¾ cup (6 ounces) Sourdough Starter (see page 90)
1 cup lukewarm water

In a small bowl, whisk the yeast into the warm water until dissolved. Let stand for 5 minutes.

In the bowl of a stand mixer or a large bowl, combine the flours, semolina, cracked rye, the ¼ cup cornmeal, the salt, and caraway seeds.

If using a stand mixer, add the yeast mixture, sourdough starter, and lukewarm water to the bowl. Mix on low speed with the dough hook for 5 minutes, or until the ingredients are combined. Increase the speed to medium and knead the dough for 5 to 7 minutes, or until it pulls away from the sides of the bowl and begins to lose its rough texture. Transfer to a lightly floured surface and knead it by hand for a few minutes, until the dough is smooth and a bit shiny.

If making by hand, add the yeast mixture, sourdough starter, and lukewarm water to the bowl. Mix with a wooden spoon until the ingredients are combined. Transfer to a lightly floured surface and knead for 10 to 15 minutes, or until the dough is smooth and a bit shiny.

Form the dough into a ball and place it in a large oiled bowl. Turn the dough over to coat it with oil. Cover the bowl with plastic wrap or a damp kitchen towel and let rise in a warm, draft-free place for 2 hours, or until increased in size by one-third.

Sprinkle a baking sheet with the 1 tablespoon cornmeal. Transfer the dough to a lightly floured surface and divide it into 2 pieces. Shape each piece into an oval (see page 28) and place on the prepared pan. Cover with a floured kitchen towel and let rise in a warm place for 1½ hours, or until a finger pressed into the dough leaves an impression.

Fifteen minutes before the bread has finished rising, remove all but the middle rack from the oven. Place a metal roasting pan on the floor of the oven and preheat the oven to 425°F. Slash the top of each loaf (see page 31) and mist them with water using a spray bottle. Wait at least 10 minutes for the slashes to begin to open.

Pour ½ cup cold water into a measuring cup and add enough ice cubes to bring the volume to 1 cup. Working quickly so that you don't lose too much heat, place the baking sheet in the oven and pour the ice water into the roasting pan. Immediately close the oven door to maintain a steamy environment.

Bake for 5 minutes, then prepare another round of ice water and repeat the process. Bake 15 minutes longer, then rotate the baking sheet front to back. Bake 20 to 25 minutes longer, for a total baking time of 40 to 45 minutes, or until the bread is deep brown and sounds hollow when tapped on the bottom. Using the spray bottle, mist the loaves to give the crust a glossy shine. Immediately close the oven door and bake for 1 minute. Transfer the loaves to a wire rack to cool.

I have learned so much here. The business is based on the idea of generosity—that is the basis of the collective and the ideals of the collective. It's a way of thinking I was very unfamiliar with.

—LAURA

Pumpernickel

This recipe makes a dark, moist loaf, our only rye bread without caraway seeds. It's not necessary to color the loaf, but the caramel coloring does make it a lovely rich brown.

MAKES 2 LOAVES
Preparation time including rising and baking: 5 hours;
active time: 45 minutes

1 teaspoon active dry yeast
¼ cup warm water
2½ cups bread flour
3½ cups medium rye flour
¼ cup pumpernickel rye flour
¼ cup semolina
¼ cup cracked rye
¼ cup plus 1 tablespoon medium-grind yellow
    cornmeal
1 tablespoon kosher salt
2 teaspoons caramel color or unsweetened cocoa
    powder (optional)
1 teaspoon blackstrap molasses
1 cup (8 ounces) Sourdough Starter (page 90)
1 cup lukewarm water

In a small bowl, whisk the yeast into the warm water until dissolved. Let stand for 5 minutes.

In the bowl of a stand mixer or a large bowl, combine the flours, semolina, cracked rye, the ¼ cup cornmeal, and the salt.

If using a stand mixer, add the yeast mixture, caramel color, molasses, sourdough starter, and lukewarm water to the bowl. Mix on low speed with the dough hook for 5 minutes, or until the ingredients are combined. Increase the speed to medium and knead the dough for 5 to 7 minutes, or until it pulls away from the sides of the bowl and begins to lose its rough texture. Transfer to a lightly floured surface and knead by hand for a few minutes, until the dough is smooth and a bit shiny.

If making by hand, add the yeast mixture, caramel color, molasses, sourdough starter, and lukewarm water to the bowl. Mix with a wooden spoon until the ingredients are combined. Transfer to a lightly floured surface and knead for 10 to 15 minutes, or until the dough is smooth and a bit shiny.

Form the dough into a ball and place it in a large oiled bowl. Turn the dough over to coat it with oil. Cover the bowl with plastic wrap or a damp kitchen towel and let rise in a warm, draft-free place for 2 hours, or until increased in size by one-third.

Sprinkle a baking sheet with the 1 tablespoon cornmeal. Transfer the dough to a lightly floured surface and divide it into 2 pieces. Shape each piece into a large round (see page 27) and place on the prepared pan. Cover with a floured kitchen towel and let rise in a warm place for 1½ hours, or until a finger pressed into the dough leaves an impression.

Fifteen minutes before the bread has finished rising, remove all but the middle rack from the oven. Place a metal roasting pan on the floor of the oven and preheat the oven to 425°F. Slash the top of each loaf (see page 31) and mist them with water using a spray bottle. Wait at least 10 minutes for the slashes to begin to open.

Pour ½ cup cold water into a measuring cup and add enough ice cubes to bring the volume to 1 cup. Working quickly so that you don't lose too much heat, place the baking sheet in the oven and pour the ice water into the roasting pan. Immediately close the oven door to maintain a steamy environment.

Bake for 5 minutes, then prepare another round of ice water and repeat the process. Bake 15 minutes longer, then rotate the baking sheet front to back. Bake 20 to 25 minutes longer, for a total baking time of 40 to 45 minutes, or until the bread is dark brown and sounds hollow when tapped on the bottom. Using the spray bottle, mist the loaves to give the crust a glossy shine. Immediately close the oven door and bake for 1 minute. Transfer the loaves to a wire rack to cool.

Marble Rye

Marble rye is two breads in one, made by combining light rye and pumpernickel doughs. When cut, the bread has dramatic swirls of dark and light. Both the light rye and the dark rye used to be baked on Tuesdays at the Cheese Board, which gave the originator of this loaf the idea to roll them together and create marble rye.

MAKES 4 LOAVES
Preparation time including rising and baking: 5³/₄ hours;
active time: 50 minutes

> 2 tablespoons medium-grind yellow cornmeal
> 1 recipe Light Rye (see page 120), prepared through
>   the first rise
> 1 recipe Pumpernickel (see page 121), prepared
>   through the first rise

Sprinkle each of 2 baking sheets with 1 tablespoon cornmeal.

Transfer the light rye dough to a lightly floured surface and roll it out with a rolling pin into a 10 by 12-inch rectangle. On a separate floured surface, roll the pumpernickel dough out into a 10 by 12-inch rectangle.

Lay the pumpernickel on top of the light rye and roll the dough up jelly roll–style (see page 29) into a cylindrical loaf 6 inches in diameter and about 12 inches long. Cut the roll into 4 pieces and carefully tuck the cut ends under. Shape each piece into a large round (see page 27), taking care to keep the light rye on the outside of the formed loaf. Place 2 loaves on each of the prepared pans and cover with a floured kitchen towel. Let rise in a warm place for 2 hours, or until a finger pressed into the dough leaves an impression.

Fifteen minutes before the bread has finished rising, arrange the oven racks in the upper and lower thirds of the oven. Place a metal roasting pan on the floor of the oven and preheat the oven to 425°. Slash the top of each loaf (see page 31) and mist them with water using a spray bottle. Wait at least 10 minutes for the slashes to begin to open.

Pour ½ cup cold water into a measuring cup and add enough ice cubes to bring the volume to 1 cup. Working quickly so that you don't lose too much heat, place the baking sheets in the oven and pour the ice water into the roasting pan. Immediately close the oven door to maintain a steamy environment.

Bake for 5 minutes, then prepare another round of ice water and repeat the process. Bake 15 minutes longer, then rotate the baking sheets front to back and trade their rack positions. Bake 20 to 25 minutes longer, for a total baking time of 40 to 45 minutes, or until the bread is deep brown and sounds hollow when tapped on the bottom. Using the spray bottle, mist the loaves to give the crust a glossy shine. Immediately close the oven door and bake for 1 minute. Transfer the loaves to wire racks to cool.

I came in the first day the Cheese Board opened. I was married to a conservative architect and had been living in Orinda for seventeen years. Berkeley was heaven to me. I'd come into Berkeley, sit in the Med, and read Pauline Kael's reviews for the Cinema Guild Studio. It was the beginning of my slow escape from suburbia.   —PAT DARROW

Sourdough Beer Rye

People often refer to this sour, dense bread with its cornmeal-coated crust as an "old country" bread. One customer described it as "perfect with a bowl of hearty borscht." Beer rye is a good keeper and can be eaten for up to a week after being baked. Our German members always claimed that it was better to wait a day before eating rye breads.

MAKES 2 LOAVES
Preparation time including rising and baking: 4½ hours; active time: 1 hour

1 teaspoon active dry yeast
¼ cup warm water
1½ cups bread flour
¾ cup medium or dark rye flour
¼ cup old-fashioned rolled oats
¼ cup medium-grind yellow cornmeal
¼ cup cracked rye
1 tablespoon kosher salt
1 tablespoon caraway seeds
1 cup (8 ounces) Sourdough Starter (page 90)
One 12-ounce bottle dark beer
½ cup coarse yellow cornmeal or polenta

In a small bowl, whisk the yeast into the warm water until dissolved. Let stand for 5 minutes.

In the bowl of a stand mixer or a large bowl, combine the flours, oats, cornmeal, cracked rye, salt, and caraway seeds.

If using a stand mixer, add the yeast mixture, sourdough starter, and beer to the bowl. Mix on low speed with the dough hook for 5 minutes, or until the ingredients are combined. Increase the speed to medium and knead the dough for 5 to 7 minutes, or until it pulls away from the sides of the bowl and begins to lose its rough texture. Transfer to a lightly floured surface and knead by hand for a few minutes, until the dough is smooth and a bit shiny.

If making by hand, add the yeast mixture, sourdough starter, and beer to the bowl. Mix with a wooden spoon until the ingredients are combined. Transfer to a lightly floured surface and knead for 10 to 15 minutes, or until the dough is smooth and a bit shiny.

Form the dough into a ball and place it in a large oiled bowl. Turn the dough over to coat it with oil. Cover the bowl with plastic wrap or a damp kitchen towel and let rise in a warm, draft-free place for 2 hours, or until increased in size by one-third.

Sprinkle a baking sheet with 2 tablespoons of the cornmeal and put the remaining cornmeal in a medium bowl. Transfer the dough to a lightly floured surface and divide it into 2 pieces. Shape each piece into a large round (see page 27). Using a spray bottle, mist the loaves with water. Roll the loaves in the bowl of cornmeal to coat them. Place the loaves on the prepared pan and slash the top of each loaf (see page 31). Cover with a floured kitchen towel and let rise in a warm place for at least 1½ hours, or until a finger pressed into the dough leaves an impression and the slashes have opened more fully.

Fifteen minutes before the bread has finished rising, remove all but the middle rack from the oven. Place a metal roasting pan on the floor of the oven and preheat the oven to 375°F. Mist the loaves again with water.

Pour ½ cup cold water into a measuring cup and add enough ice cubes to bring the volume to 1 cup. Working quickly so that you don't lose too much heat, place the baking sheet in the oven and pour the ice water into the roasting pan. Immediately close the oven door to maintain a steamy environment.

Bake for 5 minutes, then prepare another round of ice water and repeat the process. Bake 15 minutes longer, then rotate the baking sheet front to back. Bake 20 to 25 minutes longer, for a total baking time of 40 to 45 minutes, or until the bread is deep brown and sounds hollow when tapped on the bottom. Using the spray bottle, mist the loaves to give the crust a glossy shine. Immediately close the oven door and bake for 1 minute. Transfer the loaves to a wire rack to cool.

BECOMING A CHEESE BOARDER

I came out to Berkeley in the first place because I had applied for conscientious-objector status during the Vietnam War. My compatriots back in Ohio told me that once I got my conscientious-objector status in the Midwest that Berkeley was very sympathetic to objectors.

I needed to do my two years of service for my country in a civilian status, so I chose to work in Alta Bates hospital in Berkeley in the surgery department as an orderly. That brought me to Berkeley in the late sixties.

I joined the collective in 1975. I didn't join because of the business of selling food to the public, but for the political and collective nature of the business, and because of the relationships between the people. I knew a few of the members, Philip and Renate and Virginia. Interestingly enough, they got me into the collective without an interview. I wasn't even in the country when I got voted in as a member of the collective! I was in Puerto Rico, and the collective just went on the word of these three people that I would be a good person to join. So Virginia sent me a letter in Puerto Rico saying that if I wanted to work at the Cheese Board I was in, and when I got back in the country I should just come by.

They were in the middle of moving the store from the spot on Vine Street, where the Juice Bar is now, to our present location on Shattuck Avenue. I happened to be a carpenter so they wanted me to start out by remodeling the new rental space here on Shattuck. Three or four of us put the store together, and we went on from there.

—Michael

Honorary member Charlie B.

CHAPTER FIVE

HOLIDAYS

MARKING THE HOLIDAYS with special foods is a tradition that evolved at the Cheese Board as one member or another introduced baked goods that appealed to them. With so many different breads baked over a given week, the Cheese Board bread schedule is confusing at any time of year, but during holidays we add more breads to our already-packed list. Some of these baked goods are seasonal variations on standard breads, while those featured in this chapter are unique to a specific holiday.

For Valentine's Day, we make Deep Dark Chocolate Loaves and our usual shortbread cut into heart shapes and drizzled with chocolate (page 70)—that's easy. Then comes St. Patrick's Day, which we honor with our Irish soda scones. Hot cross buns are a great Easter tradition, and in summertime we put out garlic baguettes for Bastille Day (page 94). Starting in the late fall, our baking schedule becomes increasingly hectic. Holiday challah is made

for Rosh Hashanah (page 76). Fruitcakes need to be baked and aged in rum and brandy starting in October in order to be ready in December. Instead of making sweets for Halloween, we bake Halloween pizza (page 214), and the next day we make Day of the Dead Bread. Thanksgiving brings Stuffing Bread, as well as the tart surprise of cranberries in the brioche (page 61).

As the close of the year approaches, there is a palpable feeling of excitement and building momentum in the bustling store as the collective swings into high gear. We whip up cheese balls, put out the aged fruitcake for sale, and load the shelves with Florentine cookies, saffron bread, stollen, and various little sweet quick breads. Our usual days off are taken up with producing holiday goods. It is an exciting and exhausting time of year, so much so that we need to close the store for a full week after New Year's Eve in order to recuperate.

HOLIDAYS

Deep Dark Chocolate Loaves 129

Hot Cross Buns 130

Irish Soda Scones 132

Fruitcake 133

Day of the Dead Bread 134

Stuffing Bread 136

Florentines 137

Holiday Loaves 138

   Date Spread 139

   Cheese Balls 139

Saffron Bread 140

Gingerbread 141

Stollen 142

Deep Dark Chocolate Loaves

These sinful little loaves should really be called cakes. We make them for Valentine's Day, since they are perfect for a decadent dessert after a romantic dinner. The cake is so rich that frosting is superfluous—though there always is Chantilly cream.

MAKES 6 SMALL LOAVES OR 2 CAKES
Preparation time including baking: 1¼ hours

2 eggs

1 cup sour cream

1 cup strong brewed coffee, cooled

1 cup heavy cream

1 teaspoon pure vanilla extract

3 cups unbleached all-purpose flour

½ teaspoon baking soda

1 tablespoon baking powder

1⅓ cups unsweetened cocoa powder

½ teaspoon salt

1½ cups sugar

1 cup (2 sticks) cold unsalted butter, cut into
    1-inch cubes

1½ cups chocolate chips

Preheat oven to 350°F. Generously butter or spray 6 small (5 by 3-inch) aluminum loaf pans. If making this recipe into 2 cake rounds, generously butter or spray two 9-inch cake pans.

In a medium bowl, combine the eggs, sour cream, coffee, heavy cream, and vanilla. Whisk until blended.

Sift the flour, baking soda, baking powder, and cocoa powder together into the bowl of a stand mixer or a large bowl.

If using a stand mixer, add the salt and sugar to the dry ingredients and mix with the paddle attachment on low speed until combined. Add the butter and cut it in on low speed for about 4 minutes, or until it is the size of small peas. Mix in the chocolate chips. Make a well in the center and pour in the wet ingredients. Mix briefly, just until the ingredients come together.

If making by hand, add the salt and sugar to the dry ingredients and stir with a wooden spoon until combined. Add the butter and cut it in with a pastry cutter or 2 dinner knives until it is the size of small peas. Using the spoon, mix in the chocolate chips. Make a well in the center and pour in the wet ingredients. Mix briefly, just until the ingredients come together.

Fill each loaf pan three-fourths full with batter. If baking cakes, fill each pan equally with the batter. Place the pans on the middle rack of the oven. Bake for 25 minutes, then rotate the pans front to back and trade their positions. Bake 10 minutes longer, for a total baking time of 35 minutes, or until the loaves or cakes are firm and springy and a toothpick inserted in the center comes out clean. Let cool in the pans on wire racks for 10 minutes, then unmold and let cool completely.

Hot Cross Buns

Some baker years ago (who knows who) thought that including these traditional buns would be a good way to celebrate the vernal equinox. We make them the day before Easter. They are small, sweet, and spicy buns decorated with confectioners' sugar icing.

MAKES 12 BUNS

Preparation time including rising and baking: 2³/₄ hours; active time: 45 minutes

1 tablespoon active dry yeast
¹/₄ cup warm water
4 cups bread flour
¹/₂ cup granulated sugar
Grated zest of 1 orange
¹/₂ teaspoon ground cinnamon
¹/₄ teaspoon ground ginger
¹/₄ teaspoon ground nutmeg
2 teaspoons kosher salt
¹/₂ cup (1 stick) cold unsalted butter, cut into
   1-inch cubes
¹/₂ cup lukewarm water
¹/₂ cup Ricotta cheese
4 eggs
¹/₂ cup dried currants

Glaze
1³/₄ cups confectioners' sugar
¹/₄ cup warm milk

In a small bowl, whisk the yeast into the warm water until dissolved. Let stand for 5 minutes.

In the bowl of the stand mixer or a large bowl, combine the flour, sugar, orange zest, cinnamon, ginger, nutmeg, and salt.

If using a stand mixer, add the butter to the dry ingredients and cut it in with the paddle attachment on low speed for about 4 minutes, or until it is the size of small peas. Add the yeast mixture, lukewarm water, Ricotta, and 3 of the eggs, and mix on low speed until the ingredients are combined, about 2 minutes. Switch to the dough hook, increase the

mixer speed to medium, and knead for 10 minutes, or until the dough loses its rough texture and begins to acquire a satiny sheen. Add the currants and knead until the fruit is incorporated, about 1 minute. Transfer to a lightly floured surface and knead by hand for a few minutes, until the dough is smooth and elastic.

If making by hand, add the butter to the dry ingredients and cut it in with a pastry cutter or 2 dinner knives until it is the size of small peas. Add the yeast mixture, lukewarm water, Ricotta, and 3 of the eggs, and mix with a wooden spoon until the ingredients are combined. Transfer to a lightly floured surface and knead for 12 minutes, or until the dough is smooth and elastic. Flatten the dough and sprinkle with the currants. Knead until the fruit is incorporated.

Form the dough into a ball and place it in a large oiled bowl. Turn the dough over to coat it with oil. Cover the bowl with plastic wrap or a damp kitchen towel and let rise in a warm, draft-free place for 1 hour, or until doubled in size.

Line 2 baking sheets with parchment paper or baking mats. Transfer the dough to a lightly floured surface and divide it into 12 pieces. Shape the pieces into small rounds (see page 24) and place them at least 3 inches apart on the prepared pans. Cover with a floured kitchen towel and let rise in a warm place for 45 minutes, or until the buns are rounded and puffy, and a finger pressed into the dough leaves an impression.

Fifteen minutes before the buns have finished rising, arrange the oven racks in the upper and lower thirds of the oven. Preheat the oven to 375°F.

In a small bowl, whisk the remaining egg. Using a pastry brush, brush the top and sides of each bun with the beaten egg.

Bake for 15 minutes, then rotate the baking sheets front to back and trade their rack positions. Bake 15 minutes longer, for a total baking time of 30 minutes, or until the rolls are golden on the top and bottom. Line a work surface with newspaper and place a wire rack on top. Transfer the buns to the rack to cool for 20 minutes.

While the buns are cooling make the glaze: Warm the milk in a small saucepan. Add the confectioners' sugar and whisk until blended to a smooth glaze. Using a teaspoon or pastry bag, drizzle the icing onto each bun in the form of a cross.

Irish Soda Scones

For years the Cheese Board made Irish soda bread on St. Patrick's Day. Two years ago, one of our members developed an Irish soda scone recipe, taking our tradition in a new direction. These scones are triangular in shape and flakier than our regular scones. Sweetened only with golden raisins, they are perfect to split open and spread with butter and jam.

MAKES 12 SCONES
Preparation time including baking: 45 minutes

3½ cups unbleached all-purpose flour
¾ teaspoon baking soda
1 tablespoon baking powder
½ teaspoon kosher salt
¾ cup old-fashioned rolled oats
2 tablespoons caraway seeds
1¼ cups (2½ sticks) cold unsalted butter, cut into
    1-inch cubes
1 cup golden raisins
1½ cups buttermilk

Preheat the oven to 375°F. Line a baking sheet with parchment paper or a baking mat.

Sift the flour, baking soda, and baking powder together into the bowl of a stand mixer or a large bowl.

If using a stand mixer, add the salt, oats, and caraway seeds, and mix with the paddle attachment on low speed until combined. Add the butter and cut it in on low speed for about 4 minutes, or until it is the size of small peas. Mix in the raisins. Make a well in the center and add the buttermilk. Mix briefly, just until the ingredients come together; add a bit more buttermilk if the dough seems too dry. Let stand for 10 minutes to allow the oats to absorb the liquid.

If making by hand, add the salt, oats, and caraway seeds, and stir with a wooden spoon until combined. Add the butter and cut it in with a pastry cutter or 2 dinner knives until it is the size of small peas. Using the spoon, mix in the raisins. Make a well in the center and add the buttermilk. Mix briefly, just until the ingredients come together; add a bit more buttermilk if the dough seems too dry. Let stand for 10 minutes to allow the oats to absorb the liquid.

Place the dough on a generously floured surface. Using a rolling pin, roll the dough out into a 1-inch-thick rectangle. Fold the rectangle in half and roll it again until it is 1 inch thick. Repeat twice more. Your final rectangle should be approximately 5 by 9 by 1 inch thick. Divide the dough in half lengthwise and then cut each piece into 6 even triangles.

Place the scones on the prepared pan about 2 inches apart. Bake on the middle rack of the oven for 30 minutes, or until light brown. Transfer the scones to a wire rack to cool.

Working here, I feel that it's like being in a wonderful, large room. You can go to any corner of the room and somebody is there doing something in a way that you like: it could be the way that they are cutting the Parmesan or the way they are speaking to a customer. I have been given the opportunity to pull different knowledge from different people. You can change yourself here. It's a precious space.

—CARRIE

Fruitcake

Even if you don't like fruitcake, you may love these. There are no weirdly colored unidentifiable candied fruits in this recipe, only dried fruits and whole nuts. Weighing the ingredients makes for a more successful cake, but we have included cup measurements in case you don't have a scale. The most time-consuming part of making fruitcake is amassing all the ingredients.

The dried fruit needs to soak in the alcohol overnight to soften, so begin making these one day ahead. The flavor improves with age; we make our cakes in October for sale at the end of November.

MAKES 3 SMALL FRUITCAKES
Preparation time including baking: 3 hours

Fruit

    1 cup brandy

    1 cup rum

    8 ounces (1½ cups) raisins

    4 ounces (¾ cup) dried figs, coarsely chopped

    4 ounces (¾ cup) pitted dates, coarsely chopped

    4 ounces (¾ cup) dried currants

    2 ounces (1 cup) unsweetened coconut

    2 ounces (⅓ cup) dried pears, coarsely chopped

    2 ounces (⅓ cup) dried nectarines, coarsely chopped

    2 ounces (⅓ cup) dried peaches, coarsely chopped

    2 ounces (⅓ cup) dried apricots, coarsely chopped

Cake

    ½ unpeeled lemon, seeded and coarsely chopped

    ½ unpeeled orange, seeded and coarsely chopped

    1½ cups unbleached all-purpose flour

    ¾ teaspoon ground cinnamon

    ¼ teaspoon ground nutmeg

    ⅛ teaspoon ground allspice

    ⅛ teaspoon ground cloves

    ⅛ teaspoon ground ginger

    ¾ cup (1½ sticks) unsalted butter, at room temperature

    ¾ cup packed light brown sugar

    ½ teaspoon kosher salt

    ⅔ cup dark unsulfured molasses

    2 eggs

    4 ounces (¾ cup) blanched almonds, toasted (see page 23)

    2 ounces (⅓ cup) Brazil nuts, toasted

    2 ounces (⅓ cup) pecans, toasted

    2 ounces (⅓ cup) walnuts, toasted

    2 ounces (⅓ cup) hazelnuts, toasted

    Soaked dried fruits, above

Liquor

    2 tablespoons brandy

    2 tablespoons rum

To soak the fruit, combine the 1 cup brandy and 1 cup rum in a large bowl. Add the fruit and soak overnight.

The next day, preheat the oven to 275°F. Generously butter or spray with cooking spray the insides of 3 small (5 by 3-inch) aluminum loaf pans.

Chop or process the lemon and orange until they are a fine, smooth purée. Set aside.

Sift the flour and the spices together into a small bowl. Set aside.

If using a stand mixer, combine the butter, brown sugar, and salt in the bowl. With the paddle attachment on medium speed, cream the mixture together for about 4 minutes, until light and fluffy. Add the molasses and eggs and mix on low speed until blended. Add the flour mixture and mix briefly. Reserving 9 almonds, add the nuts, chopped orange and lemon, and the soaked dried fruits (and any remaining liquid), and mix until completely blended, about 2 minutes.

If making by hand, combine the butter, brown sugar, and salt in a large bowl. Cream the mixture together with a wooden spoon until light and fluffy. Add the molasses and eggs and mix until blended. Add the flour mixture and mix briefly. Reserving 9 almonds, add the nuts, chopped orange and lemon, and the soaked dried fruits (and any remaining liquid), and mix until completely blended.

Scoop the batter into the prepared pans. Smooth the tops of the batter into gentle domes that rise just over the rim of the pans. Decorate the top of each fruitcake with 3 of the reserved almonds. Place the pans on the middle rack of the oven. Bake for 1 hour, then rotate the pans front to back and trade their positions. Bake 40 minutes longer, or until a toothpick inserted in the center of the cakes comes out clean. Transfer the pans to a wire rack.

Combine the 2 tablespoons brandy and 2 tablespoons rum in a small bowl. Using a pastry brush, brush the cakes with the liquor while they are still warm. Let cool completely. Unmold the cakes. Wrap them first with plastic wrap, then with aluminum foil, and store in an airtight container in a cool place. Let age for at least 1 month before eating. We have eaten delicious fruitcake that has been aged for a year! (If you do keep the cakes this long, douse them with 2 more tablespoons each of the brandy and rum halfway through the year.)

Wednesdays, when I'm schlepping fifty-pound bags of flour and throwing them up on the shelves, and sweating and climbing up the ladder and loading up the sugar, I'm thinking that people go to the gym and work out. I'm working out *and* I'm getting paid for it!   —STU

Day of the Dead Bread

The Days of the Dead are celebrated throughout Latin America on November 1 and 2. Images of the dead in skeleton form are made as sweets to be offered and eaten in memory of the departed. Day of the Dead Bread was first made at the Cheese Board by children as a fundraiser for a local school. The students fashioned dough into the shape of people, glazed them with sweet orange icing, and decorated them with dried currants. The project inspired us to include this bread in our holiday repertoire. (You can also top the breads with brightly colored candied aniseeds, found in Indian food markets.)

MAKES 6 BREADS

Preparation time including rising and baking: 3¹/₂ hours; active time: 1 hour

    2 tablespoons active dry yeast
    ¹/₄ cup warm water
    4 ¹/₂ cups bread flour
    ¹/₂ cup granulated sugar
    2 teaspoons aniseeds
    2 teaspoons kosher salt
    ¹/₂ cup (1 stick) cold unsalted butter, cut into
        1-inch cubes
    3 eggs
    ¹/₂ cup lukewarm water
    ¹/₄ cup orange juice
    1 tablespoon dried currants

Topping

1/4 cup orange juice

2 tablespoons confectioners' sugar

2 tablespoons candied aniseeds (optional)

In a small bowl, whisk the yeast into the warm water until dissolved. Let stand for 5 minutes.

In the bowl of a stand mixer or a large bowl, combine the flour, sugar, aniseeds, and salt.

If using a stand mixer, add the butter to the dry ingredients and cut it in with the paddle attachment on low speed for 4 minutes, or until it is the size of small peas. Add the yeast mixture, eggs, lukewarm water, and orange juice, and mix on low speed until the ingredients are combined, about 2 minutes. Switch to the dough hook, increase the mixer speed to medium, and knead for 10 minutes, or until the dough loses its rough texture and begins to acquire a satiny sheen. Transfer to a lightly floured surface and knead by hand for a few minutes, until the dough is smooth and elastic.

If making by hand, add the butter to the dry ingredients and cut it in with a pastry cutter or 2 dinner knives

until it is the size of small peas. Add the yeast mixture, eggs, lukewarm water, and orange juice, and mix with a wooden spoon until the ingredients are combined. Transfer to a lightly floured surface and knead for 12 minutes, or until the dough is smooth and elastic.

Form the dough into a ball and place it in a large oiled bowl. Turn the dough over to coat it with oil. Cover the bowl with plastic wrap or a damp kitchen towel and let rise in a warm, draft-free place for 1 hour, or until doubled in size.

Line 2 baking sheets with parchment paper or baking mats. Transfer the dough to a lightly floured surface and divide it into 6 pieces. Gently form each piece into a loose round (see page 26) and cover with a floured kitchen towel. Let rest for 10 minutes. Imagining each round to be a domed clock face, make five 1½-inch cuts into the interior of the round (leaving at least 1 inch across intact in the middle of the round), at 10, 20, 30, 40, and 50 minutes (fig. A). Shape each piece of dough into a human form by gently pulling, rolling, and shaping the arms, legs, and head (fig. B). Put the shaped dough on the prepared pans, crossing the arms (fig. C).

Cover with a floured kitchen towel and let rise in a warm place for about 45 minutes, or until rounded and a finger pressed into the dough leaves an impression.

Fifteen minutes before the breads have finished rising, arrange the oven racks in the upper and lower thirds of the oven. Preheat the oven to 375°F. Decorate the figures with currants to create eyes and buttons, pressing the currants firmly into the dough (fig. D).

Bake for 15 minutes, then rotate the baking sheets front to back and trade their rack positions. Bake 15 minutes longer, for a total baking time of 30 minutes, or until the breads are a deep golden brown.

While the breads are baking, make the topping: In a small saucepan, combine the orange juice and confectioners' sugar. Stir over low heat for a few minutes to make a smooth, hot glaze.

Line a work surface with newspaper and place 2 wire racks on top. Transfer the breads to the racks. While the breads are still hot, brush the glaze onto them with a pastry brush. Sprinkle with the candied aniseeds.

Stuffing Bread (aka Turkey Bread)

Many years ago, one of our members was devoted to making this bread with homemade turkey stock. It is now a vegetarian bread, but we still use the traditional Thanksgiving flavors of sage, celery, and onions. You can use this bread for stuffing by making it a day or two ahead. It's also good for turkey sandwiches.

MAKES 2 LOAVES
Preparation time including rising and baking: 3½ hours; active time: 45 minutes

----

1 tablespoon plus 1½ teaspoons active dry yeast

¼ cup warm water

4½ cups bread flour

1 tablespoon plus 1 teaspoon kosher salt

1 tablespoon minced fresh sage, or ½ teaspoon
  dried sage

½ cup buttermilk

1½ tablespoons unsalted butter at room temperature

1⅔ cup lukewarm water

1 yellow onion, finely chopped

1 stalk celery, finely chopped

In a small bowl, whisk the yeast into the warm water until dissolved. Let stand for 5 minutes.

In the bowl of a stand mixer or a large bowl, combine the flour, salt, and sage.

If using a stand mixer, add the yeast mixture, buttermilk, butter, and lukewarm water to the bowl. Using the paddle attachment on low speed, mix until the ingredients are combined, about 2 minutes. Switch to the dough hook, increase the mixer speed to medium, and knead for 10 minutes, or until the dough is soft and sticky. Add the onion and celery and knead just until incorporated (you may need to add a bit more flour because the vegetables add moisture). Transfer to a lightly floured surface and knead by hand for a few minutes, until the dough is soft, shiny, and a little sticky.

If making by hand, add the yeast mixture, buttermilk, butter, and lukewarm water to the bowl and mix with a wooden spoon until the ingredients are combined. Transfer to a lightly floured surface and knead for 12 minutes, or until the dough is soft, shiny, and a little sticky. Flatten the dough out, sprinkle the onions and celery over the top, and roll it into a ball. Knead just until incorporated (you may need to add a bit more flour because the vegetables add moisture).

Form the dough into a ball and place it in a large oiled bowl. Turn the dough over to coat it with oil. Cover the bowl with plastic wrap or a damp kitchen towel and let rise in a warm, draft-free place for 1 to 1½ hours, or until doubled in size.

Lightly spray 2 loaf pans with cooking spray. Transfer the dough to a lightly floured surface, and divide it into 2 pieces. Gently form each piece into a loose round (see page 26) and cover with a floured kitchen towel. Let rest for 10 minutes. Shape each piece into a loaf (see page 28) and place in the prepared pans. Sprinkle flour over the tops of the loaves and spread it out evenly over the top. Cover with a floured kitchen towel and let rise in a warm place for 45 minutes, or until the loaves have risen 1 inch above the rim of the pan and a finger pressed into the dough leaves an impression.

Fifteen minutes before the loaves have finished rising, remove all but the middle rack from the oven. Preheat the oven to 375°F.

Place the loaves in the oven and bake for 25 minutes. Turn the loaf pans around front to back and switch sides left to right. Bake 25 minutes longer, for a total baking time of 50 minutes, or until the loaves are golden and sound hollow when tapped on the bottom. Unmold onto a wire rack to cool.

Years ago people seemed to think that they had to give up their other life to make the Cheese Board run. Nowadays people feel like, "It can run without me. I don't want it to run forever without me, but it's okay to be gone for a while."

—ARAYAH

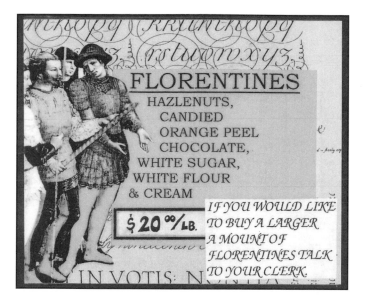

Florentines

Rich, decadent, and addictive, these cookies are almost a confection. They were first made as Christmas presents for Cheese Board members, but word leaked out, and they have become a once-a-year bakery treat. Florentines are so labor-intensive that the Christmas baking crew looks forward to making them with mingled anticipation and dread. We prefer to use a Belgian couverture chocolate (a candy grade of chocolate) such as Callebaut for dipping, as it melts more smoothly and has an intense flavor.

MAKES 48 COOKIES
Preparation time including baking: 1½ hours;
active time: 45 minutes

- 1 scant cup (4 ounces) hazelnuts, toasted, skins on (see page 23)
- ½ cup (4 ounces) candied orange peel
- ½ cup sugar
- ¼ cup unbleached all-purpose flour
- Pinch of kosher salt
- ⅔ to ¾ cup heavy cream
- 8 ounces semisweet chocolate, coarsely chopped

Arrange the oven racks in the upper and lower thirds of the oven. Preheat the oven to 350°F. Line 3 baking sheets with parchment paper.

If using a food processor, coarsely chop the nuts and then take them out of the bowl. Put the orange peel and ¼ cup of the sugar in the food processor and process until fine. Return the nuts and pulse for a few seconds until the mixture is mostly the texture of coarse sand, with some larger pieces of nuts remaining.

If chopping by hand, use a chef's knife to finely chop the nuts to the texture of coarse sand, with some larger pieces remaining. Chop the orange peel with ¼ cup of the sugar until fine.

The rest of the mixing is best done by hand. In a large bowl, combine the nuts and orange sugar mixture, the remaining ¼ cup sugar, the flour, and salt. Stir with a rubber spatula or wooden spoon until thoroughly combined. Add ⅔ cup of the cream and mix briefly to form a loose, soft dough; if the batter appears firm and stiff, add more cream by the tablespoonful until it loosens up. (This dough can be refrigerated now for up to 5 days; however, 1 to 2 tablespoons cream should be added before using.)

Place teaspoonfuls of dough 2 inches apart on the prepared pans, 16 cookies to a sheet. Fill a small bowl with water to wet your hand. Flatten the spoonfuls of dough with the wet heel of your hand until they are spread out and uniformly ⅛ inch thick or less, though not so thin that the paper shows through.

Put 2 sheets of cookies in the oven and bake for 12 to 18 minutes, watching carefully for the moment the cookies turn golden brown. Let cool on the pans for 5 minutes, then transfer to wire racks to cool completely. Bake the last sheet of cookies in the same way.

While the cookies are cooling, melt the chocolate in a double boiler over barely simmering water (see page 19).

Turn the parchment paper used for baking the cookies upside-down on the work surface. Transfer both parts of the double boiler to a heatproof spot on the counter. Dunk the cooled cookies halfway into the warm melted chocolate and place them on the parchment. (This part can get very deliciously messy! It should be done quickly so as not to get too thick a coating on the cookie.) If the chocolate begins to cool, replace the cooled water in the bottom section of the double boiler with hot water. Let the cookies set completely before storing, about 4 hours. The cookies are fragile, so stack them gently. They will keep for weeks stored in an airtight container in a cool place.

Holiday Loaves

We make small, sweet loaves from our muffin batter during the holidays. They are nice to serve on holiday mornings or to give as gifts.

MAKES 5 SMALL LOAVES
Preparation time including baking: 1¹/₄ hours

> 1 recipe Lemon Poppy Seed Muffins (page 54), Banana Mocha Chocolate Chip Muffins (page 56), Pecan Pear Muffins (page 58), or Raspberry Orange Muffins (page 58)

Preheat the oven to 350°F. Generously butter or spray with cooking spray 5 small (5 by 3-inch) loaf pans. Fill each about three-fourths full with batter.

Place the pans on the middle rack of the oven. Bake for 25 minutes, then rotate the pans front to back and trade their positions. Bake 10 minutes longer, for a total baking time of 35 minutes, or until the loaves are firm and springy and a toothpick inserted in the center comes out clean. Let cool in the pans on a wire rack for 10 minutes, then unmold and let cool completely.

Date Spread

We make this spread for the winter holidays. Sweet and cinnamony, it's good on Sunday Bread.

MAKES 1¹/₂ CUPS
Preparation time: 20 minutes

- 1 cup (¹/₂ pound) cream cheese at room temperature
- 2 tablespoons heavy cream
- ¹/₂ cup (3 ounces) Medjool dates, pitted and chopped
- 2 tablespoons dried currants
- 1 tablespoon honey
- Scant teaspoon ground cinnamon

Put the cream cheese in the bowl of a stand mixer. Using the paddle attachment, mix on medium speed until smooth, about 2 minutes. Add the heavy cream and mix on low until well blended. Add the dates, currants, honey, and cinnamon and mix on low speed just until blended. Or, use a wooden spoon to stir the ingredients in a bowl.

Serve immediately or store covered in the refrigerator for up to 1 week.

Cheese Balls

Cheese balls are a holdover from the fifties. We are almost embarrassed to be making such Mrs. Cleaver items without a gingham apron, but the fact is these are delicious. Place them on the buffet next to your molded Jell-O.

MAKES 4 CHEESE BALLS
Preparation time: 30 minutes

- 1¹/₂ pounds sharp Cheddar cheese cut into 1-inch cubes, at room temperature
- 3 tablespoons crumbled Roquefort cheese
- ¹/₂ cup plus 2 tablespoons (5 ounces) cream cheese
- 1 clove garlic, minced
- 4 cups walnut halves, toasted (see page 23)

Put the Cheddar in the bowl of a stand mixer. Using the paddle attachment, mix on medium speed until smooth, about 5 minutes. Add the Roquefort, cream cheese, and garlic, and mix on medium speed until well blended.

Wet your hands and shape the mixture into 4 balls each about the size of a softball. Using 1 cup of walnuts per ball, roll the cheese ball in the walnuts, pressing the stray nut in here and there until you cover the entire surface. Serve immediately or wrap tightly in plastic wrap and store in the refrigerator for up to 1 week.

One of the strangest, funniest things that ever happened to me was during one of our marathon periods at the Cheese Board. It was at Christmastime, and I was working more than forty hours a week. All my shifts were ten and eleven hours long. I was working extra because it was busy and lots of people were out sick, so I was really working hard. Steve called the store at the end of a Saturday, and I answered the phone—at this point I'd been on the shift for eleven hours. He wanted to know how much bread we'd sold and if there was any left over. He said, "Who is this?" and I couldn't answer. I thought, "I know my name. I've known it all my life!" But I just couldn't think to tell him who I was! He finally said, "Is this Vicki?" and I said, "Ah. Yes, that's it, yes, this is Vicki!"   —VICKI

Saffron Bread

A former member developed this fragrant bread from his grandmother's holiday recipe. This tea bread is best thinly sliced—try it served with marmalade. It also makes great toast with a spread of sweet butter. We roll the dough into a decorative braided turban created from two strands of dough.

MAKES 2 LOAVES
Preparation time including rising and baking: 3¼ hours; active time: 45 minutes

¼ teaspoon saffron threads
¼ cup hot water
1 tablespoon active dry yeast
¼ cup warm water
4 cups bread flour
¾ cup sugar
2 teaspoons kosher salt
1½ cups (3 sticks) cold unsalted butter, cut into 1-inch cubes
1½ cups lukewarm water
Grated zest of 1 lemon and 1 orange
4 eggs
½ cup dried currants

In a small bowl, stir the saffron into the hot water. Set aside to steep.

In another small bowl, whisk the yeast into the warm water until dissolved. Let stand for 5 minutes.

In the bowl of a stand mixer or a large bowl, combine the flour, sugar, and salt.

If using a stand mixer, add the butter to the dry ingredients and cut it in with the paddle attachment on low speed for 4 minutes, or until it is the size of small peas. Add the saffron mixture, yeast mixture, lukewarm water, citrus zests, and 3 of the eggs, and mix on low speed until the ingredients are combined, about 2 minutes. Switch to the dough hook, increase the mixer speed to medium, and knead for 7 minutes, or until the dough begins to lose its rough texture. Add the currants and knead until the fruit is incorporated,

about 1 minute. Transfer to a lightly floured surface and knead by hand for a few minutes, until the dough is smooth and elastic.

If making by hand, add the butter to the dry ingredients and cut it in with a pastry cutter or 2 dinner knives until it is the size of small peas. Add the saffron mixture, yeast mixture, lukewarm water, citrus zests, and 3 of the eggs, and mix with a wooden spoon until the ingredients are combined. Transfer to a lightly floured surface and knead for 10 minutes, or until the dough is smooth and elastic. Flatten the dough and sprinkle with the currants. Knead until the fruit is incorporated.

Form the dough into a ball and place it in a large oiled bowl. Turn the dough over to coat it with oil. Cover the bowl with plastic wrap or a damp kitchen towel and let rise in a warm, draft-free place for 1 hour, or until doubled in size.

Line a baking sheet with parchment paper or a baking mat. Transfer the dough to a lightly floured surface and divide it into 2 pieces. Gently form each piece into a loose round (see page 26) and cover with a floured kitchen towel. Let rest for 10 minutes. Shape each piece into a 2-stranded turban (see page 30) and place on the prepared pan. Cover with a floured kitchen towel and let rise in a warm place for 45 minutes, or until a finger pressed into the dough leaves an impression.

Fifteen minutes before the loaves have finished rising, preheat the oven to 375°F.

In a small bowl, whisk the remaining egg. Using a pastry brush, brush the top and sides of each loaf with the beaten egg. Repeat this step.

Bake on the middle rack of the oven for 20 minutes. Rotate the baking sheet front to back. Bake for 20 to 25 minutes longer, for a total baking time of 40 to 45 minutes, or until the loaves are a shiny, medium brown with bright yellow showing through at the crevices. Transfer to a wire rack to cool.

Gingerbread

Small loaves of gingerbread are the perfect winter present. This gingerbread is spicy, full of molasses flavor, and not overly sweet.

MAKES 5 SMALL LOAVES
Preparation time including baking: 1¼ hours

½ cup (4 ounces) firmly packed candied ginger

½ cup plus ¾ cup sugar

2 eggs

1¼ cups safflower or canola oil

1 cup dark unsulfered molasses

3¾ cups unbleached all-purpose flour

¾ teaspoon baking soda

1 teaspoon dry mustard

1 teaspoon ground ginger

1 teaspoon ground cinnamon

¾ teaspoon kosher salt

1½ teaspoon freshly ground black pepper

Preheat the oven to 350°F. Generously butter or spray with cooking spray 5 small (5 by 3-inch) loaf pans.

In a food processor, combine the candied ginger and the ⅛ cup sugar. Process until the ginger is finely chopped and incorporated into the sugar, about 1 minute. Set aside. Or, use a chef's knife to chop the ginger as finely as possible and combine it with the sugar.

In a medium bowl, combine the eggs, oil, and molasses. Set aside.

Sift the flour, baking soda, mustard, ginger, and cinnamon together into the bowl of a stand mixer or a large bowl.

If using a stand mixer, add the salt, pepper, ¾ cup sugar, and ginger sugar to the dry ingredients and mix with the paddle attachment on low speed until combined. Make a well in the center and pour in the wet ingredients. Mix briefly, just until blended.

If making by hand, add the salt, pepper, ¾ cup sugar, and ginger sugar to the dry ingredients and stir with a wooden spoon until combined. Make a well in the center and pour in the wet ingredients. With a few strokes of the spoon, gently combine.

Pour the batter into the prepared pans. Place the pans on the middle rack of the oven. Bake for 35 minutes, then rotate the pans front to back and trade their positions. Bake 10 minutes longer, for a total baking time of 45 minutes, or until the loaves are firm and springy. Let cool in the pans on a wire rack for 10 minutes, then unmold and let cool completely.

WILLI'S STOLLEN

The Cheese Board's stollen is adapted from my mother's recipe. I wish I had thought of naming it Willi's Stollen—her name was Wilhelmine Dilloo, but everybody called her Willi, and she was a very good cook. Stollen is a must for every house in Germany at Christmastime. There are two different kinds. Dresden style is made mostly of almonds and almost no flour; it has a layer of marzipan, and it's almost like a confection. I have never made it— it's the kind you buy in the store and it keeps forever. The kind we made at home (and we now make at the Cheese Board) has more flour and fewer almonds, and is more like a bread.

It was hard to adapt my mother's recipe for a bakery-sized recipe. The first time I made the stollen, I didn't think to order blanched almonds, so I ended up blanching them by hand, like I do at home. It was on a Sunday and, all told, I think I blanched fifteen pounds of almonds.

My special secret in making stollen is to cut the candied citron and lemon and orange peel extremely small so that they impart their flavor but you never have to bite into a piece. To do this for a huge batch was difficult because candied fruit is extremely sticky. It was terrible—it stuck to the knife, the table, my hands, everything! By the third year, I finally worked it out by grinding the candied fruit in the food processor with a little sugar and some almonds.

That was my biggest baking achievement, to come up with a way to make that complicated home recipe into an industrial-scale recipe by using a different technique. It's those little things that are the most exciting discoveries.

—Frieda Dilloo

Stollen

Making stollen, a traditional German bread, is the culmination of our holiday preparations at the store. When we plan our holiday work schedule, it is the centerpiece of the December calendar. Stollen requires every collective member's participation, because making it is a lengthy process and because we make so many of them. We bake them before our December meeting so everyone can help wrap the hundreds of sweet loaves.

This recipe was developed by one of our members from her mother's home recipe (see page 141). The last step of making stollen is creating a luxuriant confectioners' sugar crust. Be warned: this step can envelop the entire kitchen in a cloud of confectioners' sugar. This is an overnight dough.

MAKES 3 LOAVES
Preparation time including rising and baking: 15 hours; active time: 1½ hours

1 tablespoon plus 1½ teaspoons active dry yeast

¼ cup warm water

¾ cup granulated sugar

⅓ cup candied orange peel

⅓ cup candied citron

⅓ cup candied lemon peel

6 cups unbleached all-purpose flour

2½ teaspoons kosher salt

1 teaspoon ground cinnamon

1½ cups (3 sticks) cold unsalted butter, cut into
1-inch cubes

3 eggs

3 tablespoons rum

1 cup milk

¾ cup blanched slivered almonds

⅓ cup golden raisins

⅓ cup dark raisins

⅓ cup dried currants

Topping

¾ cup (1½ stick) unsalted butter

1¼ cups confectioners' sugar

In a small bowl, whisk the yeast into the warm water until dissolved. Let stand for 5 minutes.

In a food processor, combine the sugar, candied orange peel, citron, and lemon peel. Pulse for about 45 seconds, or until the candied citrus is finely chopped and incorporated into the sugar. Or, use a chef's knife to chop the candied fruit as finely as possible and combine it with the sugar.

In the bowl of a stand mixer or a large bowl, combine the flour, salt, and cinnamon.

If using a stand mixer, add the butter to the flour mixture and cut it in with the paddle attachment on low speed for about 4 minutes, or until it is the size of small peas. Add the yeast mixture, citrus sugar, eggs, rum, and milk, and mix on low speed until the ingredients are combined, about 2 minutes. Switch to the dough hook, increase the mixer speed to medium, and knead for 7 minutes, or until the dough is soft and pliable. Add the almonds, golden raisins, dark raisins, and currants, and continue to knead just until incorporated. Transfer to a lightly floured surface and knead by hand for a few minutes, until the dough is smooth and elastic.

If making by hand, add the butter to the flour mixture and cut it in with a pastry cutter or 2 dinner knives until it is the size of small peas. Add the yeast mixture, citrus sugar, eggs, rum, and milk, and mix with a wooden spoon until the ingredients are combined. Transfer to a lightly floured surface and knead for about 10 minutes, or until the dough is

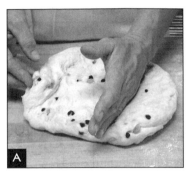
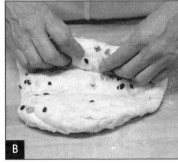
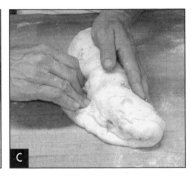

smooth and elastic. Flatten the dough and sprinkle it with the almonds, golden raisins, dark raisins, and currants. Roll it up and continue kneading for a few minutes until the fruit is incorporated.

Form the dough into a ball and place it in a large oiled bowl. Turn the dough over to cover it with oil. Cover the bowl with plastic wrap or a damp kitchen towel and let rise in the refrigerator overnight.

The next day, remove the dough from the refrigerator and let stand at room temperature for 2 hours.

Line 2 baking sheets with parchment paper or baking mats. Transfer the dough to a lightly floured surface and divide it into 3 pieces. Knead 1 piece of dough for 1 minute. Pat the dough into a 10-inch disk about 1 inch thick. Create a crease with a single karate chop positioned two-thirds of the way across the disk (fig. A). Roll the larger portion like a jelly roll tightly to the crease, leaving a 1½-inch lip (fig. B). Seal the edge with your fingers by pressing the rolled edge down toward the bottom lip (fig. C). Repeat the process with the 2 remaining pieces of dough. Place 2 stollens on a prepared pan and 1 on the second pan. Cover with floured kitchen towels and let rise in a warm, draft-free place for 2 hours, or until increased in size by one-fourth.

Fifteen minutes before the loaves have finished rising, arrange the oven racks in the upper and lower thirds of the oven. Preheat the oven to 325°F.

Bake for 20 minutes, then rotate the baking sheets front to back and trade their rack positions. Bake 50 to 60 minutes longer, or until the stollens are light brown and sound hollow when tapped. (It is important not to underbake the stollens because they will be gummy on the inside. On the other hand, if you overbake them, they will form too thick a crust and dry out too quickly.)

When the stollens are almost finished baking, melt the ¾ cup butter in a small saucepan. Line a work surface with newspaper and place 2 wire racks on top. Transfer the stollens to the racks. While the stollens are still hot, using a pastry brush, generously brush them with the melted butter. Dust the loaves with confectioners' sugar. Repeat the brushing and dusting two more times. Let the loaves cool completely.

I remember making the stollen last year. I loved the process. All the racks out and the breads on the tables and confectioners' sugar everywhere, flying around. The best part about Christmas is the camaraderie, the feeling that everybody is on the same page, doing hard work and loving it.

—PAUL

~WISCONSIN
~CHEAP/MILD
OTHER VARIETIES
OFTEN AVAILABLE
CHESHIRE
~MRS APPELBY'S 12⁰⁰
CHEVRE
GOATS
~ALPINE
~BANON
~BETHMALE
~BLEUET
~BLUE (DOMESTIC)
~BOUCHERON 12⁰⁰
~BOULE de QUERCY
~BUCHE PAILLE
~QUESO
~REDWOO
~SELLES
~TOM
CHIM
10⁵⁰
12⁰⁰
20⁰⁰
14⁵⁰
18⁰⁰
12⁵⁰
5¹⁵

CHAPTER SIX

THE CHEESE COUNTER

O Cheese

In the pantry the dear dense cheeses, Cheddars and harsh
Lancashires; Gorgonzola with its magnanimous manner;
the clipped speech of Roquefort; and a head of Stilton
that speaks in a sensuous riddling tongue like Druids.

O cheeses of gravity, cheeses of wistfulness, cheeses
that weep continually because they know they will die.
O cheeses of victory, cheeses wise in defeat, cheeses
fat as a cushion, lolling in bed until noon.

Liederkranz ebullient, jumping like a small dog, noisy;
Pont l'Evêque intellectual, and quite well informed; Emmentaler
decent and loyal, a little deaf in the right ear;
and Brie the revealing experience, instantaneous and profound.

O cheeses that dance in the moonlight, cheeses
that mingle with sausages, cheeses of Stonehenge.
O cheeses that are shy, that linger in the doorway,
eyes looking down, cheeses spectacular as fireworks.

Reblochon openly sexual; Caerphilly like pine trees, small
at the timberline; Port du Salut in love; Caprice des Dieux
eloquent, tactful, like a thousand-year-old hostess;
and Dolcelatte, always generous to a fault.

O village of cheeses, I make you this poem of cheeses,
O family of cheeses, living together in pantries,
O cheeses that keep to your own nature, like a lucky couple,
this solitude, this energy, these bodies slowly dying.

—DONALD HALL

THE CHEESE COUNTER

How Cheese Is Made **148**

From Market to Table **152**

CHEESE PLATES

Raw-Milk Cheeses **161**

Raw-Milk Cheese Plate 163

American Cheeses **164**

American Cheese Plate 165

California Cheese Plate 166

California Goat Cheese Plate 166

AOC Cheeses **168**

AOC Cheese Plate 169

. . .

Wednesday-Morning Cheese Plate . . . 171

New Year's Eve Cheese Plate 173

Stinky-Cheese Plate 174

Super Bowl Cheese Plate 175

Intimate Picnic Cheese Plate 176

Camping Cheeses 176

The Cheese Stands Alone 179

CHEESE BREADS

Cheese Onion Curry Bread 180

Greek Shepherd's Bread 181

Asiago Bread 182

Corn Onion Cheddar Bread 184

Experimental Bread No. 7,
   or X Bread 186

Provolone Olive Bread 187

OTHER CHEESE RECIPES

Raclette 189

Fondue 190

Mock Boursin 190

Hot Cheddar Spread 191

Salmon Spread 191

THE CHEESE COUNTER is where we get to know our customers. The interaction over the wooden counter is the most intimate one we have with customers in the store. Here there is time to chat and exchange ideas. Discussions range over many topics, but cheese lore is a constant. Our customers educate us, and we hope to do the same for them. Our patrons are sometimes in a hurry, but usually they value the chance to pass the time in a more leisurely way than most places outside our doors.

We have over three hundred different kinds of cheese, crammed with some logic into two venerable cheese cases that have been with us for twenty-five years. The array of cheese can seem intimidating to new customers. They often seem to think, mistakenly, that they need to know something before they can make a purchase. Nothing

could be further from the truth. That is why we offer tastes of everything we sell. The best description of a cheese pales beside the immediacy of the actual taste.

The exchange between our customers and us occurs on many levels. Between clerk and patron lies the case full of cheeses, over which we talk, advise, and consume. The talk is usually light, sometimes flirtatious, and often humorous. Sometimes (actually, quite often) our task is to identify a cheese described by a customer. They might have eaten it in the Dordogne on vacation, or it was the key ingredient in their grandmother's dish, or they had it three days ago, but the name eludes them. Other times, we are asked to help select party cheeses or figure out the best match for a recipe. All these interactions have the flavor of a treasure hunt about which we are fortunate enough to have privileged knowledge. There is a bond formed over a mutual love of food, especially cheese.

We are blessed with extraordinarily loyal customers who are very patient as they stand in long lines on busy Saturdays, and put up with shortages of fresh Mozzarella during tomato season. Seeing people advising each other about how to figure out the workings of the Cheese Board and exchanging tastes as they stand side by side is one of the things that makes clerking the cheese counter so much fun.

I love our customers. I think that they are the greatest customers in the world. I love the eccentricity of them, the worldliness of them. I mean, they are *fun*. I have always felt that if I hadn't tried to become an artist, I would have become a writer of short stories because I love the short-story form. I have always said that each customer who comes in feels like a short story to me. Some are very interesting, some are shy, some live fabulously entertaining lives, some are obviously eccentric, but they are all fascinating.   —VICKI

HOW CHEESE IS MADE

Cheese is basically a way of preserving milk. Milk spoils easily, but transformed into cheese it can be stored for long periods of time. (There is a story of a Swiss cheese, Saanen, that is eaten at the baptism of a baby and saved to be served years later at the wake of the same person.) While food preservation is no longer the issue it once was, we are left with the legacy of cheeses that were developed to address this issue.

Cheese is created by manipulating curdled milk in a variety of ways. Milk is curdled with an array of products, the most common being rennet, a coagulating agent derived from the stomach lining of calves or lambs. Many cheeses made in the United States, Scandinavia, and England now use a vegetarian equivalent—either a microbial or vegetable-based rennet. Other curdling agents, such as the sap of fig trees or an infusion of nettles, are used in traditional Sicilian and Portuguese cheese making.

After curdling, the cheese-making process continues with a variety of steps. Depending on the type of cheese, the process may include cutting the curd with different types of cutting tools; heating the curd; molding and pressing the curd to expel more of the whey; and salting the outside of the formed cheese with dry salt or immersing it in brine. The final formed and salted cheese may be rubbed with lard or oil, wrapped with cheesecloth, encouraged to form a rind, smoked, or, in the case of blue cheese, pierced with needles. (While fresh cheeses, such as cream cheese and Ricotta, employ curdling and draining, unlike aged cheeses they are not encouraged to develop a rind or to ripen.)

The three cheeses discussed below—Gruyère, Roquefort, and Taleggio—illustrate the many steps that are required to make a cheese.

Gruyère

This Swiss cheese is smooth textured, unlike the holey cheese many people expect from that country, and is sweetly nutty on the tongue. It also melts beautifully. Gruyère arrives in our store in eighty-five-pound wheels, making cutting it into smaller, easy-to-use pieces a laborious task. This cheese is made in a number of towns in the region surrounding the town of Gruyère.

THE MILK

Gruyère is made from unpasteurized milk that comes from cows fed on hay, either from mountain pastures or from hay cut and stored for winter use. The herds are not treated with hormones or antibiotics. It is possible to taste the sweetness of the hay and mountain flowers in the final product. The evening's milk is delivered to the cheese dairy, where it is held in two thousand-liter copper vats at slightly below room temperature. The morning's milking is added to the vats.

ADDING THE CULTURE AND THE RENNET

A starter culture is added to the vats of milk. This bacterial culture is grown in-house on the whey produced from the cheese-making process. Calf rennet is then added, causing the milk to curdle over a period of thirty minutes. In the last three to five minutes of this process, the milk separates into yellowish whey floating on top and whiter curds clinging together beneath the surface in a gelatinous mass. The curd is almost ready to be cut.

CUTTING THE CURD

Using a combination of experience and instinct, the cheese maker must determine the precise moment to commence the cutting of the curd; a mistake in timing even of one minute will result in an inferior final cheese. To cut the curd, metal cheese rakes that resemble gigantic egg slicers are drawn through the vat until the curd is the size of grains of wheat. This procedure takes about ten minutes. Cutting the curd allows the whey to drain more readily. Generally, the finer the curd is cut, the firmer the final product will be.

HEATING THE CURD

The temperature of the curd is then raised to 131°F over a period of forty-five minutes to achieve the classic dense, smooth texture of Gruyère. At this juncture, the cheese maker decides if the curds are the proper dryness; when sufficiently dry, the curd is pumped through stainless steel tubes into the waiting forms.

FORMING THE CURD

The curd is pumped into a two-level form made of a stainless steel bottom section and a high-sided plastic top. When enough whey has drained off that the curd is at the level of the stainless steel section, the plastic top is removed. The cheese is then marked with the dairy number, date, and mold number, which allows quality and production count to be accurately controlled.

PRESSING THE CURD

The cheese maker transfers the wheel to the press and begins the pressing to expel even more whey. Over the next two and a half hours, the pressure will increase to over two thousand pounds over the surface of the wheel. The cheese remains in the press for twenty hours.

BRINING THE WHEEL

The wheels are removed from the presses and put on a rack; the entire rack is then submerged in a brine bath for twenty hours. Half of the final amount of salt in the cheese is absorbed during this brining stage.

SALTING AND AGING

The cheese is placed on spruce wood shelving and turned and rubbed with salt water daily for ten days. The daily washings and turnings are then slowly decreased to once weekly. At three months of age, the wheel is transported to a finishing house to be aged for a minimum of five months, at which point it is cored and tested for flavor. The cheese is then either held for further aging or sold at this stage.

Roquefort

Considered an aphrodisiac by Casanova and written about by Pliny, Roquefort is still delighting blue-cheese lovers today. This cheese has a pronouncedly blue flavor overlying the sweetly delicate flavor of the sheep's milk it is produced from. It is always aged in the natural caves of the *causses* (plateaus) in the *département* of Aveyron, which provide the optimal climate for the *Penicillium roqueforti* that produces the blue veins running through the buttery interior.

THE MILK

Following centuries of tradition, Roquefort is made from unpasteurized sheep's milk produced in the Auvergne and Rouergue regions. The milk is produced by a special breed of sheep called Lacaune that are specially adapted to the dry climate and rocky terrain. AOC regulations (see page 168) restrict their feed to natural fodder in the form of pasturage or fresh-cut hay. The milk is transported to the cheese-making facility, where it is tested for quality and heated to 80°F.

RENNETTING AND CUTTING THE CURD

The milk is then curdled with lamb's rennet (some dairies use the less-expensive calf's rennet). The mixture is allowed to stand for two hours, then the curd is cut and stirred to release the whey. The curd is allowed to drain on cloth-lined flat wicker baskets. The curds are then hand ladled into perforated draining forms.

INTRODUCING THE MOLD

The *Penicillium roqueforti* that produces the blue veining in the finished cheese is grown on enormous loaves of bread—made of rye and wheat grown nearby in Lévezou—specially baked for this purpose. The loaves are allowed to sit for over two months in the same caves that the cheese will later ripen in, to become thoroughly colonized by mold. If determined by their appearance to contain the correct mold, the loaves are dried and ground into powder. This powder is then either mixed with the milk when the rennet is added or folded in by hand as the curds are ladled into the cheese forms.

DRAINING THE CHEESE

The cheese sits for two weeks in a draining room, where the forms are turned frequently (up to six times the first day) and kept at 65°F. They are then dated, marked, and transported to the caves.

Coring the cheese.

THE CAVES

The Roquefort caves have been used to age cheese for over one thousand years. The massive series of aging caves are under Combalou, the plateau near the town of Roquefort-sur-Soulzon. They are the unique product of geology and the presence of man. In some places, the caves are eleven stories deep, and they cover an area twice the size of the town of Roquefort-sur-Soulzon. The wheels of cheese are naturally cooled (with some adjustments) by chimneys, called *fleurines*, that connect the caves to the outside and allow a steady breeze for cooling and humidity control, keeping the interior climate at 90 to 95 percent humidity and below 47°F.

SALTING AND NEEDLING

Once the cheeses are transported to the caves, they are salted with a fine dry sea salt in the salting chambers. First the top and the bottom of the cheeses are salted, then salt is applied around the sides. The cheeses are pierced with needles to allow air to reach the interior of the cheese. This promotes the growth of the mold that produces the characteristic blue veins; if you examine a slice of Roquefort you will notice the streaks of blue that surround the needling marks. The cheeses are turned three times daily during this period.

SCRAPING AND AGING

After two to three weeks in the caves, a natural crust begins to form on the outside of the cheese. This layer is scraped off and the cheeses are resalted and wrapped in foil. The wrapped cheeses are held at a temperature of 40°F for a minimum of three months. At this point, the Roquefort is ready to be sold.

Taleggio

Soft (but not runny) and fragrant, Taleggio is a washed-rind cheese with a winey, sweet flavor. This cheese was served at the papal coronation banquet of Pope Clement VI in 1344 and at the wedding feast of Francesco Sforza in 1441. Originally called Stracchino, it was given the name it currently bears in the early twentieth century. It is made in its traditional production area of the Val Taleggio, near Bergamo, as well as in other provinces in the Italian Alps, the Veneto, and the Lombardy plain. Taleggio arrives in our store as a ten-inch square stamped with its distinctive emblem of four circles and wrapped with several layers of paper. Like all soft-ripened cheeses, it ripens from the outside in. The surface of the cheese is supple and pink and somewhat sticky, while the interior is creamy and sometimes doted with small holes. The raw-milk version has a firmer center and a more flowery flavor than does pasteurized Taleggio.

THE MILK

While Taleggio can be made from either raw or pasteurized milk, today most Taleggio is made from pasteurized whole cow's milk. When made in the traditional manner, the morning milk is added to the ripened evening milk. The milk is heated in cauldrons or vats to 86° to 96°F.

ADDING THE CULTURE AND RENNET

The starter culture is added to the heated milk, followed by liquid calf's rennet. After about fifteen minutes, the curds begin to form.

BREAKING THE CURD

The curd is broken into small pieces and allowed to rest for ten to fifteen minutes. At this point, the curd is stirred and crumbled into ¾-inch pieces.

FORMING THE CURD

After resting again for a period of five minutes, the curd is poured into bottomless square forms placed on mats and allowed to drain.

RIPENING THE CURD

The molds are placed in warm (75°F), humid rooms and turned repeatedly to expel whey and assist the ripening of the cheese. Depending on the acidity of the curd and the characteristics of the milk, this step takes between eight and twenty-four hours.

BRINING

The cheeses are salted either by immersion in a brine bath for eight to ten hours or by hand salting them with repeated applications of dry salt.

AGING

The cheeses are moved to ripening rooms or, in the case of one-third of the Taleggios made today, to the natural caves of the Valsassina where the temperature is kept to a low 39° to 42°F. The caves, like the Roquefort caves, have fissures in them that allow for the entrance of the *soffioni* (the mountain breezes) and maintain an ambient humidity of at least 90 percent. During the thirty- to forty-day maturation period, the cheeses are frequently turned and washed with applications of salt water, which encourages the traditional pink mold to cover the cheese.

FROM MARKET TO TABLE

How to Choose Cheese

Cheese is a living food that changes almost daily, so the best way to select cheese is by tasting it. At the Cheese Board, we hand the customer a taste on a slip of waxed paper. The customer can see the whole cheese in front of them, notice the interior and exterior condition, smell the cheese as well as taste it, and ask questions of their clerk. We find that many of our customers are not confident in their own palate and want to rely on us for cheese recommendations. While we enjoy giving recommendations, we encourage you to trust your own palate, using our recommendations as a complement to your own experimentation in developing a list of favorite cheeses.

Start by finding a market or cheese shop that has a good variety of domestic and imported cheeses, and asking the clerks to give you samples. You might also encourage the shop to lay out a table with different cheeses to be sampled each week. Once you find such a place, and clerks who make good recommendations, develop a relationship with them and explore the cheese world with their guidance.

If you don't have a vendor who is willing to let you taste a cheese before you buy it, then you will have to rely on the look, smell, and feel of the cheese.

LOOK AT THE CHEESE

The appearance of cheese tells a lot about it; its outward condition, outer rind, and color are just a few of the clues. The exterior of a soft-ripened cheese such as Brie or Camembert should be supple and soft, not sunken or slimy. Cheese grows mold, and many will have amazing-looking molds growing on the outside. In the case of an aged goat cheese, the brainlike spiraling mold is a healthy sign of proper aging. Aged cheese can also have very funky-looking rinds. The rind on a Tomme de Savoie, a raw-cow's-milk cheese from France, is crusty, like someone left it under a rock for years; but the inside will have a golden *pâte* (the interior part of the cheese, also known as the *paste* or *pasta*) with tiny, even holes throughout. Such a rind protects the interior ripening during the aging process, and in many cases the rind is essential to the growth of the bacteria needed to properly age the cheese. For example, the rinds of cheeses rubbed with salt, or washed with brines, wine, or beer (known as *washed-rind cheeses*), create a suitable environment for specific bacteria to grow on the outside. The microbes then penetrate to the interior of the cheese, giving the cheese its strong, deep taste—such as in the case of Fournols, a more powerful cousin of Chaumes. Some microbial growths, however, are not desirable; pink or yellow mold on a fresh cheese like Ricotta, for example, is a sign of spoilage. Cheese should always be free of mold on the cut surface.

The pâte of a cheese is another important visual indicator. Aging a cheese—which so enhances the flavor and texture of such varieties as Swiss Gruyère and Emmental; Italian Parmigiano-Reggiano and domestic Parmesan; Asiago; and Dutch Gouda—often results in crunchy bits of crystallized whey that appear as whitish spots in the interior of the cheese. These spots are a unique characteristic of the pâte of some aged cheeses. Soft-ripened cheeses, such as a Reblochon, a raw-cow's-milk cheese from Savoie, should have a pâte that looks moist, smooth, and luxurious. No pâte should appear grayish brown, which indicates that the rind has eaten too far into the interior, usually resulting in a bitter taste.

SMELL THE CHEESE

Even at the grocery store, you can lift up a cheese and have a sniff. Find the smells that attract you. If you like mild cheese, search out a sweet, faintly fermented cheese aroma. If you like strong cheese, the smell should still attract you. If the cheese has a flat or bitter smell, or an odor of decay (which is called a "dead" smell), trust your senses—the cheese has probably been mishandled or is past its prime.

FEEL THE CHEESE

Touch can also help you choose a cheese. If it's Brie, give it a little squeeze. Is it the texture you are longing for? Do you like young, firm Brie or gooey, ripe Brie? Open the Camembert box and feel the surface. A ripe Camembert or Brie should be plump, with an overall pliable, soft texture. It shouldn't be dry or hard and wrinkled along the edges.

Find out how long the shop allows their cut pieces of cheese to stay on the shelf. If it's more than a few days, purchase your cheese somewhere else.

After a while you will be able to tell a lot about whether cheese is at its peak or over-the-hill. So back to the question: How do you choose cheese? Let the cheese talk, and just listen.

A NEW LOVE

As a new cheese clerk twelve years ago, I was confronted with the daunting task of learning the names of over three hundred cheeses. To add to that, I would hear my coworkers tell a little story—sometimes fact, sometimes myth—to their hungry customers about the cheese they were sampling. How was I ever going to remember all that? It didn't take me long to realize who my most significant teacher of all was: my palate. Once tasted, each cheese was so different, speaking to me immediately of its essential characteristic, whether pungent, creamy, sensual, grassy, herbal, crunchy, sweet, milky, or fruity. From there, just as with someone you are drawn to, the cheese's lingering taste would lead me to find out where in the world it came from, who were the people who made it, how old it was, and the story of its lineage.

I'd overhear pieces of coworkers' and customers' conversations about cheese lore; there was always a story. I'd reach back to the small bookshelf behind our cheese cases to learn what little town in Europe or the States a particular cheese was made in. My relationship with the cheeses was becoming more and more intimate.

The story of cheese is centuries old, while my involvement is only twelve years old—I couldn't possibly be an expert. I only know that I won't be the one to end this relationship.

—Lisa

Slicing with a cheese plane.

Cheese Tools

Having the right tool for the job is as important for tasting and serving cheese as it is for hammering a nail. Our customers often wonder, "You know, cheese always tastes better here than at home. Why is that?" There are many factors involved—the surrounding smells (see page 174) and the marketplace environment are two—but one of the main reasons is that when a customer is considering a cheese to buy, we offer a wafer-thin sample sliced off with our trusty cheese plane. There are only two tools at our cheese counter: a sharp, long-bladed knife for making cheese cuts and a cheese plane for shaving samples for the customers. Both tools are inexpensive and readily obtainable, and will increase your tasting pleasure tenfold.

A cheese plane is designed to cut thin, uniform shavings from a piece of cheese, a firm cheese in particular. Whereas a cube or a hunk of cheese tends to have a gummy consistency, a thin slice (less than $\frac{1}{16}$ inch thick) melts on the tongue, opening up its flavors. A good cheese plane (that means one made in Norway or Holland) will help you appreciate the sometimes subtle, other times pronounced, flavor variations from one cheese to the next.

Dividing Gruyère with an English wire cheese cutter.

For softer cheeses like Reblochon, Brie, Camembert, Saint-Nectaire, or Oka, you can try using a cheese plane by turning the wedge onto one of its cut sides and delicately slicing it. If the cheese is ripe, ready, and runny, it is best to use a sharp, longer-bladed knife, taking care not to make the slices too thick.

Extremely runny cheeses can be kept in a container and spooned out or scooped out with a short, wide, flat-bladed knife. For very hard cheeses, such as Italian Parmigiano-Reggiano, Mimolette from France, or California dry Monterey Jack, you can use the cheese plane, pulling off a thin curl of the aged cheese. At the store, if we pull the cheese plane across the top of a Parmigiano-Reggiano and it curls into a perfect ribbon, then we know we have a great wheel. Parmigiano-Reggianos are traditionally broken into chunks with a chisel-like tool and a small mallet so that the sharp blade of a knife doesn't damage the whey crystals so integral to this cheese's character. When selling Parmigiano, however, we bow to our cus-tomers' desire for a uniform block of cheese and lay the knife upon it.

For the bigger jobs of dividing large wheels or blocks of cheese, the Cheese Board has the advantage of one tool that most homes do not have: the English wire cheese cutter, a platform made of stainless steel transected by heavy-gauge wire attached to a handle. A large piece or wheel of cheese is set on the platform and the wire is positioned and pulled to smoothly cut the cheese. We keep two English wire cutters near the cheese counters, one for the blues like English Stilton and French Roquefort, the other for English Cheshires, French goat logs, or any of the crumbly cheeses.

Storing Cheese

Many customers ask us, "What is the best way to store cheese?" Cheese Boarders have brought cheeses home and stored them in the refrigerator in various ways—waxed paper, cellophane, aluminum foil, plastic wrap, recycled

CHEESE CUTS

I was staying with some friends recently and brought them some cheese as a gift. They seemed really happy to see my gift and me. The next morning we toasted some good bread and the cheese was duly brought out to the table. The only implement to get at the cheese was a sharp, pointed knife. My friends each took a big 3/4-inch slab off the front end of the cheese and bit into it. They looked pleased, but not terribly interested otherwise. When I asked if they had a cheese plane they looked puzzled, and replied no after my short explanation. I turned the cheese wedge on its side, and with the same knife cut off a few *very* thin slices. I ate one right off and then put the rest of them on my toasted bread. My friends watched with rapt attention and followed suit. They were delighted at the difference in the taste. The cheese had suddenly turned delicious with the simple "new way" to cut it. I said, "You should taste the same cheese when cut with a cheese plane!"

—Lisa

waxed cereal bags, a glass cheese box with a water well on the bottom—all of which keep the cheese in good shape. Though there may not be a clear set of rules for cheese storage, there are some general guidelines.

While cut cheese should not be overexposed to air, it does need to be able to breathe; cheese is a living food, and wrapping it in heavy plastic wound tightly around the cheese over and over will harm its texture and flavor. At the cheese counter, we wrap large pieces of cheese in plastic wrap for display; because we are constantly unwrapping and wrapping the cheeses as we give tastes and sell pieces to customers, the stored cheese has a chance to breathe. (If a cheese has been wrapped for a period of time, we trim it before giving a taste.) At home, using a loosely wrapped layer of paper surrounded by plastic wrap allows sufficient air to circulate around the cheese, as does

heavy waxed paper, well folded to seal the edges. There are also products specifically designed for wrapping cheese, some with an outer paper layer and a cellophane liner, others made of cellophane perforated with tiny holes. If you have a good cheese shop in your area, request that your cheese be wrapped in one of these.

Regardless of the method you choose, it is important to keep the cheese freshly wrapped. Do not reuse the same plastic or paper wrap.

Home Ripening

Some customers are interested in ripening cheese at home. Experimentation is the best method; many of the most successful experiments at the Cheese Board have been the result of mistakes or surprises. A particular wheel of Baita Friuli (a hard Italian cheese) comes to mind. One spring we received a mediocre wheel, so when the next shipment arrived, we put that one in our *cave* (a cool, humid cupboard we use for aging cheeses) to ripen, or in this case, to be forgotten. One year later, someone brought it out to the cheese counter and cored it. (This is done with a corer, a long half tube inserted into the middle of the cheese, turned several times, and carefully drawn out so the taster can check the innermost part of the paste to see if it's ready to consume; see illustration, page 150). We were treated to magnificently fruity, sharp Baita Friuli. It was gone after two days in the shop—good news travels quickly. We've also had our share of failures, such as the unwaxed young Gouda we took out of the Cryovac and put in the *cave* unwrapped. When we checked on the wheel after two weeks, there were big fissures and a lot of serious interior mold. Had we taken the time to wrap it in foil, we might have been more successful.

Ripening a cheese to perfection at home requires a controlled environment—usually moist, cool, and cavelike. The type of cheese you choose for further home ripening should be a whole cheese; it's really not possible to ripen a cut piece of cheese. One good cheese to try would be a Camembert, or another small, soft-ripened cheese, as this type of cheese is often sold when immature and firm. A small block of waxed Cheddar would be ideal to experiment with; simply remove the wax and replace it with foil, sealing it tightly. Two hard cheeses—Petit Agour, a small round of sheep's milk cheese from the French Pyrénées, and young Tête de Moine, a small, round raw-milk Swiss cheese—benefit from longer aging, as they develop a grainier texture and a fuller flavor. Keep the cheese in a cardboard box that is a little bigger than the cheese itself to allow moist air to settle around it.

If you are serious about ripening cheeses at home you should purchase a combination temperature-and-humidity gauge. Below is a guide to the conditions that certain styles of cheese need in order to ripen. Find an environment in your home that meets these conditions, such as the vegetable drawer in your refrigerator, or a basement (making sure that it is out of reach of animals). Try ripening a softer cheese, like Camembert, for 24 to 48 hours, or try a hard block of Cheddar wrapped in foil for a month or so, turning it from one side to another inside the cardboard box every few days. As with sourdough bread making, there is only so much you can read about aging cheese—the rest is trial and error.

CHEESE	TEMPERATURE	RELATIVE HUMIDITY
Edam	53.6° to 57°F (12° to 14°C)	75 to 80 percent
Brie	50°F (10°C)	85 to 90 percent
Camembert	53.6° to 55.4°F (12° to 13°C)	90 to 95 percent
Coulommiers	50°F (10°C)	90 percent
Hard Swiss-style	59° to 68°F (15° to 20°C)	90 to 95 percent
Mini Stilton	44.6°F (7°C)	80 to 90 percent
Soft-ripened/chèvres	53.6° to 55.4°F (12° to 13°C)	90 to 95 percent
Gouda	50° to 59°F (10° to 15°C)	80 percent
Limburger	59°F (15°C)	90 to 95 percent
Hard sheep's cheese	59° to 64°F (15° to 18°C)	75 to 80 percent
Pont l'Evêque	57° to 68°F (14° to 20°C)	85 to 90 percent
Cheddar	44.6° to 53°F (7° to 12°C)	80 to 85 percent

Based on information from a chart courtesy of Mariano Gonzalez, Fiscalini Cheese Company, Modesto, California.

Presented at the conference "Aging Gracefully: The Art and Science of Ripening," under the auspices of the California Milk Advisory Board.

There are some sweet older customers that have been coming here long before I started working here. They are so wonderful, so special to me. It's such a joy to see them. We have a 104-year-old customer who is so hilarious and fun. You can barely see her over the counter, she's so short.

—ERIN

Selling cheese to someone, you actually get into their head and figure out what their needs are. They have a question and you are trying to fulfill their party needs, or they are trying to impress someone or just want to enjoy something they have never enjoyed before, and you are completely free to follow any lead. It's like some kind of mind meld: having a conversation without having to figure out any big issues. You are just trying to match them with some cheese.

—JOHN

CHEESE FACTS (OR FICTION)

At the Cheese Board, we have a vibrant oral tradition of stories and techniques handed down from one generation to another. As these get handed down they change; baking techniques get modified and generally improved, as do many of our stories, often to the point where even we can't tell if they are fact or fiction. This is especially true of many of the "cheese facts" that we have told customers only to later discover that we had it all wrong.

For example, there was the story that Vacherin Mont d'Or, a French winter cheese, was produced from the milk of pregnant cows. When a clerk waited on someone who wrinkled her nose in distaste at this morsel of information, we investigated a little and discovered that it was *false*.

Then there are the much-vaunted claims that Caesar had it for lunch and Pliny wrote about it: this includes the cheeses Sbrinz, Roquefort, and Taleggio. Pliny wrote a lot: *true*. Did Caeser eat it? *Maybe*.

Valençay has the most delightful shape, a small, truncated pyramid. Did Talleyrand (a French statesman) actually lop off the top of this originally pyramid-shaped goat cheese to satiate Napoleon's lust for revenge after losing his Egyptian campaign? Who knows, but it's great copy.

Halafalouki is a mythical cheese that exists only to terrify new clerks. Many collectivists actually claim that this story is theirs——who knows? Maybe it happened more than once. Here is the tale. A customer approaches the cheese counter and curtly announces, "Halafalouki." The new clerk, already feeling disadvantaged in comparison to the more knowledgeable clerks surrounding her as well as the numerous confident customers, decides this cheese must be of Balkan extraction—possibly Greek. Rooting around in the Greek sheep's-milk section, she gives up and turns to a comrade to ask, "Where can I find Halafalouki cheese?" She is met with a burst of laughter, "Oh, that isn't a cheese—that is Mr. Luekke and he is here to pick up his challah—challah for Luekke!"

Is Cacio di Fossa actually lowered into a well near a graveyard in a small Italian village? So we were told by a customer. *False*. Actually, following an eight-hundred-year-old method of preservation and aging, Cacio di Fossa is put in burlap bags and buried in hollows in the tufa near Sogliano al Rubicone during August and drawn out again in November. The pressure of the stacked cheeses reduces the moisture and size of this sheep's-milk cheese and makes it engagingly distorted and rustic in appearance.

A *cave* for aging cheese can become bewitched. *True*. An exorcism was held to cleanse a *cave* in France that had become infested with the wrong kind of microorganism. The presence of this microorganism was preventing the cheese from developing properly, so a priest was called in and the ritual was performed.

Henry IV bought some Maroilles for four sols, and this cheese was served to Louis XI, Charles VI, and Francis I. It has been around so long that a mass for its one-thousand-year birthday was celebrated in 1961 in the Abbey of Maroilles. *True, at least the last part.*

Amalthée—a goat that suckled the abandoned baby Zeus, keeping him from starving, or the name of a soft-ripened goat cheese from France? The second is *true*.

Le Tétoun de Santa Agata is a breast-shaped goat cheese made in southern France to honor the martyrdom of St. Agatha. *True and delicious.*

· CHEESE PLATES ·

One of our favorite tasks at the cheese counter is helping customers create interesting and unique cheese plates. When their number is called, they hand us their card and the conversation begins. "I'm having people over and I'd like to serve a cheese plate; can you give me some advice?"

While scanning the case with its huge selection of cheeses, we respond with questions of our own: "What types of cheese do you like?" "How many people are you serving and how adventurous are they?" "What is the occasion?" "How many types of cheese would you like to serve?" We'll pull a cheese out of the case we think that they might like and give them a taste of it. From then on we are guided by their responses.

Our rule of thumb for the amount of cheese to serve is based on the number of people invited. For hors d'oeuvres, 1 to 2 ounces of cheese per person is sufficient. If the cheese is the centerpiece of a gathering or a meal, the amount should be 3 to 5 ounces per person. For a pre-dessert or dessert cheese course, a light 1-ounce serving per person is usually enough.

There are an almost infinite number of ways a cheese plate can be composed. Whether the selection is for a before-dinner cheese board, a cheese course preceding dessert, or a platter at a wedding reception, there are no hard-and-fast rules. The main things to keep in mind are that there should be variety and the cheeses should go well together.

Generally, we advise customers to select three to five cheeses for a cheese plate. You should love the cheeses you are buying, and the flavors should complement one another; from there the choices are endless. Customers have chosen the all-Italian cheese plate, a blue cheese sampler, a mixed-milk cheese plate (one cow's milk, one goat's milk, and one sheep's milk cheese), or a same-milk cheese plate. Sometimes they just choose the cheese for aesthetic value: by shape and color. Your cheese selection should match your event, budget, and desires.

Baguettes, fruit, and simple crackers are ideal companions to cheeses. Choose other foods as a supporting cast to the cheeses and avoid overwhelming flavors. When serving wine with cheese, we feel that the rule is very simple: The wine should stand up to the flavors of the cheese and enhance them without overpowering them.

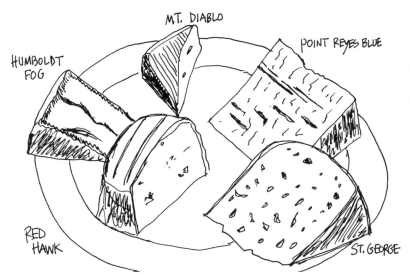

MT. DIABLO

POINT REYES BLUE

HUMBOLDT FOG

RED HAWK

ST. GEORGE

I personally like three cheeses on a plate. When advising a customer on a cheese plate, I always like to suggest two tried-and-true crowd-pleasers that I know most everyone will like. As a third cheese, I like to slip in a surprise by including one showstopper: an unusual, unfamiliar, or unique choice, or something that is exceptionally good that day, or a cheese that's hard to find, or one that is new on the scene.

—CATHY

Plan to take the cheese plate out of the refrigerator an hour before serving it, as the flavor of cheese is more apparent at room temperature, and the texture, especially of soft cheeses, is more luxurious.

In this section you will find a variety of cheese plates based on different themes. The selections are chosen not only for their complementary flavors, but also because they represent some of our favorite cheeses. The descriptions provide a little information about each cheese, and some serving and individual cooking suggestions are included here and there.

RAW-MILK CHEESES

Some of the world's greatest cheeses are made with raw (unpasteurized) milk. Our customers request and crave these unique and flavorful cheeses; for many people, these cheeses are an experiential connection to the farmyard and a particular piece of countryside.

Raw-milk cheeses are usually made on a small scale with local raw milk, which has a complexity of flavor that is absent from the pasteurized product. The flavor of raw-milk cheese reflects the local geologic conditions that create the pasturage, weather conditions, and methods used to produce the cheese. These cheeses have what is called a "long" taste—that is, a taste that has many stages, each developing into distinct flavors that evolve and linger.

Many of these cheeses are rooted in history. Cheese is an ancient food, and its origins are documented as far back as seven thousand years. For example, English Cheshire has two thousand years of history behind it, and the Romans originally made Portuguese Serra da Estrela. These cheeses are not only delicious but are a venerable food that supports a connection to a particular place and way of life.

The difference between raw and pasteurized cheese is that while raw-milk cheeses vary in the method of production, they all use milk that has not been heated to eliminate the native microflora. It is this diversity of microflora in raw-milk cheeses that results in their complex flavor. Both raw- and pasteurized-milk cheeses are inoculated with a starter culture of bacteria. In raw-milk cheeses, adding the starter culture to the lactic-acid bacteria that naturally exists in milk gives the cheese maker greater control of the fermentation process. With pasteurized-milk cheeses, it is necessary to replenish the lactic-acid bacteria killed during pasteurization (in addition to its flavor attributes, this bacteria plays a vital role in the curdling and aging of the cheese). But since the starter culture has no connection to the microbes previously present in the raw milk, it produces a blander, more uniform flavor in the cheese. The ripening process is slower for pasteurized-milk cheese, which again produces a milder, less complex flavor.

In the United States, cheeses made with pasteurized milk became the standard during World War II for a variety of reasons. A shortage of experienced cheese makers and an increased market for cheese resulted in a rising amount of factory-made cheese. Large-scale production required the use of milk from many sources, which in turn required holding large amounts of milk for an extended period of time. Pasteurization met the needs of the marketplace.

The incidence of food poisoning from cheese is low, especially compared to other protein food products such as meat or eggs. However, all cheese makers know the importance of observing strict hygiene when producing milk or milk products, whether pasteurized or not. The aging process naturally eliminates pathogens in cheese. Most reported outbreaks of disease relating to cheese products are due to contamination from other sources than the cheese-making process, such as handling after the cheeses are made, something that causes problems in raw and pasteurized cheeses alike.

FDA regulations state that raw-milk cheese is an acceptable and safe food as long as it is aged for more than sixty days. However, the FDA is currently considering banning all raw-milk cheese in the United States. If the FDA enacts such a ban, not only would it be impossible for us to eat our locally produced as well as imported raw-milk cheeses, it would encourage the EU to enact a similar ban, a step it is unfortunately considering taking. A few years ago, most traditional European cheeses arrived in our store as raw-milk products. Today, more and more of them are being produced as pasteurized simulacra, greatly impacting their flavor and texture. Cheese producers are either going out of business or adjusting to the new regulations as best they can.

The fact that the existence of traditionally made cheese is threatened is partially due to a misinformed concern that raw-milk cheese is a source of health problems. However, the bigger cause is the globalization of food industries. The pasteurization standards will eliminate many of the small to midlevel cheese factories, particularly the farmstead dairies, leaving the field to the big factories. In the last decade alone, Italy has lost close to half of its native cheeses *forever*—they simply are not being made any longer, and the methods of production have been lost. Soon, when visiting a foreign country you may find the same mass-produced products you see at your local supermarket. A huge loss of variety and flavor, as well as traditional products and ways of life, will be the result.

Note: While we believe carefully made raw-milk cheese is a safe food, consumers with special health needs, such as pregnant women, people with compromised immune systems, and the elderly, should consult their doctor in order to make an informed decision about eating it.

Raw-Milk Cheese Plate

SELLES-SUR-CHER

With its black wood-ash exterior contrasting with a white interior, this is one of the prettiest of the French goat cheeses. When young, Selles-sur-Cher is firm, sweet, and cakey. As it ages, the surface becomes wrinkled, and it softens and develops even more flavor. The cheese has been made in the Loire River Valley since the nineteenth century.

REBLOCHON

This cheese is made in the Haute-Savoie on the French side of the Alps, just over the mountains from where Italian Fontina is made. A rich, creamy, soft-ripened cheese, Reblochon has a pleasing delicacy of flavor and is a wonderful contrast or alternative to a Camembert. It is delicious eaten with grapes.

TOMME DE SAVOIE

Made in the same region as Reblochon, Tomme de Savoie is firm and more aromatic. It has a gray feltlike exterior, and fine holes dot the smooth, pale gold interior. Not overly assertive, its flavor is pleasantly nutty. Look for raw-milk versions with no cracks or signs of dryness.

EMMENTAL

This is the holey cheese everyone has in mind when they ask for Swiss cheese. The real thing, however, is a far cry from the bland, Cryovac-wrapped supermarket version. When well aged, it is one of the world's great cheeses—hard, with a nutty flavor that has winey overtones and a beautiful dark rind. Emmental is also excellent when eaten with a hot mustard on rye.

BERKSWELL

A most welcome newcomer, Berkswell has the presence of a grande dame. An English farmhouse cheese, its flavor is deep, mellow, and sweet, with a flaky texture. Made from ewe's milk, the cheese gives off the fragrance of pasture if you sniff the rind. Berkswell has a beautiful shape, a graceful seven-pound dome with the basket-weave imprint of the cheese mold decorating the surface. The amber color of the cheese glows on the plate.

RAW-MILK CHEESES: A PARTIAL LIST

Ami du Chambertin	Lincolnshire Poacher
Appenzeller	Manchego
Azecitão	Maytag Blue
Beaufort	Parmigiano-Reggiano
Berkswell	Point Reyes Original Blue
Bleu d'Auvergne	
Bleu de Gex	Port l'Evêque
Comté	Reblochon
Crottin de Chavignol	Redwood Hill Goat Feta
Emmental	
English Farmhouse Cheddar	Roquefort
Farmhouse Cheshire	Sainte Maure de Touraine
Fiscalini Bandage Wrapped Cheddar	Selles-sur-Cher
Fleur du Maquis	Serra da Estrela
Fontina Valle d'Aosta	Shelburne Farms Vermont Cheddar
Gruyère	Tomme de Savoie
Hoch Ybrig	Vacherin du Haut-Doubs/Mont d'Or
Idiazabal	
Langres	Vallée d'Aspe
Le Maréchal	Vigneron

CAN I EAT THE RIND?

This is a question we hear often. We used to tell customers that in most cases it is a matter of personal discretion, and that most rinds are edible (but that doesn't necessarily make them *eatable*). This is true of all soft-ripened cheeses. The flavor of an Affidelices au Chablis, Munster, or Epoisses is dependent on the entire cheese, including the rind. In the case of Brie, it depends entirely on your preference; the same is true for many chèvres. The molds on the outside of some cheeses might look scary, but they won't hurt you; however, they don't always taste great.

In the case of harder cheeses and factory-made blue cheeses, it is more difficult to give clear advice. Recently, many cheeses (particularly Italian and French sheep's-milk cheeses) have been arriving in our store with "Do Not Eat" warnings on the label concerning the rind. This is because they are being treated with natamycin (a preservative derived from milk). While according to the FDA this substance is not harmful to consume, we consider the warnings on the European cheeses significant enough to relay to our customers.

AMERICAN CHEESES

In the last twenty years, something new and delightful has appeared on the cheese plate: American artisanal cheeses. Before the advent of dependable refrigeration and efficient transportation, almost every dairy farm in the country produced cheese as a way to use surplus milk. Many of these cheeses have been lost to modernization and the centralization of cheese production in America, but a reversal of this trend began in the seventies and eighties when a number of dedicated and talented pioneers decided to turn their hand to cheese making. In California, Jennifer Bice of Redwood Hill Farms, Laura Chenel of chèvre fame, Cindy and Liam Callahan of Bellwether Farms, and Mary Keehn of Cypress Grove are just a few of a new wave of cheese makers. Outside our own region, the renaissance has been supported by old stalwarts: Maytag Dairy Farms, Grafton Village Cheese Company, and Cabot Creamery, who have been joined by enthusiastic new cheese makers such as Cynthia and David Major of Major Farms in Vermont, Allison Hooper and Bob Reese of the Vermont Butter and Cheese Company, and Judy Schad of Capriole. We have been happy to watch (and taste!) their cheeses develop into dependably delicious products over the years. It seems as if every week another cheese maker or sales representative visits our store with a new domestic cheese for us to taste. While we are proud of the breadth and quality of the European cheese selection we offer, we are even more excited to be able to sell cheese made by small farmsteads and dairies here in the United States.

Making cheese is time-consuming, hard work, and it requires a significant initial financial outlay. Most important of all, it requires a profound passion for the product. After years of accepting bland, factory-made cheeses, Americans today are interested in eating flavorful, handmade cheeses. There is a lot of excitement surrounding the renaissance of domestic artisanal cheeses. What has caused us to suddenly be so much more interested and educated in our food choices? Perhaps it was the original organic food movement of the sixties that made us examine more closely the authenticity and quality of the foods we consume. Perhaps it is our increased exposure to high-quality artisanal products from abroad, or a combination of both.

Whatever the reasons, the Cheese Board is now faced with the happy problem of choosing from an increasingly large selection of domestic handmade cheeses. Below you will find three suggested cheese plates, one featuring American cheeses and two others focusing on cheeses made in California.

American Cheese Plate

NANCY'S HUDSON VALLEY CAMEMBERT

Made by Old Chatham Sheepherding Company, this cheese—a combination of sheep's and cow's milk—is velvety smooth and rich. Almost like a triple cream in its unctuous texture, its flavor is similar to Explorateur in that you are lulled by a creamy richness to be later surprised by the piquancy of the aftertaste. This two-pound cheese is also made in a one-pound size called Tom's Hudson Valley Camembert.

BONNE-BOUCHE

Meltingly soft, with a rippled, soft rind when fully ripe, Bonne-Bouches are small, ash-covered disks made from goat's milk by the Vermont Butter and Cheese Company. The fact that the makers include cheese-handling instructions in each box of this cheese for the retailer is indicative of the level of care these tasty morsels are made with. If cut in half when fully ripe, the cheese instantly runs out of the rind. These little goat cheeses are simultaneously sweet and piquant, made to be slathered on a baguette.

TUMELO TOMME

Made in central Oregon, this is a raw-milk farmhouse goat cheese made in four-pound wheels. Although a firm cheese, it is silky in texture, with a pleasing tartness of flavor. Hand washing the cheeses with a brine solution produces a rust-colored exterior that provides a nice contrast with the off-white pâte. Unique.

GRAND CRU

This is an extraordinarily good American Gruyère, with a deep flavor and a luscious, densely smooth texture. Grand Cru is produced in eighteen-pound wheels in Wisconsin dairy country. Although a factory cheese, Grand Cru is carefully made with lots of hands-on time during making and aging. The Roth Käse factory has ties to Switzerland, and their knowledge of what a good Gruyère should taste like is apparent. Unlike the Swiss original, Grand Cru is made with vegetarian rennet.

MAYTAG BLUE

This well-established American blue is made in Newton, Iowa. A rich, crumbly blue, it is handmade and aged for six months. Its pronounced flavor, characterized by an initial sharp bite followed by a sour-cream flavor, is due to the fact that it is a raw-milk cheese. This cheese has a fanatical following, which is probably why the dairy sells over 800,000 pounds of it yearly.

BELLWETHER FARMS SHEEP RICOTTA

This Ricotta from Sonoma County, California, is just firm enough to slice. It has a creamy sweetness reminiscent of Italian sheep's-milk Ricotta. It arrives in the store weeping whey, in a domelike shape from the form. Seasonally available, it is sometimes hard for us to obtain because the local chefs snap it up, but it is worth waiting for. Perfect for splurging on a superlative lasagna or as a simple dessert of Ricotta drizzled with honey and served with fresh fruit.

California Cheese Plate

HUMBOLDT FOG

With its fresh, earthy flavor, this is the star of domestic goat cheeses. A tall five-pound round, it is a dramatically beautiful cheese resembling a cheesecake. The fluffy white interior, transected by a decorative band of vegetable ash, varies from slightly crumbly to melting around the edges, depending on the stage of ripeness. Its flavor stays on the tongue for a long, satisfying period of time, during which different flavors emerge. It is tart and sweet and never overwhelmimgly goaty.

RED HAWK

Triple cream, vegetarian (curdled with vegetable rennet), and organic—how California can you get? This cheese is the New World answer to Epoisses (page 171). Made in Marin County by Cowgirl Creamery, it breaks the flavor barrier for organic cheese and is delightfully pungent when allowed to ripen until soft and tender. Buy it when the surface yields under a gentle squeeze.

ST. GEORGE

Authoritative and sharp when aged, with a distinctive edgy tang, this raw-cow's-milk cheese is similar to a medium-strength Cheddar when young. The Matos family in Santa Rosa makes it on a small scale, modeled on the Portuguese São Jorge. The age of the wheels varies a lot, as does its flavor. When well aged, this is one of the greats.

FISCALINI BANDAGE WRAPPED CHEDDAR

This newcomer has an ancient look: wrapped in cloth, the sixty-pound wheels are covered in a bluish mold that assists in the aging process. It is made from raw cow's milk and aged for at least eighteen months. (We have held a wheel for an additional six months in our *cave* to allow it to develop even more character.) The flavor is sharp and complex, reminiscent of the English Farmhouse Cheddars it is modeled on. Produced by the Fiscalini family farm in Modesto, this cheese is lovingly handmade.

POINT REYES ORIGINAL BLUE

Another local hero, from a family venture that produces this raw-milk blue from a Holstein herd in Marin County. It is a rich blue with a pronounced flavor of buttermilk. The wheels come into the Cheese Board sharper and more aged than they were in the first year of production. The Giacomini family claims that the proximity of their farm to the salty coast fog contributes to the flavor of the cheese.

California Goat Cheese Plate

There are just too many lovely and unique goat cheeses made here in California for them all to fit on a California cheese plate, so here is a plate devoted exclusively to California goat cheeses.

CAMELLIA

Redwood Hill Farms in Sebastopol makes this creamy goat Camembert. The company crafts its cheese from its own fresh goat's milk, which gives the products a particularly sweet taste, as the milk is used almost straight from the animal, leaving it no time to develop the unpleasantly strong flavors and odors so often associated with goat cheese. The pretty, white Camellia is a mold-ripened cheese that softens as it matures. The edible crust is supple and thin, and the interior is meltingly mild, with flowery overtones. On a warm day, it oozes out of the shell of its rind when cut, as if seeking a fresh, warm baguette.

CALIFORNIA CROTTIN

This sweet tasting Crottin, also made by Redwood Hill Farms, has the classic wrinkled exterior, but it is usually sold at an earlier point in its development than the French original. At the Cheese Board, we order this cheese without the wrapper so that we can continue the aging process at the store. We usually age these Crottins for two weeks to allow a lovely, flaky consistency and a complex caramel-like flavor to develop (for instructions on home aging, see page 157). Young or aged, this Crottin has the unique flavor of northern California grassland.

CAPRICIOUS

This cheese is made from pasteurized milk, but until recently we were under the impression that it was a raw-milk cheese, as its flavor is so deep and earthy. We sell it as a very aged (over ten months) hard goat cheese, so firm that it needs to be shaved in paper-thin slices. Made by My Time Dairy near Eureka, in coastal northern California, Capricious is sold in roughly shaped seven-pound disks. Its handmade appearance adds to its presentation; every fold of the cheesecloth used to make it is imprinted on its surface.

LAURA CHENEL TAUPINIÈRE

Taupinière means "molehill" in French, and describes the truncated-column shape of this ash-gray California cheese from Sonoma. When fully ripe, this cheese is forthright and honest about is goaty origins. Not for the faint of heart! At its perfect point of readiness, it is tart and cakey in the center and runny and tasty on the outside. Serve with grapes and crusty sourdough.

AOC CHEESES

The French system of Appellation d'Origine Contrôlée, or AOC, regulates the production and labeling of certain food products with ties to specific geographic regions in France. Currently, there are thirty-eight cheeses bearing an AOC label, as well as numerous wines, several butters, olives and olive oils, and a lentil.

The producers of any product with a distinctive history, a recognizable style of production, and firm roots in the agricultural traditions of any region in France can organize to apply for an AOC label. If they are successful, the use of a particular name will be reserved exclusively for those producers and products adhering to strict production guidelines. The right to use this name is legally protected, and violators can be prosecuted for fraud.

The AOC system was originally conceived as a means of regulating the production and labeling of wines. The wine trade had traditionally been awash in fraud and adulterated products, but at the turn of the nineteenth century, the explosion of the Champagne trade generated particularly intense rivalries among the vineyardists and vintners of the Marne and the Aube, both of whom tried to claim exclusive use of the name "Champagne." By 1911, there were widespread riots and mass resignations of local governmental officials across northeast France. To prevent a recurrence of violence, after the First World War the National Assembly set in place the centralized structure of the AOC system. Other countries, such as Italy and Spain, followed suit and enacted similar (though not as thorough and far-reaching) legislation to protect their own national food products. Even the United States has enacted some laws regulating the labeling of certain American wines.

AOC regulations are typically quite detailed. For cheeses, they specify the species and breed of animal, frequency of milking, type and minimum acres of pasturage, kind of hay or other supplemental feed, as well as myriad details of the cheese-making process itself, such as the temperature to which the curd is heated; how the curd is cut, ladled, and pressed or drained; the washing or inoculation of the rind; the material on which the cheese is aged; and the frequency of turning.

The AOC system helps consumers reliably identify great wines, cheeses, and other foods. It also plays a vital role in preserving traditional rural industries and communities, and helps to sustain a diverse population of animals and plants that might not otherwise be considered economically viable.

In the seventies, the cheese section was certainly smaller, especially as far as the lesser-known French cheeses. The artisanal American cheeses weren't there at all. We had only six or seven goat cheeses. It was so different how people bought cheese then. People would come in and buy one pound of Dill Havarti, two pounds of Cheddar, and a half pound of Brie. That's what they would serve before their dinner party—they'd plunk down pounds of cheese. Now, customers are more discerning.

—FRIEDA

AOC Cheese Plate

VALENÇAY

You will be delighted by the unique look of this small, ash-covered truncated pyramid, but it is the flavor that will utterly seduce you. This cheese is wonderful consumed when young and moist, as well as when it is aged. Young, it is very white inside and delicate in flavor; as it ages, the outer edge of the cheese becomes softer and darker while the core remains firm, providing contrasts in flavor as well as texture.

OSSAU-IRATY

Made in both pasteurized and raw-milk versions, Ossau-Iraty, from the Pyrénées region, is a firm and smooth-textured Basque sheep's-milk cheese sold in fifteen-pound wheels. We carry a pasteurized type called Istara that has a smooth, warm flavor—an instant crowd-pleaser. We also sell a handmade raw-milk Ossau-Iraty under the name Vallée d'Aspe. It has a slightly gamey scent, and the flavor is sweet, heavy, and a little more pungent than that of its pasteurized cousin.

BLEU D'AUVERGNE

Rich and soft, Bleu d'Auvergne is a flavorful, sharp blue that is not overly salty (as is the case with so many other blues). Even though this raw-cow's-milk blue is usually factory made, it has a unique clean tang that contrasts nicely with many other flavors.

BEAUFORT

The Beaufort *d'eté* (summer Beaufort) or *d'alpage* (made in the mountains) are the ones to look for. This moist, firm alpine cheese made from raw cow's milk has a grassy, flowery flavor that is beautifully balanced by its smooth texture. Perhaps more than any other, this cheese

THE CHEESE AND SOURDOUGH CONNECTION

In my spare time, I like to read up on the cheeses we offer at the Cheese Board. Last fall I was reading about Parmigiano-Reggiano. One day while replenishing the Cheese Board's sourdough starter to be used in our next day of dough making, I was suddenly struck by the similarity of technique between making sourdough bread and making certain cheeses. In each case, you reserve a portion of natural starter to be used for future bread or cheese making. At that moment, the connection between bread and cheese became crystal clear to me.

Parmigiano-Reggiano has been made in the same ritualistic manner for at least eight hundred years. It has a DOC status (much like the French AOC designation), which ensures the continuation of the ancient method of cheese making. Each requirement—origin and method of manufacture, time of year made, kind of milk, brining and aging techniques—culminates in a amazingly noble seventy-five-pound wheel of cheese.

Recently, I stayed after hours at the Cheese Board to watch a 2½-year-old Rocca Parmigiano-Reggiano be opened by one of my coworkers. The entire outside rind was stamped in vertical rows with the words *Parmigiano-Reggiano*. The date of the cheese making and where it was made were also included in an oval stamp on the side of the wheel. The rind of a Parmigiano is thick and hard, so Dan scored the center with a razor blade. Then, following his scoring with a very sharp knife, he made a one-inch cut around the fat center of the cheese. Finally, he turned the wheel onto its side, took a cheese wire, and placed it in the one-inch crevasse. With good leverage and bracing, he gracefully drew the wire through the wheel of cheese. The halves fell away from each other, and we both grabbed a cheese plane to slice off and taste a piece of the newly opened wheel.

At times like this I feel so lucky. In the Midwest, where I grew up, the only kind of Parmesan cheese we ever had came in a green can. We would sprinkle it on spaghetti, pizza, and sometimes salad. I had no idea that this was a feeble imitation of a dignified cheese. That yellow, powdery, salty cheese is unrecognizable as true Parmigiano. The opened wheel was golden inside and tasted like fruit and meadows. Its texture was hard and grainy, but when we tasted it, the pâte melted in our mouths. I am filled with respect for the cheese makers who for centuries have carried on their traditional practices.

What is the connection between Parmigiano-Reggiano and sourdough bread making? There is the obvious one of the use of a saved starter from one day to the next, but less obvious is the lesson in history that you receive from tasting the finished product. There is historical continuity in the simple act of making bread and cheese, and this is peacefully satisfying.

—Cathy

has a lingering flavor—you can still taste summer in an alpine meadow more than five minutes after eating it. It is made in enormous wheels that use the entire day's milking from a herd of forty-five cows. Beaufort is a fabulous melter.

EPOISSES DE BOURGOGNE

Almost lost forever after World War I, this sticky, pungent soft cheese is a deep mahogany red-brown in color and creamy and sweet on the inside. Originally created in the sixteenth century by Cistercian monks, its distinctive coloration is a result of frequent washings by hand that encourage the local bacteria to spread and grow. During the final days of the *affinage* (aging process), the small rounds are washed in Marc de Bourgogne, a spirit of the region. When well ripened, this cheese should be soft to the touch and fill its round spruce container.

I really enjoy the interaction with the customer. Working the cheese counter is a *very* different thing than baking; it's all about being gracious with the customer and being available to them.

—MARTHA

• • •

Wednesday-Morning Cheese Plate

LE LINGOT DU QUERCY

This French raw-goat's-milk cheese looks like a rectangular piece from a children's miniature play set of wooden blocks. It is pale gold in color and has a slightly wrinkled, edible soft skin. When young, it is a firm, cake-like cheese with a subtly sweet flavor of grass and blossoms. Aged, it becomes increasingly soft, verging on liquescent. As this happens, the flowery sweetness is overtaken by an almost caramel-like flavor.

TOMME DU LÉVEZOU

Made by the same French cooperative that makes the Lingot, this cheese is a hard, aged raw-sheep's-milk round. It has a dusty gray exterior that, when sliced, reveals a white interior that is slightly flaky and grainy. The cheese doesn't immediately reveal itself when eaten, but it has a long, slow buildup that surprises and rewards with a gentle authority of flavor.

AFFIDELICES AU CHABLIS

The gentle cousin of Epoisses. Also French, this is a cow's-milk cheese that is washed with Chablis, which causes the rind to become a deep red-brown in color. When perfectly ripened, it should be eaten with a spoon, which is why it comes in a small, round wooden box that it is almost impossible to remove from. The flavor of Affidelices stops short of the musky funkiness of its other relatives from Alsace, but it delivers a potent briny hit with a sensuous texture. Perfect with a baguette.

VENTO D'ESTATE

This is a hard, dense cheese from the Veneto region of Italy. Vento d'Estate (which means "summer's wind") is aged in a barrel packed with hay. It is made with a variety of milks, and we have never quite figured out what determines the milk selection, the cheese maker's whim or availability. (Its label states that it is either cow's or sheep's milk, with goat cultures.) Whatever the composition, it is a memorable cheese with a high, bright flavor and sweet-wine overtones. Its straw-colored, lopsided roundish shape, covered in wisps of hay, has a rustic appeal. This cheese is good with a wheat bread like the Suburban (page 109) or drizzled with Italian olive oil.

EVERY WEDNESDAY MORNING

Every Wednesday morning, I ready my box cutter, pens, and stickers and start unpacking wooden crates and cardboard boxes from the United States, France, Italy, England, Portugal, Canada, and Spain. I lift out handmade cheeses from farms and small towns thousand of miles away. I love reading the labels and imagining the far-off places the cheeses come from, like the Majorero, a Spanish goat cheese made on the Canary Islands off the coast of Africa. Each cheese comes with a story, sometimes from a recent era, other times rooted in the past, even in antiquity. For example, Azeitão, a Portuguese sheep's-milk cheese, was made in Roman times and is still curdled with an infusion made from nettles rather than the usual rennet.

Some labels make for very good reading, such as that of Abbaye de Tamié, a semisoft washed-rind cheese from France. The waxed-paper wrapping surrounding it recounts the entire history of its makers, an order of monks, starting from the founding of the monastery by a grateful count centuries ago. I have often been so swept up by the contents of a shipment that I've wasted precious time on busy morning shifts trying to decipher labels with coworkers, using our rusty high-school French or Italian.

The cheeses that interest me the most are the ones with lumpy, hoary, mold-encrusted exteriors, such as Brin d'Amour, a sheep's-milk cheese from Corsica that is covered with rosemary and overgrown with a mold so hairy that it looks like a cashmere sweater. The scarier-looking a cheese, the more interesting I find it. Sadly, an increasing number of traditional cheeses are coming into the store interred in Cryovac, with no possibility of breathing, an essential requirement for cheese.

As I open the boxes, different scents float up and mingle with the smells of bread baking from the nearby ovens. Each cheese has a different bouquet, and the aromas range from sweet to grassy to downright funky barnyard. The odor of a cheese, interestingly enough, does not always predict its taste. A strong-smelling Munster may actually be mild and flowery in flavor, belying its industrial-strength gaminess on the nose.

Some of the cheeses we receive are made from the milk of very small herds of animals and are not easily available, even in their own country of origin. One such cheese is Bleu de Termignon, from the Rhône Alps in France. Made by one farmer from the milk of a herd of only nine cows, it is a crumbly white cheese, lightly edged with a naturally occurring blue mold. The mold in this cheese is not injected into the interior as it is in most blues, but allowed to settle on the exterior and grow inward by itself. Another is Hoch Ybrig, a Swiss cow's-milk cheese imported by a passionate cheese enthusiast in Florida. This firm mountain cheese is made from raw milk and has sweet combinations of flavor that linger for an exceptionally long time on the tongue.

Then there are all the new cheeses, many of which are local. It is gratifying to see these brand-new creations arrive. The cheeses are often wonderful from the start, and it is fun to observe how they change as their makers gain knowledge and have the time and resources to experiment with and age their new creations. One such new cheese is Point Reyes Original Blue from Marin County, California, which has a unique buttermilk flavor underlying a blue bite that is faintly reminiscent of another domestic great, Maytag Blue. (This isn't too surprising, as the cheese maker helping to develop this blue came to Marin County from Iowa, where he worked in the Maytag factory.)

The most fun and exciting moments are when I get to unpack cheeses that I've never seen before. Our purveyors comb the countrysides of the Old World and the New, searching for novel and traditional cheeses to market. When a cheese is introduced to us, we all try to taste it and comment on it. Hopefully, the cheese is at its best at that moment, because first impressions determine whether or not clerks will offer the cheese for tastes at the counter.

When I unpack the crates of cheese, the feeling is like that of a hurried version of Christmas morning. As with everything else at the Cheese Board, doing a task in a detailed manner is balanced against doing it efficiently. I have to finish unpacking the order. It is time to date the cheeses, price and label them, and put them away. I am always amazed that an hour and a half has passed so quickly, and it is now time to wait on customers. I get to tell them all about the new lovelies we have just received, and offer tastes of my favorites.

—Ursula

LINCOLNSHIRE POACHER

This raw-cow's-milk cheese from England has a real presence. Uncut, it is a large cylinder covered in cheesecloth and discolored by mold. The firm interior is a beautiful deep creamy yellow, edged with cracks and fissures where the mold has made incursions into this dignified cheese. Its flavor has the highly prized bite desired by the Cheddar enthusiast, coupled with a slow, complex flowering of taste uniquely its own. Flaky in texture, it is a real pleasure to shave into wafer-thin slices and eat with crisp apples.

New Year's Eve Cheese Plate

The busy holiday season culminates with New Year's Eve, when the most common question asked is, "What should I serve with Champagne?" Everything tastes good with Champagne, but for New Year's Eve you want especially rich, usually forbidden cheeses.

BRILLAT-SAVARIN

You don't need to make your New Year's resolutions until January 1, so enjoy this triple-cream cow's-milk cheese that is at least 75 percent butterfat. It has a soft, "bloomy" rind that resembles white velvet. Rich and creamy, this cheese will bring you closer to heaven. If you have a hard time finding Brillat-Savarin, ask for a St. André or an Explorateur.

LE MARÉCHAL

The floral aroma of mountain meadows precedes the taste of this rich Swiss cheese made from raw cow's milk. The interior is smooth, with a firm texture a little softer

LANGRES

For a romantic (and private) New Year's Eve celebration, I'd bring home a small Langres. It's a French cow's-milk cheese from the high plains of Langres in Champagne. The outside is orange in color, sticky, and smelly. It has a strong yeasty flavor and a smooth, oozy texture. Langres is shaped like a cylinder with a well in the top. Traditionally, Champagne is poured into the well. You really don't need any other cheeses or a lot of company.

—Cathy

PS: Because it is unpasteurized and ready to eat before the U.S. regulation of sixty days of aging for raw-milk cheeses, Langres is rarely found here. If you ever see it at your local cheese shop, toss your planned menu and surprise everyone with your discovery.

than that of Gruyère. The herbs rubbed on the dark outside of this cheese make its flavor quite different from any other. It ranges from sweet and mild when young (four or five months) to earthy and strong when aged.

SAINT-AGUR

This sophisticated blue cheese made from cow's milk has beautiful blue-marbled veins running throughout and an assertive flavor that is simultaneously sweet, salty, and sharp. It tastes smooth and rich, complementing Champagne and leaving your palate with a fragrant, clean finish.

THE SCENT OF CHEESE

My first memories of working at the Cheese Board are impressed in the membrane cells of my nose. I had just moved back to Berkeley and was so happy to be working at the store. On Friday nights, my job was to restock and clean the cheese case. After my shift, I would stay and wash up with lemon juice, scrubbing to my elbows and wondering why I could still smell the stinkness as if I hadn't washed at all. I would sniff my clothes—they seemed okay, but the smell coming from me was unbearable. When I eventually got home, my boyfriend would move toward me to give me a welcome-home kiss, but never make it to my lips before sending me off to the shower with a "Phew!"

It took years of experience (and meeting another man) for me to discover exactly what causes this unpleasant occurrence. It is the random piece of cheesy substance that hides itself on the unsuspecting clerk. Sometimes you just have to touch the end of your nose with a cheesy hand, and there it is! All day you keep sniffing around, washing your hands, but it is right there at the end of your nose the whole time.

It might have been when you cut a ripe Taleggio, and a wee bit of the perfuming rind was flung onto the side of your apron. Once you accidentally wipe it onto your fingertip, which then barely brushes the seam of your pants, you keep smelling something potent. You wash your hands, and by now you have learned to wash your face and nose too. You even change your apron, but you just keep smelling it. You know it's somewhere nearby—maybe it's your coworkers—no, it's still there as you politely move away from them.

One occasion I'll never forget. A customer called needing a low-fat cheese that she could get only at our store. I rarely have time to do this, but in this instance, I agreed to ship it to her. So I packed the box carefully with ice packs so the cheese would not spoil or smell, and ran up to a little shipping store a block from the Cheese Board. Standing in line for several minutes, I noticed something odiferous. When it was my turn, I was eager to share this information, so I leaned forward toward the young man behind the counter (a regular customer at our store), and murmured, "Hey, you know it smells pretty funky in here, you should open the door." When he glanced at me and said, "It smells like cheese," I shrunk to the size of a mini Stilton, meowed "I'm sorry," hurriedly completed my business, and quickly left.

—Lisa

Stinky-Cheese Plate

In the case of most stinky cheeses, the bark is bigger than the bite. The smell of the perfumey rind is part of the eating experience, but in most cases it will not override the smooth, strong, sometimes even sweet flavor of the cheese.

FONTINA D'AOSTA

This is a semisoft cheese from the Valle d'Aosta, a large valley at the foot of Monte Bianco. While this cheese is pungent, its flavor should be assertive but not overwhelming. It has a silky smoothness of texture and melts beautifully, making it a great addition to baked polenta or pizza.

MUNSTER

Though Maroilles and Livarot are also candidates, Munster is unique in its stinkiness. Munster's history dates back over a thousand years, to A.D. 960. A good ripe Munster will perfume your refrigerator to the point where you won't open the door unless you have to. This French Alsace cheese and its twin from Lorraine, Géromé, are washed-rind cheeses with an interior reminiscent of a creamy, malty Trappist beer (which, incidentally, is its perfect accompaniment, along with a chewy dark rye with caraway seeds).

GORGONZOLA

There is a story about one of our past members opening the plastic bag that the Gorgonzola comes in and drinking the liquid therein. True? Who knows, but we still tell the story to all our new cheese clerks. Gorgonzola juice is so smelly—everyone at the Cheese Board knows it as one of the main culprits of Stinky Hand Syndrome—but let your cheesemonger worry about that part. With its flavors of toasted pistachios, cream, and salt, all in one wonderful mouthful, this cheese is too good to miss.

Super Bowl Cheese Plate

Super Bowl parties are the complete opposite of New Year's Eve celebrations. Instead of cheeses to match with Champagne, select cheeses to eat with beer. Everyone always talks about matching cheese and wine, but beer has been a long-time companion to cheese. Below are a few suggestions for armchair football players.

TALEGGIO

Maybe Italians don't watch American football, but Taleggio could easily be on a World Cup cheese plate. The pinkish rind is slightly gooey, with heavy yeasty overtones that do not mask the luscious sweetness of this cheese. (For a discussion of the making of Taleggio, see page 151.)

ROOMANO GOUDA

Made in Holland from cow's milk, Old Amsterdam Gouda is aged for a minimum of two years, during which time it develops a deep golden color, a firm smooth texture, and a butterscotch flavor. Sweet white crystals throughout the pâte add a crunchy texture to each bite.

BEERKAESE

This is an American factory-made cow's-milk cheese fashioned after a Danish Esrom. If aged long enough, it has a wonderful stinky quality and a deep flavor with hints of caraway. The paste is creamy in color and semisoft in texture, with small irregular holes.

GUBBEEN

Made in County Cork, Ireland, in two- to three-pound wheels, this pungent cow's-milk cheese has a soft interior and an assertive flavor. It is a perfect cheese to eat while drinking stout.

COTSWOLD

This factory-made English cow's-milk cheese is a mixture of Double Gloucester and chives. Orange in color with green specks throughout, it has a texture that is firm and smooth. The chives add a mild onion flavor to the cheese, which is delicious with beer and chips.

I love the variety of the cheeses. I like to know how they are made, where they come from, what they are eaten with, and how they are traditionally eaten. I love seeing the way a wheel of cheese changes. I can taste a wheel of cheese and think, "Oh, this is nothing compared to the way it usually is." Or, "Wow, this is by far the best wheel of this cheese we've ever had." I eat cheese here, at the store, more out of a sense of responsibility than because I love it so much. I feel like I should taste all the cheese.

—ADAM

It's weird, but when it's the turn for my next customer, my favorite customers are often the next in line. Hardly anyone else ever gets to wait on them. It's my fate to wait on them again and again. They go from being customers to being friends in no time.

—LISA

The very first Saturday I worked at the Cheese Board, a woman came in with her tiny baby. Now when I see that baby grown into a boy, it makes me so happy. Every time I see him it reminds me of my first day—he marks my tenure in the collective.

—CATHY

Intimate Picnic Plate

Whether the location is a meadow, a beach, or your living room floor, an intimate picnic implies romance and requires a simple and elegant selection of small cheeses. These cheeses travel well, whatever your destination, and reflect the mood of the occasion.

PICANDOU

This petite fresh goat cheese comes in two-ounce round disks that are perfect to share. It has a tart, floral flavor and a creamy texture. Serve it with fresh cherries and a glass of white wine.

CAMEMBERT

Sold in the familiar eight-ounce round wooden boxes, Camembert is made from cow's milk that is hand ladled into molds and aged for three weeks. It has a bloomy white rind and the pâte is the color of straw. The rich, mellow flavor of Camembert is sensual and satisfying.

PETIT AGOUR

This one-pound Tomme is made from raw sheep's milk from the Pyrénées. The small size of the cheese is perfect for cutting in half. The flavor is smooth, nutty, and bright, perfect with a light red wine.

Camping Cheeses

People often come into the store and ask for advice about what types of cheese would hold up to the rigors of camping. Some people will be car camping with a cooler, while others will only have a small space at the bottom of a backpack. In both cases they are looking for a cheese that is sturdy as well as tasty. Since cheese was developed mainly as a way of preserving milk before refrigeration existed, there are many types that are eminently suited to the exigencies of outdoor living. Our recommended cheeses are all well aged, and they will hold their shape and keep their flavor even when they are tossed around in a backpack, and heated by the sun at high altitudes. Most cheeses will sweat a combination of moisture and oil if left unrefrigerated; while the look may not be pleasing, usually no harm is done to the cheese. If cheeses are allowed to get hot, a more significant change of texture will occur; again, not always pretty, but usually edible. (Discard any cheese with a rank smell or brightly colored molds on the surface.) To keep cheese unrefrigerated, wrap it in a layer or two of cheesecloth and seal it tightly in two plastic bags.

DRY JACK

This California cheese is made in an eight-pound disk; its dark exterior is rubbed with oil and cocoa powder. It has a warm, mellow flavor that is pleasing on a sandwich or grated over a dinner dish. The extra-aged variety has a flaky quality and a sweet flavor.

PARMIGIANO-REGGIANO

Simply put, this is one of the best and most versatile cheeses around. Its use as a grating cheese is well-known, but it has been overlooked as an excellent cheese eaten out of hand. It may seem like a luxury, but as a backpacking cheese Parmigiano is hard to beat. It's good with crackers and will make your high-altitude vermicelli taste great.

THE NASAL TOUR

"Why does my cheese taste stronger when I get it home?" is a frequently asked question at our cheese counter. The answer is partially due to how enthusiastic we are about strong cheeses—so much so that we influence our customers' choices. But mostly it has to do with the store itself, which produces such an olfactory overload that the sense of taste is overwhelmed; as a result, robust-tasting cheeses seem mild. Here is a nasal tour of our store, featuring a few of the aromas that compete with an accurate assessment of cheeses.

The two cheese cases, arranged in an L shape, produce a wonderful array of musty aromas. Wandering over to the goat cheese section, centrally displayed on wooden risers, you instantly get a whiff of the barnyard. A little farther along the same case, you find the French cheeses. Take a snort of the Munster and what can you say except, "Ah, stinky feet"? Of course, not all of the cheeses are so stinky. Walk around the protruding corner of the first case and you will discover the sheep cheeses; rather than reeking, they more often have a scent of caramel candy, rich and sweet. (An exception would be a liquidy Brin d'Amour melting on an unseasonably hot June day.) Many of these cheeses, such as the Beaufort, have a subtle fragrance that is experienced as both a bouquet and a delicious, complex flavor.

Mingled with the delightfully cheesy aroma of the store is the scent of hot bread fresh from the oven. The seductive smell is so strong that the last portion of my three-block stroll to work could probably be accomplished by following my nose with my eyes closed. From half a block away, I can tell whether or not cheese rolls are coming out of the oven. The fragrance of hot baked goods assaults the prospective cheese buyers, surrounding them in waves rising from the nearby baskets.

Other smells intertwine with the cheese and bread odors. In the back of the kitchen, near the Hobart bread mixer, lives the sourdough starter. Beware of the potent emanation coming from the buckets that house the starters. If a top is bulging, don't ever make the mistake of putting your nose right over it when you open it, lest the pent-up gas escape with a hiss and rush up your nose. You'll gasp, and tears will come to your eyes as the acidic fumes overload your sinuses. During warm weather, the sourdough starters frequently rise to the top of the buckets and push off their lids, foaming over onto the steel tray where they rest, forming a pool of odiferous white muck.

The espresso cart and coffee urns by the front window contribute a comforting mellowness to the surroundings that belies the jolt they provide a tired baking crew and busy customers on the way to work. The huge coffee urn remains hot and fragrant hours after it has been shut off and the Morning Bakery has closed down.

There are also those moments in our olfactory history we'd like to forget about, such as the time various staff members intermittently noticed acrid fumes of burning wood. A few days later, we figured out that our huge walk-in oven had succeeded in burning through the floor, and had started charring the joists underneath it!

The lesson: When tasting cheese, be aware that your nose is part of the experience, and adjust your selections accordingly!

—Ursula

Everybody is transformed as a person by working in the collective. Working at the Cheese Board, I really learned how important it is to include everybody, I learned generosity there for sure. It definitely extended my family—it kind of made the whole community my family. I'd be a completely different person if I hadn't worked at the Cheese Board.

—TESSA

PECORINO TOSCANO RISERVA

Made by the Il Forteto cooperative in Tuscany, this is a well-aged sheep's-milk cheese the color of pale straw. With a warm, sweet flavor and a flaky texture that never seems dry, it is suitable for shaving over dinner with a Swiss Army knife or eating with apples and bread.

MANCHEGO

This Spanish sheep's-milk cheese from La Mancha has a design on the rind that resembles a woven basket. It is a rich cheese with the flavor of caramel. Choose one aged at least six months for camping and ask for a taste, as the varieties differ quite a bit in flavor.

SBRINZ

At the Cheese Board, we receive two versions of this Swiss cheese. One is a hard rectangular block, also called Swiss hard mountain cheese, and the other is a hefty round. Both versions are smooth, dense aged cheeses that are ideal for camping. Sbrinz is sweet and satisfying—a nice mountain cheese to be enjoyed in an alpine meadow anywhere.

Now that I've learned how to be a doula, I describe my life as "bread and babies." I go for interviews with prospective parents who are about to hire me to assist at a birth, and when they find out that I work at the Cheese Board, the interview turns into, "Oh, what is the collective really like?" It turns into a conversation more about the Cheese Board than about them changing their life and turning into parents! It's very funny.   —ERIN

MEXICAN-STYLE CHEESES

As we are unable to obtain imported Mexican cheeses, we sell only American-made Mexican-style cheeses at the Cheese Board. While these cheeses may share a name with their Mexican counterparts, don't expect them to taste the same as the originals. For the most part, these cheeses are quite young and mild, suitable for cooking and for topping any number of dishes. They are especially handy for making *bocadillos* (sandwiches or snacks).

QUESO PANELA

This is a fresh, white cheese with a texture slightly softer than loaf Mozzarella. Mild and salty, it can be crumbled on top of Spanish rice, refried beans, or tostadas, and also makes a very good grilled cheese sandwich. Sliced, rolled in cornmeal, and cooked on top of a griddle, it holds its shape and becomes delectably crispy around the edges and soft on the inside. In the state of Michoacán, this cheese is often sold as an strong-smelling aged cheese.

QUESO DOBLE CREMA

While richer and sweeter than Queso Panela, this cheese also holds its shape when baked or grilled. It comes in a large, white round that is still weeping whey when cut for sale. Use it for stuffing *chiles rellenos* and crumble it on top of tostadas.

QUESO FRESCO

When crumbled, Queso Fresco has a fine-grained texture somewhat like that of Feta; however, it is a moister cheese, milder in flavor, and less salty. It is delicious crumbled on top of black beans.

QUESO COTIJA

Dry and salty, this cheese is almost as flavorful as an Italian Romano. It can be used as a grated cheese on top of pastas, and as a topping for *bocadillos.*

The Cheese Stands Alone

Sometimes, serving one cheese by itself is more dramatic than a plate of three or more cheeses; in other cases, a cheese is so pungent it is better served by itself. The cheeses below are all eminently suitable for a solo appearance. We have included two of our favorite blues in this list, as they are particularly good for a cheese course or dessert offering.

VACHERIN DU HAUT-DOUBS/MONT D'OR

Round, with a rumpled-looking top, this cheese comes banded by spruce bark, which imparts a woodsy flavor to the body of the cheese. When perfectly ripened, it should be spooned out for eating. This rich, liquid delicacy is available from November through February (during the summer months, the milk is used to make French Comté). For the best flavor, buy raw-milk Vacherin (the French ones are usually made from raw milk, while the Swiss ones are often pasteurized).

STILTON

Classic and *stately* are two words to describe this English blue. It is firm textured, with a thin brown rind enclosing a creamy yellow interior striated by bands of blue mold radiating out from the center. It is a unique blue, almost more like Cheddar in texture and background flavor. Stilton is buttery, spicy, and less salty than most blues.

CABRALES

Spanish blues are very distinctive in look and flavor. In its coat of dark brown leaves, this Spanish blue looks like a chocolate cake, while inside its veining is dense and dark green in color. The leaves add a faint forest astringency to the intensely blue flavor, as well as helping to hold the crumbly, moist cheese together. Similar cheeses are Picon and Valdeon.

RUSTICHELLA

If you love truffles, this is the cheese for you; and though many of us at the Cheese Board don't care for truffle-flavored cheese, we love this one. Rustichella is an imposing, tall Italian sheep's-milk wheel with a brown, rustic basket-weave exterior. It is firm and moist. Though the truffles definitely take center stage, the background flavor is pleasing and clean.

• CHEESE BREADS •

Cheese Onion Curry Bread (aka Salzbrot, aka Hobrot)

This bright yellow bread was the first to be developed at the bakery. It is a great way to use up those odd bits of cheese that would otherwise languish unwanted in your refrigerator; in fact, this is the reason we developed it. Originally called Cheese Onion Curry Bread, it was renamed Salzbrot in honor of the collectivist who for years managed to knead this giant dough by hand. After we finally started making it in the Hobart mixer, it was renamed Hobrot. We also make a sort of English muffin out of this dough called a Berkeley Bun. The cheese you use to make this bread will influence its final flavor; be as daring as you like.

MAKES 2 LOAVES AND 8 BERKELEY BUNS
Preparation time including rising and baking: 4 hours;
active time: 40 minutes

- 2 teaspoons active dry yeast
- 1/2 cup warm water
- 4 cups plus 1 tablespoon bread flour
- 1 1/2 teaspoons finely ground black pepper
- 2 tablespoons curry powder
- 2 teaspoons kosher salt
- 1 1/4 cups lukewarm water
- 1 yellow onion, coarsely chopped
- 1 pound mixed cheeses such as Cheddar, Gouda, and Fontina, cut into 3/4-inch cubes
- Medium-grind yellow cornmeal for sprinkling
- 1 egg, beaten

In a small bowl, whisk the yeast into the warm water until dissolved. Let stand for 5 minutes.

In the bowl of a stand mixer or a large bowl, combine the 4 cups flour, the pepper, curry powder, and salt.

If using a stand mixer, add the yeast mixture and lukewarm water to the bowl. Using the paddle attachment on low speed, mix until the ingredients are combined, about 2 minutes. Switch to the dough hook, increase the mixer speed to medium, and knead for 8 minutes, or until the dough is silky and a bit shiny. In a small bowl, toss all but 1/4 cup of the chopped onion with the 1 tablespoon flour. Add the onion to the dough and continue to knead on medium speed until well incorporated, about 2 minutes. Transfer the dough to a lightly floured surface. Flatten it into a 1-inch-thick round and place the cheese in the center. Gather the dough around the cheese and knead just until the cheese is evenly distributed, taking care not to break it up.

If making by hand, add the yeast mixture and lukewarm water to the bowl and mix with a wooden spoon until the ingredients are combined. Transfer to a lightly floured surface and knead for at least 12 minutes, or until the dough is silky and a bit shiny. In a small bowl, toss all but 1/4 cup of the chopped onion with the 1 tablespoon flour. Flatten the dough into a 1-inch-thick round and place the onion in the center. Gather the dough around the onion and knead until well incorporated, about 2 minutes. Flatten the dough once again and add the cheese, kneading just long enough to evenly distribute the cheese throughout the dough, taking care not break it up.

Form the dough into a ball and place it in a large oiled bowl. Turn the dough over to coat it with oil. Cover the bowl with plastic wrap or a damp kitchen towel and let rise in a warm, draft-free place for 1 1/4 hours, or until doubled in size.

Generously sprinkle 2 baking sheets with cornmeal. Transfer the dough to a lightly floured surface and divide it

into 3 pieces. Gently form 2 of these pieces into loose rounds (see page 26) and cover with a floured kitchen towel. Let rest for 10 minutes. Shape the 2 pieces into large rounds (see page 27) and place the loaves on a prepared pan. Cover with a floured kitchen towel and let rise in a warm place for 1¼ hours, or until increased in size by one-half and a finger pressed into the dough leaves an impression.

While the loaves are rising, prepare the third piece of dough for the Berkeley Buns. On a floured surface, roll the dough out into a 12 by 6 by ½-inch-thick rectangle. Using a 3-inch floured round cookie cutter or a floured drinking glass, cut out 8 disks and place them on the second prepared pan. Discard the scraps. Cover with a floured kitchen towel and let rise for 45 minutes, or until puffy and increased in size by one-fourth. Preheat a large cast-iron skillet or griddle over medium-low heat for at least 5 minutes. Sprinkle cornmeal on the heated pan; if the cornmeal pops and burns, the pan is too hot and should be cooled for a minute. Place the buns in the preheated pan and cook for 8 to 10 minutes on each side, or until a dark golden brown.

Fifteen minutes before the loaves have finished rising, preheat the oven to 450°F.

Using a pastry brush, brush the top of each loaf with the beaten egg. Gently place the reserved ¼ cup chopped onions on top of each loaf.

Bake the loaves on the middle rack of the oven for 10 minutes. Lower the oven temperature to 400°F and bake 10 minutes longer. Rotate the baking sheet left to right and bake 25 to 30 minutes longer, for a total baking time of 35 to 40 minutes, or until the loaves are nicely browned and sound hollow when tapped on the bottom. Transfer to a wire rack to cool.

We always taste the cheese to make sure it's good. On any given day, you'll find a bunch of clerks standing around tasting a cheese that might be weird or bitter or gross, and you are walking by and someone will say to you, "Try this cheese, it's awful!"

—OLIVIA

Greek Shepherd's Bread

We make this bread with pitted Kalamata olives and Kefalo-graviera, a Greek sheep's-milk cheese with a salty, assertive flavor. Every Tuesday afternoon it is a Cheese Boarder's job to stand at the prep table and check the olives so that no stray pits find their way into the dough.

MAKES 3 LOAVES
Preparation time including rising and baking: 4¾ hours; active time: 30 minutes

- 2 teaspoons active dry yeast
- ½ cup warm water
- 3½ cups plus 1 tablespoon bread flour
- 2 teaspoons kosher salt
- ¾ cup lukewarm water
- 1 small yellow onion, coarsely chopped
- ½ pound Kefalograviera cheese (or any firm sheep's-milk cheese), cut into ½-inch cubes
- ½ cup pitted Kalamata olives, coarsely chopped
- 1 egg, beaten
- 3 tablespoons sesame seeds

In a small bowl, whisk the yeast into the warm water until dissolved. Let stand for 5 minutes.

In the bowl of a stand mixer or a large bowl, combine the 3½ cups flour and the salt.

If using a stand mixer, add the yeast mixture and luke-warm water to the bowl. Using the paddle attachment on low speed, mix until the ingredients are combined, about 2 minutes. Switch to the dough hook, increase the mixer speed to medium, and knead for 7 minutes, or until the dough is smooth, silky, and elastic. In a small bowl, toss the chopped onion with the 1 tablespoon flour. Add the onion to the dough and continue to knead on medium speed until well incorporated, about 2 minutes. Transfer the dough to a lightly floured surface. Flatten it into a 1-inch-thick round and place the cheese and olives in the center. Gather the dough around the cheese and olives and knead just until they are evenly distributed. (Kneading the dough too long will break up the cheese, and the olives will turn the dough a muddy color.)

If making by hand, add the yeast mixture and lukewarm water to the bowl and mix with a wooden spoon until the ingredients are combined. Transfer to a lightly floured surface and knead for at least 12 minutes, or until the dough is smooth, silky, and elastic. In a small bowl, toss the chopped onion with the 1 tablespoon flour. Flatten the dough into a 1-inch-thick round and place the onion in the center. Gather the dough around the onion and knead until well incorporated, about 2 minutes. Flatten the dough once again, add the cheese and olives, and knead just until they are evenly distributed. (Kneading the dough too long will break up the cheese, and the olives will turn the dough a muddy color.)

Form the dough into a ball and place it in a large oiled bowl. Turn the dough over to coat it with oil. Cover the bowl with plastic wrap or a damp kitchen towel and let rise in a warm, draft-free place for about 1½ hours, or until doubled in size.

Lightly dust 2 baking sheets with flour. Transfer the dough to a lightly floured surface and divide it into 3 pieces. Gently form each piece into a loose round (see page 26) and cover with a floured kitchen towel. Let rest for 10 minutes. Shape each round into a 2-stranded turban (see page 30). Place 2 of the loaves on a prepared pan at least 4 inches apart, and place the third loaf in the center of the second pan. Cover with a floured kitchen towel and let rise in a warm place for 1½ hours, or until doubled in size and a finger pressed into the dough leaves an impression.

Fifteen minutes before the loaves have finished rising, arrange the oven racks in the upper and lower thirds of the oven. Preheat the oven to 375°F.

Using a pastry brush, brush the tops of the loaves with the beaten egg and sprinkle them with the sesame seeds.

Bake the loaves for 20 minutes. Rotate the baking sheets top to bottom and front to back. Bake 20 minutes longer and rotate the loaves again. Bake 10 to 15 minutes longer, for a total baking time of 50 to 55 minutes, or until the bread is a golden brown and sounds hollow when tapped on the bottom. Transfer to a wire rack to cool.

Asiago Bread

We make this bread on Thursday mornings. Half of the batch is dedicated to loaves, and the other half is formed into small rolls or rolled into sticks (or "schticks," as we call them). These three different shapes satisfy different needs: the sandwich, the easy lunch, and the light snack.

MAKES 2 LOAVES AND 6 STICKS
Preparation time including rising and baking: 3½ hours;
active time: 30 minutes

  2 teaspoons active dry yeast
  ½ cup warm water
  3 cups plus 1 tablespoon bread flour
  2 teaspoons kosher salt
  2 teaspoons dried marjoram
  1 cup lukewarm water
  1 yellow onion, coarsely chopped
  1 pound Asiago cheese, cut into ¾-inch cubes
  1 egg, beaten
  2 tablespoons sesame seeds

In a small bowl, whisk the yeast into the warm water until dissolved. Let stand for 5 minutes.

In the bowl of a stand mixer or a large bowl, combine the 3 cups flour, the salt, and marjoram.

If using a stand mixer, add the yeast mixture and lukewarm water to the bowl. Using the paddle attachment on low speed, mix until the ingredients are combined, about 2 minutes. Switch to the dough hook, increase the mixer speed to medium, and knead for 7 minutes, or until the dough is smooth, silky, and elastic. In a small bowl, toss the chopped onion with the 1 tablespoon flour. Add the onion to the dough and continue to knead on medium speed until well incorporated, about 2 minutes. Transfer the dough to a lightly floured surface. Flatten it into a 1-inch-thick round and place the cheese in the center. Gather the dough around the cheese and knead just until the cheese is evenly distributed, taking care not to break it up.

If making by hand, add the yeast mixture and luke-warm water to the bowl and mix with a wooden spoon until the ingredients are combined. Transfer to a lightly floured surface and knead for at least 12 minutes, or until the dough is smooth and elastic. In a small bowl, toss the chopped onion with the 1 tablespoon flour. Flatten the dough into a 1-inch-thick round and place the onion in the center. Gather the dough around the onion and knead until well incorporated, about 2 minutes. Flatten the dough once again and add the cheese, kneading just long enough to evenly distribute the cheese throughout the dough, taking care not to break it up.

Form the dough into a ball and place it in a large oiled bowl. Turn the dough over to coat it with oil. Cover the bowl loosely with plastic wrap or a damp kitchen towel and let rise in a warm, draft-free place for about 1 hour, or until doubled in size.

Lightly dust 2 baking sheets with flour. Transfer the dough to a lightly floured surface and divide it into 3 pieces. Gently form each piece into a loose round (see page 26) and cover with a floured kitchen towel. Let rest for 10 minutes. Shape 2 of the rounds into 2-stranded turbans (see page 30) and place 3 inches apart on a prepared pan. Cover the loaves with a floured kitchen towel.

To shape the sticks, divide the remaining ball of dough into 6 pieces. Roll them by hand into long, skinny 6-inch lengths and place 2 inches apart on the second pan. Cover with a floured kitchen towel.

Let the loaves and sticks rise in a warm place for 1 hour, or until a finger pressed into the dough leaves an impression.

Fifteen minutes before the dough has finished rising, arrange the oven racks in the upper and lower thirds of the oven. Preheat the oven to 400°F.

Using a pastry brush, brush the tops of the loaves with the beaten egg and sprinkle them with the sesame seeds.

Bake the sticks for 25 to 30 minutes, or until golden brown. Bake the loaves for 20 minutes, then rotate the baking sheet left to right. Bake 20 minutes longer, for a total baking time of 40 minutes, or until the loaves are golden brown and sound hollow when tapped on the bottom. Transfer to a wire rack to cool.

Being in this environment in the United States is a thrill. I am so proud to be working here, owning my own business. In Guatemala, we survive by doing things collectively. It would be hard for a single person to survive there because of the economy, the regime; the system is *so* different from the United States. There is no Social Security, no food stamps—people who don't work don't eat. So, working together, people always pull the ones from the bottom up and keep them afloat. It's how we survive—we all work together, we push each other up. That's why I love it here in the collective—because it's a family, and I know that if I need help, everyone is here for me, and if somebody else needs help, I'll be there for them. I grew up that way.

—JESÚS

Corn Onion Cheddar Bread

This round yeasted corn bread is full of corn kernels and has melted pieces of Cheddar cheese dotting its crust. Don't be alarmed by the stickiness of the dough—that is what it is supposed to be like. It makes a quick grilled-cheese sandwich when sliced and toasted. Canned corn has always been used in this bread (the recipe was developed with a sixties aesthetic). The canned corn has the benefits of being more strongly flavored than fresh corn and providing more liquid.

MAKES 3 LOAVES
Preparation time including rising and baking: 4¹/₂ hours; active time: 40 minutes

2 teaspoons active dry yeast

¹/₄ cup warm water

4 cups plus 1 tablespoon bread flour

³/₄ cup plus ¹/₂ cup polenta or coarse yellow cornmeal

1 cup finely ground yellow cornmeal

1³/₄ teaspoons kosher salt

1 can (15 ounces) yellow corn kernels with liquid

1 egg

¹/₂ cup buttermilk

¹/₄ cup dark unsulfured molasses

1 yellow onion, coarsely chopped

1 pound orange Cheddar cheese, cut into ³/₄-inch cubes

In a small bowl, whisk the yeast into the warm water until dissolved. Let stand for 5 minutes.

In the bowl of a stand mixer or a large bowl, combine the 4 cups flour, the ³/₄ cup polenta, the fine cornmeal, and salt.

If using a stand mixer, add the yeast mixture, corn (with liquid), egg, buttermilk, and molasses to the bowl. Using the paddle attachment on low speed, mix until the ingredients are combined, about 2 minutes. Switch to the dough hook, increase the mixer speed to medium, and knead for 7 minutes, or until the dough is smooth and elastic. In a small bowl, toss the chopped onion with the 1 tablespoon flour. Add the onion to the dough and continue to knead on medium speed until well incorporated, about 2 minutes. Transfer the dough to a lightly floured surface. Flatten it into a 1-inch-thick round and place the cheese in the center. Gather the dough around the cheese and knead just until the cheese is evenly distributed, taking care not to break it up.

If making by hand, add the yeast mixture, corn (with liquid), egg, buttermilk, and molasses to the bowl. Mix with a wooden spoon until the ingredients are combined. Transfer to a lightly floured surface and knead for at least 12 minutes, or until the dough is smooth and elastic. In a small bowl, toss the chopped onion with the 1 tablespoon flour. Flatten the dough into a 1-inch-thick round and place the onion in the center. Gather the dough around the onion and knead until well incorporated, about 2 minutes. Flatten the dough once again and add the cheese, kneading just long enough to evenly distribute the cheese throughout the dough, taking care not to break it up.

Form the dough into a ball and place it in a large oiled bowl. Turn the dough over to coat it with oil. Cover the bowl with plastic wrap or a damp kitchen towel and let rise in a warm, draft-free place for about 1³/₄ hours, or until doubled in size.

Sprinkle each of 2 baking sheets with 1 tablespoon of the ¹/₂ cup polenta and put the rest of the polenta into a medium bowl. Transfer the dough to a lightly floured surface and divide it into 3 pieces. Cover with a floured kitchen towel and let rest for 10 minutes. Shape each piece into a large round (see page 27). One at a time, toss each round in the bowl of polenta, turning to coat it with polenta. Place 2 loaves on a prepared pan at least 3 inches apart, and place the third loaf in the center of the second pan. Cover the loaves with a floured kitchen towel and let rise in a warm place for 1½ hours, or until a finger pressed into the dough leaves an impression.

Fifteen minutes before the loaves have finished rising, arrange the oven racks in the upper and lower thirds of the oven. Preheat the oven to 450°F.

Bake the loaves for 15 minutes. Lower the oven temperature to 400°F and rotate the baking sheets top to bottom and front to back. Bake 20 to 25 minutes longer, for a total baking time of 35 to 40 minutes, or until the loaves are nicely browned and sound hollow when tapped on the bottom. Transfer to a wire rack to cool.

Where is the framework for the bread making? It's written in our book of recipes. But that's just a guide, in a way. It's an oral, spoken framework that you learn over time. It's probably a different framework for every person.

—PAUL

Experimental Bread No. 7, or X Bread

Strange name, huh? We were trying to develop a new bread on the Friday-morning shift. For months, we put out experimental cheese breads for sale, labeled experimental bread No. 1, experimental bread No. 2, and so on. The bread kept changing until it reached its seventh incarnation; we were so happy with this spicy bun we decided it was a keeper.

MAKES 12 ROLLS
Preparation time including rising and baking: 3½ hours; active time: 45 minutes

1 tablespoon active dry yeast
¾ cup warm water
4 cups plus 1 tablespoon bread flour
½ cup sugar
2 teaspoons kosher salt
½ cup (1 stick) unsalted butter, cut into ½-inch cubes, at room temperature
½ cup Ricotta cheese
3 eggs
2 large jalapeño chiles, seeded and coarsely chopped
3 green onions, chopped (including green parts)
1 pound Cheddar cheese, cut into ½-inch cubes
¼ cup extra-virgin olive oil
3 tablespoons grated Parmesan cheese

In a small bowl, whisk the yeast into the warm water until dissolved. Let stand for 5 minutes.

In the bowl of a stand mixer or a large bowl, combine the 4 cups flour, the sugar, and salt.

If using a stand mixer, add the butter to the dry ingredients and cut it in with the paddle attachment on low speed for 4 minutes, or until it is the size of small peas. Add the yeast mixture, Ricotta cheese, and eggs, and mix on low speed until the ingredients are combined, about 2 minutes. Switch to the dough hook, increase the mixer speed to medium, and knead for 6 minutes, or until the dough is smooth, silky, and elastic. In a small bowl, toss the jalapeños and green onions with the 1 tablespoon flour. Add the jalapeños and green onions to the dough and continue to knead on medium speed until well incorporated, about 2 minutes. (The vegetables will add moisture to the dough, and you may need to adjust for this by adding a tablespoon or more of flour.) Transfer the dough to a lightly floured surface. Flatten it into a 1-inch-thick round and place the Cheddar cheese in the center. Gather the dough around the cheese and knead just until the cheese is evenly distributed, taking care not to break it up.

If making by hand, add the butter to the dry ingredients and cut it in with a pastry cutter or 2 dinner knives until the size of small peas. Add the yeast mixture, Ricotta cheese, and eggs, and mix with a wooden spoon until the ingredients are combined. Transfer to a lightly floured surface and knead for 10 minutes, or until the dough is smooth, silky, and elastic. In a small bowl, toss the jalapeños and green onions with the 1 tablespoon flour. Flatten the dough into a 1-inch-thick round and place the jalapeños and onions in the center. Gather the dough around the vegetables and knead until well incorporated, about 2 minutes. (The vegetables will add moisture to the dough, and you may need to adjust for this by adding a tablespoon or more of flour.) Flatten the dough once again and add the Cheddar cheese, kneading just long enough to evenly distribute the cheese throughout the dough, taking care not to break it up.

Form the dough into a ball and place it in a large oiled bowl. Turn the dough over to coat it with oil. Cover the bowl with plastic wrap or a damp kitchen towel and let rise in a warm, draft-free place for 1¼ hours, or until doubled in size.

Lightly dust 2 baking sheets with flour. Transfer the dough to a lightly floured surface and divide it into 12 pieces. Cover with a floured kitchen towel and let rest for 10 minutes. Shape each piece into a small round (see page 27) and place each at least 3 inches apart on the prepared pans. Gently flatten the rolls with the palm of your hand. Cover with a floured kitchen towel and let rise in a warm place for 45 minutes, or until doubled in size and a finger pressed into the dough leaves an impression.

Fifteen minutes before the rolls have finished rising, arrange the oven racks in the upper and lower thirds of the oven. Preheat the oven to 375°F.

Bake for 15 minutes. Rotate the baking sheets top to bottom and front to back. Bake 15 minutes longer, for a total baking time of 30 minutes, or until the rolls are golden on the top and bottom. Transfer to a wire rack. While still hot, brush the rolls with the olive oil and sprinkle them with the Parmesan cheese. Let cool.

Being in the collective has to be more than a job. I've gotten so irritated with it on and off over the years and I'm still here. I think it has to be more than a job—it's a calling!

—VICKI

Provolone Olive Bread

This braided loaf, full of big green California olives and cubes of sharp Provolone, is the first cheese bread we developed with a particular cheese in mind. Until then, cheese bread had just been a vehicle for using up odd cheese ends, but with the creation of this loaf, the door was opened for developing the numerous cheese breads we now serve.

MAKES 3 LOAVES
Preparation time including rising and baking: 3½ hours;
active time: 30 minutes

2 teaspoons active dry yeast

½ cup warm water

3½ cups plus 1 tablespoon bread flour

2 teaspoons kosher salt

1 cup lukewarm water

1 yellow onion, coarsely chopped

1 pound sharp Provolone cheese, cut into ¾-inch cubes

½ cup pitted green olives, coarsely chopped

1 egg, beaten

2 tablespoons sesame seeds

In a small bowl, whisk the yeast into the warm water until dissolved. Let stand for 5 minutes.

In the bowl of a stand mixer or a large bowl, combine the 3 cups flour and the salt.

If using a stand mixer, add the yeast mixture and lukewarm water to the bowl. Using the paddle attachment on low speed, mix until the ingredients are combined, about 2 minutes. Switch to the dough hook, increase the mixer speed to medium, and knead for 7 minutes, or until the dough is smooth, silky, and elastic. In a small bowl, toss the chopped onion with the 1 tablespoon flour. Add the onion to the dough and continue to knead on medium speed until well incorporated, about 2 minutes. Transfer the dough to a lightly floured surface. Flatten it into a 1-inch-thick round and place the cheese and olives in the center. Gather the dough around the cheese and olives and knead just until they are evenly distributed. (Kneading the dough too long will break up the cheese, and the olives will turn the dough a muddy color.)

If making by hand, add the yeast mixture and lukewarm water to the bowl and mix with a wooden spoon until the ingredients are combined. Transfer to a lightly floured surface and knead for at least 12 minutes, or until the dough is smooth, silky, and elastic. In a small bowl, toss the chopped onion with the 1 tablespoon flour. Flatten the dough into a 1-inch-thick round and place the onion in the center. Gather the dough around the onion and knead until well incorporated, about 2 minutes. Flatten the dough once again, add the cheese and olives, and knead just until they are evenly distributed. (Kneading the dough too long will break up the cheese, and the olives will turn the dough a muddy color).

Form the dough into a ball and place it in a large oiled bowl. Turn the dough over to coat it with oil. Cover the bowl with plastic wrap or a damp kitchen towel and let rise in a warm, draft-free place for about 1 hour, or until doubled in size.

Lightly dust 2 baking sheets with flour. Transfer the dough to a lightly floured surface and divide it into 3 pieces. Gently form each piece into a loose round (see page 26) and cover with a floured kitchen towel. Let rest for 10 minutes. Shape the rounds into 3-stranded braids (see page 29). Place 2 of the loaves on a prepared pan at least 4 inches apart, and place the third loaf in the center of the second pan. Cover with a floured kitchen towel and let rise in a warm place for 45 minutes, or until increased in size by one-third and a finger pressed into the dough leaves an impression.

Fifteen minutes before the loaves have finished rising, arrange the oven racks in the upper and lower thirds of the oven. Preheat the oven to 400°F.

Using a pastry brush, brush the tops of the loaves with the beaten egg and sprinkle them with the sesame seeds.

Bake for 20 minutes. Rotate the baking sheets top to bottom and front to back. Bake 20 minutes longer, for a total baking time of 40 minutes, or until the loaves are golden brown and sound hollow when tapped on the bottom. Transfer to a wire rack to cool.

One Saturday afternoon I was in the back of the store washing dishes and the phone rang. I answered it, and on the other end of the line there was a little voice saying, "You seem to have a lot of new people working there." I said, "Yes, what seems to be the problem?" "Well, I was waited on by somebody today. I ordered Ricotta, and as they served me, they dropped a little piece of it on the counter, and then they picked it up with their fingers and put it in my container. I was so upset by it that I didn't say anything at the time. I was going to buy more cheese, but I didn't. I went home. When I got home I took that Ricotta and I threw it out!" So I said, "Oh, I'm so sorry that happened and it upset you, and, of course, you should come back in and I'll replace the cheese for you. Please tell me what that person looked like, and I'll talk to them about that." She said, "Well, she was blond, and she wore glasses, and she was heavyset." All of a sudden, I realized that was *me*. (Oh—my—God, I'm *heavyset!*) I briskly told her, "Okay, I'll talk to that person." Then my better side got to me and I confessed, "I've got to tell you, that was me." She got really embarrassed and said, "Oh, I'm so embarrassed, oh, oh!" I said, "Don't be embarrassed, it's fine. And actually, I'm not new here—I've been here twelve years." "Oh? I've never seen you; I come there every Saturday." I thought, "My God, how can you miss me, I'm so *heavyset!*"

I kept waiting for her, and finally two weeks later she did arrive, and I replaced her cheese and promised her I would never do that again. I was very sorry and embarrassed about it. I did assure her that I wash my hands all the time. It's true—we aren't perfect. —ERIN

• OTHER • CHEESE RECIPES

Raclette

Raclette is a cheese made in the Valais region of Switzerland. Buttery and flowery in flavor, with pungent overtones, it melts beautifully and is the basis for a very simple but luxurious dish of the same name. The word raclette *is derived from the French verb for "to scrape." Traditionally, the dish is made by cutting an entire wheel of Raclette in half and melting it by propping it up facing a fire. As the cheese melts, the bubbling, softened portion of the cheese is scraped off, chewy rind and all, and spread over potatoes or bread. This is repeated until the entire half of a wheel is consumed. This method is a little hard to follow at home, but with a few modern modifications, it is an enjoyable and easy dish to prepare. All you need is a baking sheet set on the lowest rack of your broiler. If you love this dish, you can buy a Raclette grill that sits on the table. This device enables you to do the scraping as soon as a portion of the cheese is melted, and ensures a steady supply through the course of the meal. This dish is traditionally served with potatoes, pickled onions, and cornichons.*

SERVES 6
Preparation time: 15 minutes

1 pound small red potatoes, boiled with their skins on
1/2 pound asparagus or broccoli, blanched
1 cup cornichons
1/2 cup pickled onions
1 pound Swiss Raclette cheese (French Raclette is good, too)
1/2 loaf rye or sourdough bread, sliced

Place the broiler tray as far from the heat source as possible. Preheat the broiler.

Arrange the vegetables and condiments on a platter and set aside. Cut the Raclette in half, leaving as much of the rind on as possible. Peel off any paper on the outside of the cheese and place both halves on a baking sheet. Broil for 5 minutes. Remove the pan if most or all of the cheese is melted and serve immediately, accompanied with the vegetables and condiments. If some of the Raclette is still firm, scrape the melted portion onto the vegetable platter and return the Raclette to the broiler for 3 minutes while you sit down to eat. (It is important to eat melted Raclette immediately, as it is most delicious eaten directly from the oven.)

Fondue

This is a very basic recipe that you can vary by experimenting with different kinds of cheese. While Gruyère and Emmental are traditional, any well-aged alpine cheese, such as Appenzeller, Comté, Tête de Moine, and Hoch Ybrig, will work as they are relatively low in moisture and full of flavor. The key to making fondue is patience, so be careful not to hurry the process. Each handful of cheese needs to fully melt into the wine or the fondue will separate. Fondue pots make it possible to keep the fondue warm at the table and melting while you eat it. Thrift stores are a great place to find old fondue pots.

SERVES 4 AS A MAIN COURSE, 8 AS AN APPETIZER
Preparation time: 30 minutes

2 tablespoons unbleached all-purpose flour
2 cups (1/2 pound) shredded Gruyère cheese
2 cups (1/2 pound) shredded Emmental cheese
1 clove garlic, lightly crushed
2 cups dry white wine
2 crusty baguettes

Preheat the oven to 400°F.

In a large bowl, toss the flour and shredded cheese together until the cheese is evenly coated with the flour.

Rub the garlic over the bottom and sides of a large, heavy saucepan and discard the garlic. Add the wine and bring to a simmer over medium heat. Stir in the shredded cheese by the handful (about 1/2 cup). Wait for the cheese to thoroughly melt before adding the next handful; the mixture will begin to simmer vigorously again about the same time the handful

of cheese has melted. Stir the fondue fairly frequently to keep the cheese from scorching on the bottom. When 2 handfuls of cheese are remaining, place the baguettes in the oven to heat for 5 minutes. Ready your fondue pot. After the last handful of cheese has melted into the fondue, turn the flame as low as it will go. Cube the baguettes. Pour the fondue into the pot and place it on the table. Using forks or wooden skewers, skewer the bread and dip it into the hot fondue.

Fondue Trouble-Shooting: If the fondue separates while cooking and won't smooth out, mix 1 teaspoon cornstarch with 1 tablespoon cold water in a small bowl. Gradually stir the mixture into the cooking fondue; the fondue should return to a consistent texture within a few minutes.

Mock Boursin

This is the original Cheese Board spread, which we have been selling for thirty years. It was invented as a fresh version of a French triple-cream cheese. This spread has half the fat of cream cheese because it is made with baker's cheese, a curdless fresh cheese with only .5 percent fat, as well as cream cheese. It qualifies as a low-fat cheese and a garlic-lover's favorite.

MAKES 2 CUPS SPREAD
Preparation time: 30 minutes

1 1/4 cups (3/4 pound) cream cheese
3/4 cup (1/3 pound) baker's cheese
1 clove garlic, minced
2 tablespoons minced fresh flat-leaf parsley
2 green onions, finely chopped (including green parts)
3/4 teaspoon kosher salt

In the bowl of a stand mixer, combine the cheeses. Using the paddle attachment, mix on low speed for 30 seconds, or until smooth. Do not overmix, or it will turn watery. Add all the remaining ingredients and mix on medium speed for about 1 minute. Or, mix by hand in a medium bowl with a wooden spoon. For the fullest flavor, cover and refrigerate for 24 hours. Store in the refrigerator for up to 1 week.

Hot Cheddar Spread

This orange-colored spread is spicy and Cheddary, good on bread or as a dip. Farmer's cheese, a fresh dry-curd cheese similar to dry cottage cheese, is a key ingredient for this recipe. Use your discretion when adding the jalapeño chile; it can sneak up and bite you.

MAKES 2 CUPS SPREAD
Preparation time: 30 minutes

3/4 pound sharp Cheddar cheese, cubed, at room temperature
1/2 cup (1/4 pound) farmer's cheese
1/4 cup buttermilk
1 small jalapeño chile, seeded and minced (about 1 tablespoon)
2 green onions, finely chopped (including green parts)

In the bowl of a stand mixer, combine the cheeses. Using the paddle attachment, mix on medium speed until very smooth, about 5 minutes. Add the buttermilk and mix until incorporated. Add the jalapeño and green onions and mix for about 1 minute, or until incorporated. Let stand for 30 minutes for the full flavor to emerge. Use right away, or cover and refrigerate for up to 1 week.

Salmon Spread

This is your basic lox spread. The quality of cream cheese is important; it should be a natural cream cheese with no stabilizers or thickeners. Look for this in good cheese stores and natural food stores. Traditional with bagels, this spread is also good on a baguette.

MAKES 2 CUPS SPREAD
Preparation time: 10 minutes

2 cups (1 pound) natural cream cheese
1/2 pound lox

Put the cream cheese in the bowl of a stand mixer or a large bowl. Using the paddle attachment or a wooden spoon, mix on medium speed or by hand until smooth, about 1 minute. Add the lox and mix for 30 seconds, or until the lox has broken down into small pieces and is incorporated. Use right away, or cover and refrigerate for up to 5 days.

I remember it was a Sunday in the early seventies when I found out that I had been accepted into the collective. I went over to the house next door and they were playing "I Ain't Gonna Work on Maggie's Farm No More," and I kept singing it. It was the symbolic song for my change. It was, belatedly for me, a step into the counterculture. —FRIEDA

Oy, Cheese

In the pantry the young cheeses; aging daily
but maybe not fast enough, they are
Camemberts and Reblochons and are at odds
with the truly old and wise cheeses—seated there
for twelve years or more—the Reggiano that speaks
with quick, decisive words, full of
knowledge and warning, like a Jewish mother.

Oy, cheeses of frustration, cheeses of timing,
cheeses pregnant with children and cutting
back on their hours. Young cheeses full of commitment,
cheeses of cooperative effort—will you ever
change the world?

Cambozola, smooth and cunning like a good worker;
Asiago, determined and always with a joke
to tell; Teleme running too fast and drinking another espresso;
Gammelost, stinky and disgusting.

Oy, cheeses, gossiping in the walk-in,
standing on a new epoxy floor,
cheeses that mingle and share a beer or a little
reefer after work—
or maybe diligently jumping up and down in
the dumpster instead.

Oy, cooperative of cheeses, I give you this jest,
cheeses that know each other all too well, rich in troubles
and death—these cheeses know it will be a success.

—JONAS OSMOND, FORMER MEMBER

• the cheese counter •

CHAPTER SEVEN

THE PIZZERIA

AS AN EMPLOYEE-OWNED BUSINESS, we are limited only by our imaginations. In most workplaces, you rely on the owner to come up with new ideas and innovations. Conversely, many business owners are constrained from innovating by reluctant or uncooperative workers. At the Cheese Board, if you have an idea and can convince the rest of the group of its value (not always an easy task), you can run with it. That is how the pizza business started.

In the early eighties, we would occasionally make pizzas out of our sour baguette dough for our own enjoyment. One day someone started selling slices of it during lunch. Soon people on other shifts incorporated pizza making into the baking schedule. Eventually, several members thought it would be fun to make pizzas on Friday night. We finished our normal shift at seven and then sold take-out pizzas from seven to nine. We started out by making thirty pies on Friday night and sold them all just by word of mouth. Soon people were lining up to get hot pies, and it became something of a community event; there was a certain magic to the informal nature of the process. Even-

tually, the Friday-night pizza routine grew to the point where we were selling 240 pies in 2½ hours, with a line that snaked out the door and around the corner.

Pizza was a product of several people wanting to experiment, and the larger group having enough of a spirit of adventure to take a relatively undeveloped idea and let it fly. So much of what we do comes from this organic process. There were no market studies or consultants—we just did what interested us and seemed like fun.

Nowadays, the pizzeria is a quasi-separate entity from the cheese store and bakery. It is housed in a storefront just down the block from the other store. There is a connecting walkway between the two sites that is full of travel during the day: pizza dough being rolled back to the pizzeria and half-baked pizzas being carried to sell at the bakery (not to mention all the members who need a quick hello and a nosh of something on the "other side"). While pizzeria members don't arrive as early as the bread bakers, their shifts are long and end only after the dinner crowds have been fed.

THE PIZZERIA

Pizza Preamble 197

Sourdough Pizza Dough 198

Yeasted Pizza Dough 201

Tomato Pizza with Lemon Zest 201

Zucchini and Feta Cheese Pizza with

    Sun-Dried Tomato Pesto 203

Roasted Red Bell Pizza with Feta

    and Olive Tapenade 204

Tomato Pizza with Fresh Greens

    and Goat Cheese 206

Corn Zucchini Pizza with Lime

    and Cilantro 208

Heirloom Tomato Pizza with Goat

    Cheese and Fresh Herbs 209

Three-Onion, Four-Herb, and Four-

    Cheese Pizza 210

Fresh Mushroom Pizza with Sun-Dried

    Tomato Pesto 211

Roasted Eggplant Pizza with Red

    Peppers and Feta Cheese 213

Potato Pizza 214

Red Cabbage Pizza with Gorgonzola

    and Nuts 216

Roasted Wild Mushroom Pizza with

    Goat Cheese 217

Sauce Pie. 219

Calzone. 220

PIZZA PREAMBLE

All of our pizzas are variations on a theme. We build most of our pies by layering the ingredients in the following order: Mozzarella, onions, other vegetables, more Mozzarella, a different variety of cheese, and, after baking, the application of a flavored olive oil and an herb garnish.

Follow the steps below for a successful and simple pizza.

CRUST

The Cheese Board pizza is made with a sourdough crust that is very similar to the baguette dough. For convenience and variety, we have also included a recipe for a yeasted dough that is quicker to make than the sourdough recipe. Both pizza crust recipes are pretty forgiving; they can sit for a while after being stretched out and built if you are getting behind in the baking step. There are two key factors for successfully shaping pizza rounds: you need a soft dough that is wetter than a bread dough, and you must let the loose rounds rest a sufficient amount of time before shaping. In shaping pizzas, this resting step is 20 minutes, longer than in most of our bread recipes.

To shape pizza dough, transfer the risen dough to a lightly floured surface and divide it into 3 pieces. Form the dough into loose rounds (see page 26) and cover with a floured kitchen towel. Let rest for 20 minutes. Scatter fine cornmeal or flour onto 3 inverted baking sheets. Sprinkle more flour on the work surface and pat each round out into a disk. Starting about 2 inches in from the edge of the disk, use your fingertips to work the dough out toward the edge, almost like you are typing but with a very firm touch (fig. A). If the dough is resistant or springs back immediately, allow the round to rest for another 5 minutes. Once you have made it around the circle of dough, move toward the center of the disk and work the dough out in the same manner. Sprinkle the work surface with more flour, flip the disk over (fig. B), and continue to pat out the entire disk into an 8-inch round. Next, flour the back of your hands and place your right hand, formed into a loose fist, under the flattened round. Lift the disk off the work surface and place the back of your left hand under the flattened disk as well (fig. C). Rotate the disk a couple of times by alternating your fists with a slight pulling out motion. Place the disk on the prepared baking sheet and pat and push it into a finished 10-inch round (fig. D). The disk should be about ⅛ inch thick at the center and slightly thicker at the edge. Repeat the process for the other 2 rounds.

MOZZARELLA

The total amount of Mozzarella doesn't vary much from one type of pizza to another, though there is some variation in how much goes in the first layer and how much goes in the second layer. More Mozzarella is placed under

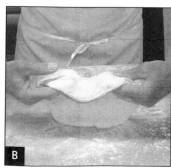
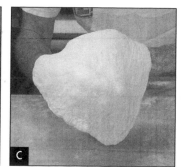
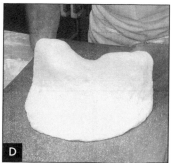

wetter vegetables such as tomatoes, and less on top, to keep the crust from getting soggy by sealing it and letting some of the moisture cook off during baking. In the case of a partially cooked vegetable (such as roasted eggplant, peppers, or potatoes), we distribute an even amount of Mozzarella on the top and bottom.

VEGETABLES

We choose vegetables by what is seasonally available and what suits our fancy. We typically use one or two varieties of vegetables per pizza recipe, plus onions. Some vegetables are used fresh, some are roasted first, and some are tossed with various condiments (salt, pepper, vinegar, and oil). If using vegetables that are full of moisture, such as tomatoes or cabbage, you will need to bake the pizzas for about 5 minutes longer.

TOPPING CHEESE

The top layer of cheese is most often a fresh goat cheese that is moist and tangy (as opposed to a harder, aged variety), or a salty Feta or Gorgonzola.

BAKING

For the home baker, we have developed a pizza-baking method that approximates what we do at the pizzeria. This involves keeping a close eye on the bake and rotating the pizzas to different levels in the oven. We recommend using a baking stone (see page 17) for two reasons: it ensures that the bottom of the crust will be crisp—the hallmark of a Cheese Board pizza—and the stone gives you an additional level for your bake, which means you can produce pizzas more quickly for your hungry crowd. If you do decide to use a baking stone, be sure to preheat your oven with the baking stone on the oven floor for 45 minutes before you bake. Before removing the pizza from the oven, peer underneath at the bottom of the pizza; you want a crisp, well-browned crust with a golden brown top.

OILS

The olive oil hitting the hot crust just after it has been taken out of the oven creates the perfume of the pizza. The flavoring of the oil (usually garlic) imparts an aroma that suits the components of each pizza.

GARNISHES

The garnishes are usually fresh herbs; sometimes we use pesto made from basil or sun-dried tomatoes. We also sometimes use tapenade.

Sourdough Pizza Dough

This recipe makes a moist, soft dough that is easy to stretch. With the addition of toppings, it will taste good no matter what. Making it overnight allows for more time on the day that you build your pizza and gives you a lighter dough.

MAKES THREE 10-INCH PIZZA CRUSTS
Preparation time including rising: 8 hours
(unless rising overnight); active time: 1 hour

3 to 3¼ cups (15 to 16 ounces) bread flour
1½ cups cool water
1½ teaspoons kosher salt
½ cup (4 ounces) Sourdough Starter (page 90)

Put 3 cups of the flour in the bowl of a stand mixer or a large bowl.

If using a stand mixer, add the water to the bowl and mix on low speed with the paddle attachment until the ingredients are thoroughly combined, about 3 minutes. Let rest for 10 minutes. Add the salt and sourdough starter. Switch to the dough hook, increase the mixer speed to medium, and knead for 12 minutes, or until the dough is slightly tacky and soft. (After a couple of minutes, the dough should gather around the hook; you can add extra flour by the tablespoonful if the dough does not pull away from the sides of the bowl.) Transfer to a lightly floured surface and knead by hand for about 5 minutes (see page 25), or until the dough is smooth, shiny, and passes the windowpane test.

If making by hand, add the water to the bowl and mix with a wooden spoon until the ingredients are thoroughly combined. Let rest for 10 minutes. Add the salt and sourdough starter and mix until all the ingredients are combined. Transfer to a lightly floured surface and knead for 15 minutes (see page 25), adding flour by the tablespoonful as necessary to keep the dough from sticking. The kneading is complete when the dough is smooth, shiny, and passes the windowpane test.

Form the dough into a ball and place it in a large oiled bowl. Turn the dough over to coat it with oil. Cover the bowl with plastic wrap or a damp kitchen towel and let rise in a cool place for 6 to 8 hours, or until the dough is doubled in size. Or, put the dough into the refrigerator and let it rise overnight; the next day, let it stand at room temperature for 2 hours befor ceeding with the recipe.

When I got the application and filled out the form, they called me for an interview. My wife dropped me off. When I came in, everybody was here, talking all about pizza, and I said, "You know I've never made pizza before, but I eat pizza." They said, "Oh, it's no problem, you'll learn." So when I went home, I told my wife and she said, "Yes, you can manage it." When I went to work the first day I asked, "Do we use a rolling pin or what?" I thought they rolled out the pizza dough! Now I know how to spin it.

—DWIGHT

You don't notice it so much when you're working, but you smell like onions and cheese. I know this because when I go to the bank to get change for the register, they all know exactly where I came from. They smell me and look up, saying, "Oh, what kind of pizza is there today?" So you know everyone else can smell it as well. I used to have a leather jacket that I wore to work. Apparently this leather jacket picked up all these aromas. My wife makes me keep it in a plastic garbage bag.

—ARTHUR

Yeasted Pizza Dough

This dough is easy to make, quick rising, and a fast and simple alternative to the sourdough crust. The dough is sweet and flaky, and a little lighter than the sourdough. The choice of olive oil used in the crust will influence the flavor of the dough. We recommend a strong-flavored olive oil, such as extra-virgin California or Italian oil.

MAKES THREE 10-INCH PIZZA CRUSTS
Preparation time including rising: 2 hours
(unless rising overnight); active time: 20 minutes

1 tablespoon active dry yeast
1¹/₂ cups warm water
2 tablespoons extra-virgin olive oil
1¹/₂ teaspoons kosher salt
3¹/₂ to 4 cups bread flour

In the bowl of a stand mixer or a large bowl, whisk the yeast into the warm water until dissolved. Let stand for 5 minutes.

If using a stand mixer, add the olive oil, salt, and 2 cups of the flour to the bowl. Using the paddle attachment on low speed, mix for 5 minutes to form a wet dough. Switch to the dough hook, add 1½ more cups of the flour, and mix on medium speed for 5 minutes. Add the remaining ½ cup flour by the tablespoonful as needed to form a soft dough with a nice sheen; it should be a little sticky, but not too wet.

If making by hand, add the olive oil, salt, and 2 cups of the flour to the bowl. Using a wooden spoon, mix for at least 5 minutes to form a wet dough. Pour 1½ cups of the flour onto a work surface, place the dough on top of it, and knead for about 8 minutes to form a soft dough with a nice sheen; it should be a little sticky, but not too wet. If the dough sticks to the work surface, rub a little olive oil on it. If the dough is impossibly sticky, add the remaining ½ cup flour by the tablespoonful as needed.

Form the dough into a ball and place it in a large oiled bowl. Turn the dough over to coat it with oil. Cover the bowl with plastic wrap or a damp kitchen towel and let rise in a warm, draft-free place for 1 hour, or until doubled in size. Or, put the dough in the refrigerator and let it rise overnight; the next day, let it stand at room temperature for 2 hours before proceeding with the recipe.

Tomato Pizza with Lemon Zest

At the pizzeria, we sell only one kind of pizza on a given day, so we say the only choice you have is how much you get. However, people call all the time and ask for this pizza more than any other. We use Bulgarian Feta, as its tang complements the cilantro and lemon zest garnish. Like other tomato pizzas, this pizza takes longer to bake and requires delicacy in handling.

MAKES THREE 10-INCH PIZZAS
Preparation time: 1³/₄ hours
(not including making the pizza dough)

1 clove garlic, minced
2 tablespoons extra-virgin olive oil
1 recipe Sourdough Pizza Dough (page 198) or
    Yeasted Pizza Dough (opposite)
Fine yellow cornmeal or flour for sprinkling
4 cups (1 pound) shredded Mozzarella cheese
¹/₂ yellow onion, thinly sliced
5 tomatoes, thinly sliced
3 ounces sheep's-milk Feta, crumbled (about ³/₄ cup)
Grated zest of 1 lemon
¹/₂ cup loosely packed fresh cilantro leaves, coarsely
    chopped
Juice of 1 lemon

Arrange the oven racks in the upper and lower thirds of the oven. Preheat the oven to 450°F. If using a baking stone, place it on the floor of the oven and preheat the oven for 45 minutes.

In a small bowl, combine the garlic and olive oil. Set aside.

To shape the pizzas, transfer the dough to a lightly floured surface and divide it into 3 pieces. Gently form each piece into a loose round (see page 26) and cover with a floured kitchen towel. Let rest for 20 minutes. Scatter cornmeal over 3 inverted baking sheets. Shape each round into a 10-inch disk (see page 197).

Divide the Mozzarella into 2 piles, one about two-thirds the total amount and the other one-third. Line up the 3 pizzas for assembly. Scatter the larger amount of Mozzarella over the 3 pizzas, leaving a ½-inch rim. Layer the onion on top of the cheese and place the sliced tomatoes over the onion, leaving a bit of space between each slice. Distribute the remaining Mozzarella on top of the tomatoes. Sprinkle with the Feta.

If using a baking stone, place a baking sheet with a pizza on the lower oven rack and bake for 10 minutes. Rotate the pizza to the upper rack, place the second pizza in the oven on the lower rack, and continue baking for 10 minutes. Then, finish baking the first pizza by sliding it off the pan directly onto the baking stone. Rotate the second pizza to the upper rack and put the third pizza in the oven on the lower rack. Bake the pizza on the stone for 4 to 8 minutes to crisp the bottom until well browned. Finish baking the second and third pizzas in the same manner.

If using baking sheets only, place a baking sheet with a pizza on the lower oven rack and bake for 10 minutes. Rotate the pizza to the upper rack, place the second pizza in the oven on the lower rack, and continue baking for 10 minutes. Then, finish baking the first pizza by sliding it off the pan directly onto the lower oven rack. Rotate the second pizza to the upper rack. Bake the pizza on the lower rack for 4 to 8 minutes to crisp the bottom until well browned. Finish baking the second and third pizzas in the same manner.

Immediately after removing each pizza from the oven, brush the garlic oil onto the rim. Garnish with lemon zest and cilantro. Sprinkle lemon juice sparingly over the top.

Zucchini and Feta Cheese Pizza with Sun-Dried Tomato Pesto

This is a colorful pizza with a faint spiciness. Use sun-dried tomatoes that are plump and soft for the pesto, as they rehydrate more quickly and have more flavor than the harder, drier variety. We think that Corsican Feta best suits the zucchini, but any sheep's-milk Feta will work well.

MAKES THREE 10-INCH PIZZAS
Preparation time: 1³/₄ hours
(not including making the pizza dough)

- ¹/₄ cup sun-dried tomatoes
- 2 cloves garlic, minced
- 4 tablespoons extra-virgin olive oil
- 1 recipe Sourdough Pizza Dough (page 198) or Yeasted Pizza Dough (page 201)
- Fine yellow cornmeal or flour for sprinkling
- Pinch of freshly ground black pepper
- Pinch of red pepper flakes
- ¹/₄ teaspoon kosher salt
- ¹/₂ yellow onion, thinly sliced
- 4 cups (1 pound) shredded Mozzarella cheese
- 1 small green zucchini, thinly sliced
- 1 small golden summer squash, thinly sliced
- 4 ounces sheep's-milk Feta, crumbled (about 1 cup)
- ¹/₂ cup loosely packed fresh flat-leaf parsley, coarsely chopped

Put the sun-dried tomatoes in a small bowl and cover with hot water. Let soak for 20 to 30 minutes, or until hydrated.

Arrange the oven racks in the upper and lower thirds of the oven. Preheat the oven to 450°F. If using a baking stone, place it on the floor of the oven and preheat the oven for 45 minutes.

In a small bowl, combine half of the garlic with 2 tablespoons of the olive oil. Set aside.

To shape the pizzas, transfer the dough to a lightly floured surface and divide it into 3 pieces. Gently form each piece into a loose round (see page 26) and cover with a floured kitchen towel. Let rest for 20 minutes. Scatter cornmeal over 3 inverted baking sheets. Shape each round into a 10-inch disk (see page 197).

Drain the tomatoes, reserving the liquid. In a food processor, combine the tomatoes, ¹/₄ cup of the reserved liquid, the remaining garlic, the remaining 2 tablespoons olive oil, the black pepper, red pepper flakes, and salt. Purée until smooth and thick, adding more of the reserved liquid as needed. Toss the onion with the pesto.

Line up the 3 pizzas for assembly. Scatter half of the Mozzarella over the 3 pizzas, leaving a ¹/₂-inch rim. Scatter the onion mixture on top of the cheese. Place the sliced zucchini and squash over the onion so that the pizzas are evenly and entirely covered. Spread the remaining Mozzarella on top of the squash. Sprinkle with the Feta.

If using a baking stone, place a baking sheet with a pizza on the lower oven rack and bake for 8 minutes. Rotate the pizza to the upper rack, place the second pizza in the oven on the lower rack, and continue baking for 10 minutes. Then, finish baking the first pizza by sliding it off the pan directly onto the baking stone. Rotate the second pizza to the upper rack and put the third pizza in the oven on the lower rack. Bake the pizza on the stone for 4 minutes to crisp the bottom until well browned. Finish baking the second and third pizzas in the same manner.

If using baking sheets only, place a baking sheet with a pizza on the lower oven rack and bake for 8 minutes. Rotate the pizza to the upper rack, place the second pizza in the oven on the lower rack, and continue baking for 8 minutes. Then, finish baking the first pizza by sliding it off the pan directly onto the lower oven rack. Rotate the second pizza to the upper rack. Bake the pizza on the lower rack for 5 minutes to crisp the bottom until well browned. Finish baking the second and third pizzas in the same manner.

Immediately after removing each pizza from the oven, brush the garlic oil onto the rim. Garnish with the parsley.

Roasted Bell Pepper Pizza with Feta and Olive Tapenade

A tapenade garnish finishes this rich pizza. You can substitute chopped olives for the tapenade. Roasting the peppers and onions together blends the flavors nicely and heightens their sweetness. For quick assembly of the pizzas, roast the vegetables ahead of time while the pizza dough rises.

MAKES THREE 10-INCH PIZZAS
Preparation time: 1³/₄ hours
(not including making the pizza dough)

1 clove garlic, minced

5 tablespoons extra-virgin olive oil

1 cup Kalamata olives, pitted

¹/₈ teaspoon freshly ground black pepper

¹/₈ teaspoon red pepper flakes

1 large yellow onion, sliced into ¹/₈-inch-thick rings

2 red bell peppers, seeded, deribbed, and cut into
    ¹/₈-inch-thick slices

1 recipe Sourdough Pizza Dough (page 198) or
    Yeasted Pizza Dough (page 201)

Fine yellow cornmeal or flour for sprinkling

4 cups (1 pound) shredded Mozzarella cheese

4 ounces sheep's-milk Feta, crumbled
    (about 1 cup)

6 tablespoons minced fresh flat-leaf parsley

Arrange the oven racks in the upper and lower thirds of the oven. Preheat the oven to 450°F. If using a baking stone, place it on the floor of the oven and preheat the oven for 45 minutes.

In a small bowl, combine the garlic and 2 tablespoons of the olive oil. Set aside.

To make the tapenade, combine the olives, black pepper, pepper flakes, and 1 tablespoon of the olive oil in a food processor or blender. Process until almost smooth, adding more oil by the teaspoonful as needed to make a loose purée.

Line a baking sheet with parchment paper. Toss the onion and bell peppers in the remaining 2 tablespoons olive oil and spread them over the prepared pan. Bake on the upper rack of the preheated oven for 5 to 8 minutes, or until the peppers are wilted and give off their liquid. Set aside to cool.

To shape the pizzas, transfer the dough to a lightly floured surface and divide it into 3 pieces. Gently form each piece into a loose round (see page 26) and cover with a floured kitchen towel. Let rest for 20 minutes. Scatter cornmeal over 3 inverted baking sheets. Shape each round into a 10-inch disk (see page 197).

Divide the Mozzarella into 2 piles, one about two-thirds the total amount and the other one-third. Line up the 3 pizzas for assembly. Scatter the smaller amount of Mozzarella over the 3 pizzas, leaving a ¹/₂-inch rim. Scatter the roasted onion and peppers on top of the cheese. Distribute the remaining Mozzarella on top of the onion and peppers. Sprinkle with the Feta.

If using a baking stone, place a baking sheet with a pizza on the lower oven rack and bake for 8 minutes. Rotate the pizza to the upper rack, place the second pizza in the oven on the lower rack, and continue baking for 8 minutes. Then, finish baking the first pizza by sliding it off the pan directly onto the baking stone. Rotate the second pizza to the upper rack and put the third pizza in the oven on the lower rack. Bake the pizza on the stone for 4 minutes to crisp the bottom until well browned. Finish baking the second and third pizzas in the same manner.

If using baking sheets only, place a baking sheet with a pizza on the lower oven rack and bake for 8 minutes. Rotate the pizza to the upper rack, place the second pizza in the oven on the lower rack, and continue baking for 8 minutes. Then, finish baking the first pizza by sliding it off the pan directly onto the lower oven rack. Rotate the second pizza to the upper rack. Bake the pizza on the lower rack for 5 minutes to crisp the bottom until well browned. Finish baking the second and third pizzas in the same manner.

Immediately after removing each pizza from the oven, brush the garlic oil onto the rim. Garnish with pea-sized dots of the tapenade and the parsley.

There are always those moments when the customers will just have to wait. I tell people, "That's why we hire the musicians—listen to the music, relax!" The only time we really fall behind is when it's really slow, and we don't put a lot of pizzas in the oven. It's slow, it's slow, it's slow, and then all of a sudden we get slammed and there's a line around the corner. That happens all the time, and it happens to everybody, and there is nothing you can do about. —ARTHUR

Tomato Pizza with Fresh Greens and Goat Cheese

The fresh greens on top of this tomato pizza make it a balanced meal all in one slice. You can use mixed baby greens, arugula, or spinach, but we prefer arugula for the hint of spice it adds. As with other tomato pizzas, this pizza takes longer to bake and requires more delicacy in handling.

MAKES THREE 10-INCH PIZZAS
Preparation time: 1³/₄ hours
(not including making the pizza dough)

2 cloves garlic, minced

6 tablespoons extra-virgin olive oil

4 teaspoons balsamic vinegar

¹/₄ teaspoon salt

Pinch of freshly ground black pepper

1 recipe Sourdough Pizza Dough (page 198) or
    Yeasted Pizza Dough (page 201)

Fine yellow cornmeal or flour for sprinkling

4 cups (1 pound) shredded Mozzarella cheese

¹/₂ small red or yellow onion, thinly sliced

4 heirloom tomatoes or 5 Roma tomatoes, thinly sliced

4 ounces fresh goat cheese

3 cups loosely packed young greens (arugula, baby
    lettuce, or baby spinach)

Arrange the oven racks in the upper and lower thirds of the oven. Preheat the oven to 450°F. If using a baking stone, place it on the floor of the oven and preheat the oven for 45 minutes.

In a small bowl, combine half of the garlic with 2 tablespoons of the olive oil. Set aside.

In another small bowl, whisk together the remaining garlic, the remaining 4 tablespoons olive oil, the balsamic vinegar, salt, and pepper. Set aside.

To shape the pizzas, transfer the dough to a lightly floured surface and divide it into 3 pieces. Gently form each piece into a loose round (see page 26) and cover with a floured kitchen towel. Let rest for 20 minutes. Scatter cornmeal over 3 inverted baking sheets. Shape each round into a 10-inch disk (see page 197).

Divide the Mozzarella into 2 piles, one about two-thirds the total amount and the other one-third. Line up the 3 pizzas for assembly. Scatter the larger amount of Mozzarella over the 3 pizzas, leaving a ¹/₂-inch rim. Scatter the onion over the cheese. Place the sliced tomatoes over the onion, leaving a bit of space between each slice. Sprinkle the remaining Mozzarella on top of the tomatoes. Crumble the goat cheese into almond-sized pieces and distribute it evenly over the pizzas.

If using a baking stone, place a baking sheet with a pizza on the lower oven rack and bake for 10 minutes. Rotate the pizza to the upper rack, place the second pizza in the oven on the lower rack, and continue baking for 10 minutes. Then, finish baking the first pizza by sliding it off the pan directly onto the baking stone. Rotate the second pizza to the upper rack and put the third pizza in the oven on the lower rack. Bake the pizza on the stone for 4 to 8 minutes to crisp the bottom until well browned. Finish baking the second and third pizzas in the same manner.

If using baking sheets only, place a baking sheet with a pizza on the lower oven rack and bake for 10 minutes. Rotate the pizza to the upper rack, place the second pizza in the oven on the lower rack, and continue baking for 10 minutes. Then, finish baking the first pizza by sliding it off the pan directly onto the lower oven rack. Rotate the second pizza to the upper rack. Bake the pizza on the lower rack for 4 to 8 minutes to crisp the bottom until well browned. Finish baking the second and third pizzas in the same manner.

Immediately after removing each pizza from the oven, brush the garlic oil onto the rim. Whisk the vinaigrette and toss it together with the greens in a medium bowl. Distribute a handful of greens over each pizza.

I love to do the baking. Baking all those pizzas and keeping up with the line of customers—it makes me feel like I'm *doing* something. When I bake I like to do it fast. Let's go!

—DWIGHT

• the pizzeria •

Corn Zucchini Pizza with Lime and Cilantro

This pizza recipe is great for hot summer evenings. The bright flavor of the lime enhances the sweetness of the corn and zucchini, and the cilantro gives this pie a Mexican taste.

MAKES THREE 10-INCH PIZZAS
Preparation time: 1³/₄ hours,
(not including making the pizza dough)

- 1 clove garlic, minced
- 2 tablespoons extra-virgin olive oil
- 1 recipe Sourdough Pizza Dough (page 198) or Yeasted Pizza Dough (page 201)
- Fine yellow cornmeal or flour for sprinkling
- ³/₄ cup fresh corn kernels (about 1 ear of corn)
- Pinch of freshly ground black pepper
- ¹/₂ teaspoon red pepper flakes
- 4 cups (1 pound) shredded Mozzarella cheese
- ¹/₂ yellow onion, thinly sliced
- 3 small zucchini, thinly sliced
- 6 ounces sheep's-milk Feta, crumbled (about 1¹/₂ cups)
- ¹/₂ cup loosely packed fresh cilantro leaves, coarsely chopped
- 2 limes, cut into quarters

Arrange the oven racks in the upper and lower thirds of the oven. Preheat the oven to 450°F. If using a baking stone, place it on the floor of the oven and preheat the oven for 45 minutes.

In a small bowl, combine the garlic and olive oil. Set aside.

To shape the pizzas, transfer the dough to a lightly floured surface and divide it into 3 pieces. Gently form each piece into a loose round (see page 26) and cover with a floured kitchen towel. Let rest for 20 minutes. Scatter cornmeal over 3 inverted baking sheets. Shape each round into a 10-inch disk (see page 197).

In a small bowl, toss the corn kernels with the black pepper and pepper flakes. Line up the 3 pizzas for assembly. Scatter half of the Mozzarella over the 3 pizzas, leaving a ¹/₂-inch rim. Place the onion over the cheese and spread the zucchini over the onion. Scatter the remaining Mozzarella over the onion and zucchini. Sprinkle with the Feta and corn.

If using a baking stone, place a baking sheet with a pizza on the lower oven rack and bake for 8 minutes. Rotate the pizza to the upper rack, place the second pizza in the oven on the lower rack, and continue baking for 8 minutes. Then, finish baking the first pizza by sliding it off the pan directly onto the baking stone. Rotate the second pizza to the upper rack and put the third pizza in the oven on the lower rack. Bake the pizza on the stone for 4 minutes to crisp the bottom until well browned. Finish baking the second and third pizzas in the same manner.

If using baking sheets only, place a baking sheet with a pizza on the lower oven rack and bake for 8 minutes. Rotate the pizza to the upper rack, place the second pizza in the oven on the lower rack, and continue baking for 8 minutes. Then, finish baking the first pizza by sliding it off the pan directly onto the lower oven rack. Rotate the second pizza to the upper rack. Bake the pizza on the lower rack for 5 minutes to crisp the bottom until well browned. Finish baking the second and third pizzas in the same manner.

Immediately after removing each pizza from the oven, brush the garlic oil onto the rim. Garnish with the cilantro. Squeeze lime juice over the top of the pizzas.

Probably the worst thing I ever did was to forget to put salt into a pizza dough. Later that evening, about 10 P.M., I suddenly realized I had forgotten the salt. I told my wife that I had to go back to the store. She asked, "Why at this time of night?" and I said that there would be no pizza at lunch if I didn't make a new dough.

—ARTEMIO

Heirloom Tomato Pizza with Goat Cheese and Fresh Herbs

When tomato season is at its height, use a mix of heirloom tomatoes for this pizza. Pick different colors, shapes, and sizes for a bright and cheerful pizza.

MAKES THREE 10-INCH PIZZAS
Preparation time: 1³/₄ hours
(not including making the pizza dough)

1 clove garlic, minced

2 tablespoons extra-virgin olive oil

1 recipe Sourdough Pizza Dough (page 198) or
Yeasted Pizza Dough (page 201)

Fine yellow cornmeal or flour for sprinkling

4 cups (1 pound) shredded Mozzarella cheese

¹/₂ small red or yellow onion, thinly sliced

5 or 6 assorted heirloom or Roma tomatoes, thinly sliced

4 ounces fresh goat cheese

¹/₂ cup loosely packed mixed fresh marjoram, oregano, thyme, and flat-leaf parsley, minced

Arrange the oven racks in the upper and lower thirds of the oven. Preheat the oven to 450°F. If using a baking stone, place it on the floor of the oven and preheat the oven for 45 minutes.

In a small bowl, combine the garlic and olive oil. Set aside.

To shape the pizzas, transfer the dough to a lightly floured surface and divide it into 3 pieces. Gently form each piece into a loose round (see page 26) and cover with a floured kitchen towel. Let rest for 20 minutes. Scatter cornmeal over 3 inverted baking sheets. Shape each round into a 10-inch disk (see page 197).

Divide the Mozzarella into 2 piles, one about two-thirds the total amount and the other one-third. Line up the 3 pizzas for assembly. Scatter the larger amount of Mozzarella over the 3 pizzas, leaving a ¹/₂-inch rim. Scatter the onion on top of the cheese. Place the sliced tomatoes over the onion,

leaving a bit of space between each slice. Sprinkle the remaining Mozzarella on top of the tomatoes. Crumble the goat cheese into almond-sized pieces and distribute it evenly over the pizzas.

If using a baking stone, place a baking sheet with a pizza on the lower oven rack and bake for 10 minutes. Rotate the pizza to the upper rack, place the second pizza in the oven on the lower rack, and continue baking for 10 minutes. Then, finish baking the first pizza by sliding it off the pan directly onto the baking stone. Rotate the second pizza to the upper rack and put the third pizza in the oven on the lower rack. Bake the pizza on the stone for 4 to 8 minutes to crisp the bottom until well browned. Finish baking the second and third pizzas in the same manner.

If using baking sheets only, place a baking sheet with a pizza on the lower oven rack and bake for 10 minutes. Rotate the pizza to the upper rack, place the second pizza in the oven on the lower rack, and continue baking for 10 minutes. Then, finish baking the first pizza by sliding it off the pan directly onto the lower oven rack. Rotate the second pizza to the upper rack. Bake the pizza on the lower rack for 4 to 8 minutes to crisp the bottom until well browned. Finish baking the second and third pizzas in the same manner.

Immediately after removing each pizza from the oven, brush the garlic oil onto the rim. Garnish generously with the herbs.

One April Fool's Day, for a joke, Arturo ordered a Domino's pizza for us. There was a long line of customers out the door, and there was the Domino's guy standing out front with a pizza, looking around. I said, "No way, man; I'm not paying for that pizza." And then out popped Arturo from behind the garbage can. He stood up and said, "Awww, come on, pay the guy." So I paid for it, and then I fed it to everybody waiting in the line!

—SLOAN

We talk a lot over the table, spinning and building pizzas. Rolling out and spinning takes at least an hour and a half. Then two or three people will start building the pizzas, which takes anywhere from an hour and a half to two hours. Over the table sometimes it's very lighthearted, sometimes it's quiet, and sometimes we listen to music. **—ARTHUR**

Three-Onion, Four-Herb, and Four-Cheese Pizza

Our unlimited access to the cheese counter and the array of different imported cheeses led to this version of quattro formaggio *pizza. When fresh produce is scarce during the winter months, this is a hearty recipe that satisfies the pizza urge. Fontal is a semisoft Italian cheese that melts beautifully. Leave it in the refrigerator until just before grating, or it will bunch up and melt on the grater.*

MAKES THREE 10-INCH PIZZAS
Preparation time: 1¾ hours
(not including making the pizza dough)

1 clove garlic, minced
2 tablespoons extra-virgin olive oil
1 recipe Sourdough Pizza Dough (page 198) or
   Yeasted Pizza Dough (page 201)
Fine yellow cornmeal or flour for dusting
3 cups (12 ounces) shredded Mozzarella cheese
1½ cups (6 ounces) shredded Italian Fontal or
   Italian Fontina cheese
¼ yellow onion, thinly sliced
¼ red onion, thinly sliced
2 green onions, coarsely chopped (including
   green parts)
2 ounces Gorgonzola cheese, crumbled
   (about ½ cup)
½ cup grated Parmigiano-Reggiano cheese
1 tablespoon chopped fresh marjoram
1 tablespoon chopped fresh flat-leaf parsley
1 tablespoon chopped fresh thyme
1 tablespoon chopped fresh oregano

Arrange the oven racks in the upper and lower thirds of the oven. Preheat the oven to 450°F. If using a baking stone, place it on the floor of the oven and preheat the oven for 45 minutes.

In a small bowl, combine the garlic and olive oil. Set aside.

To shape the pizzas, transfer the dough to a lightly floured surface and divide it into 3 pieces. Gently form each piece into a loose round (see page 26) and cover with a floured kitchen towel. Let rest for 20 minutes. Scatter cornmeal over 3 inverted baking sheets. Shape each round into a 10-inch disk (see page 197).

Toss the Mozzarella and Fontal together in a medium bowl. Divide the cheese mixture into 2 piles, one about two-thirds the total amount and the other one-third.

Line up the 3 pizzas for assembly. Distribute the larger amount of the cheese mixture over the pizzas, leaving a ½-inch rim. Scatter the onions on top of the cheese. Dot the top of the pizzas with small clumps of the Gorgonzola. Sprinkle with the remaining cheese.

In a small bowl, mix the Parmigiano and herbs together. Set aside.

If using a baking stone, place a baking sheet with a pizza on the lower oven rack and bake for 8 minutes. Rotate the pizza to the upper rack, place the second pizza in the oven on the lower rack, and continue baking for 8 minutes. Then, finish baking the first pizza by sliding it off the pan directly onto the baking stone. Rotate the second pizza to the upper rack and put the third pizza in the oven on the lower rack. Bake the pizza on the stone for 4 minutes to crisp the bottom until well browned. Finish baking the second and third pizzas in the same manner.

If using baking sheets only, place a baking sheet with a pizza on the lower oven rack and bake for 8 minutes. Rotate the pizza to the upper rack, place the second pizza in the oven on the lower rack, and continue baking for 8 minutes. Then, finish baking the first pizza by sliding it off the pan directly onto the lower oven rack. Rotate the second pizza to the upper rack. Bake the pizza on the lower rack for 5 minutes to crisp the bottom until well browned. Finish baking the second and third pizzas in the same manner.

Immediately after removing each pizza from the oven, brush the garlic oil onto the rim. Sprinkle the herb mixture over the top of each pizza.

Fresh Mushroom Pizza with Sun-Dried Tomato Pesto

This is our most traditional all-American pizza recipe, though of course we still use goat cheese. It further veers from the norm by the addition of sun-dried tomato pesto as a topping. (As we were saying, this is the closest we could get to a typical American-style pizza.)

MAKES THREE 10-INCH PIZZAS
Preparation time: 1³/₄ hours
(not including making the pizza dough)

- ¼ cup sun-dried tomatoes
- 2 cloves garlic, minced
- 4 tablespoons extra-virgin olive oil
- 1 recipe Sourdough Pizza Dough (page 198) or Yeasted Pizza Dough (page 201)
- Fine yellow cornmeal or flour for sprinkling
- Pinch of freshly ground black pepper
- Pinch of red pepper flakes
- ¼ teaspoon kosher salt
- ²/₃ pound white button or cremini mushrooms, thinly sliced
- ½ yellow onion, thinly sliced
- 1 green bell pepper, seeded, deribbed, and thinly sliced
- 4 cups (1 pound) shredded Mozzarella cheese
- 4 ounces fresh goat cheese
- ½ cup loosely packed fresh flat-leaf parsley, coarsely chopped

Put the sun-dried tomatoes in a small bowl and cover with hot water. Let soak for 20 to 30 minutes, or until hydrated.

Arrange the oven racks in the upper and lower thirds of the oven. Preheat the oven to 450°F. If using a baking stone, place it on the floor of the oven and preheat the oven for 45 minutes.

In a small bowl, combine half of the garlic with 2 tablespoons of the olive oil. Set aside.

To shape the pizzas, transfer the dough to a lightly floured surface and divide it into 3 pieces. Gently form each piece into a loose round (see page 26) and cover with a floured kitchen towel. Let rest for 20 minutes. Scatter cornmeal over 3 inverted baking sheets. Shape each round into a 10-inch disk (see page 197).

Drain the tomatoes, reserving the liquid. In a food processor, combine the tomatoes, ¼ cup of the reserved liquid, the remaining garlic, the remaining 2 tablespoons olive oil, the black pepper, red pepper flakes, and salt. Purée until smooth and thick, adding more of the reserved liquid as needed. Toss the sliced mushrooms with the pesto.

Line up the 3 pizzas for assembly. Scatter half of the Mozzarella over the 3 pizzas, leaving a ½-inch rim. Scatter the onion on top of the cheese. Place the mushroom mixture and bell pepper over the onion. Layer the remaining Mozzarella on top. Crumble the goat cheese into almond-sized pieces and distribute it evenly over the pizzas.

If using a baking stone, place a baking sheet with a pizza on the lower oven rack and bake for 8 minutes. Rotate the pizza to the upper rack, place the second pizza in the oven on the lower rack, and continue baking for 8 minutes. Then, finish baking the first pizza by sliding it off the pan directly onto the baking stone. Rotate the second pizza to the upper rack and put the third pizza in the oven on the lower rack. Bake the pizza on the stone for 4 to 8 minutes to crisp the bottom until well browned. Finish baking the second and third pizzas in the same manner.

If using baking sheets only, place a baking sheet with a pizza on the lower oven rack and bake for 8 minutes. Rotate the pizza up to the upper rack, place the second pizza in the oven on the lower rack, and continue baking for 8 minutes. Then, finish baking the first pizza by sliding it off the pan directly onto the lower oven rack. Rotate the second pizza to the upper rack. Bake the pizza on the lower rack for 4 to 8 minutes to crisp the bottom until well browned. Finish baking the second and third pizzas in the same manner.

Immediately after removing each pizza from the oven, brush garlic oil onto the rim. Garnish with the parsley.

Roasted Eggplant Pizza with Red Peppers and Feta Cheese

The dark skin of the eggplant contrasts beautifully with the red peppers on this roasted-vegetable pizza. The eggplant, onion, and peppers can be roasted earlier in the day; this makes the building of the pizza quicker, and it is easier to handle the vegetables when they are cool.

MAKES THREE 10-INCH PIZZAS

Preparation time: 1¾ hours

(not including making the pizza dough)

3 cloves garlic, minced

4 tablespoons extra-virgin olive oil

1 large eggplant, halved lengthwise and cut into
⅛-inch-thick half-moons

2 teaspoons kosher salt, plus a pinch

1 yellow onion, thinly sliced

2 red bell peppers, seeded, deribbed, and cut into
¼-inch-thick slices

⅛ teaspoon freshly ground black pepper

¼ teaspoon red pepper flakes

1 recipe Sourdough Pizza Dough (page 198) or
Yeasted Pizza Dough (page 201)

Fine yellow cornmeal or flour for sprinkling

4 cups (1 pound) coarsely shredded Mozzarella

6 ounces sheep's-milk Feta, crumbled
(about 1½ cups)

¼ cup minced fresh flat-leaf parsley

Arrange the oven racks in the upper and lower thirds of the oven. Preheat the oven to 450°F. If using a baking stone, place it on the floor of the oven and preheat the oven for 45 minutes.

In a small bowl, combine the garlic and olive oil. Set aside.

In a colander, toss the sliced eggplant with the 2 teaspoons salt and let stand for 10 minutes to draw out moisture and bitterness. Wipe off the salt and excess moisture from the eggplant by blotting it with a paper towel. Line 2 baking sheets with parchment paper. Spread the eggplant in one layer over one of the prepared pans and bake until soft and tender, about 15 minutes. Let cool.

While the eggplant is baking, spread the onion and bell peppers on the other prepared pan. Bake the onion and peppers for 5 to 8 minutes, or until the onions are soft. Let cool.

Toss the cooked eggplant with 2 tablespoons of the garlic olive oil and season with the black pepper, pepper flakes, and pinch of salt.

To shape the pizzas, transfer the dough to a lightly floured surface and divide it into 3 pieces. Gently form each piece into a loose round (see page 26) and cover with a floured kitchen towel. Let rest for 20 minutes. Scatter cornmeal over 3 inverted baking sheets. Shape each round into a 10-inch disk (see page 197).

Line up the 3 pizzas for assembly. Scatter half of the Mozzarella over the 3 pizzas, leaving a ½-inch rim. Layer the onion and bell peppers on top of the cheese, followed by the eggplant. Distribute the remaining Mozzarella over the vegetables. Sprinkle with the Feta.

If using a baking stone, place a baking sheet with a pizza on the lower oven rack and bake for 8 minutes. Rotate the pizza to the upper rack, place the second pizza in the oven on the lower rack, and continue baking for 8 minutes. Then, finish baking the first pizza by sliding it off the pan directly onto the baking stone. Rotate the second pizza to the upper rack and put the third pizza in the oven on the lower rack. Bake the pizza on the stone for 4 to 8 minutes to crisp the bottom until well browned. Finish baking the second and third pizzas in the same manner.

If using baking sheets only, place a baking sheet with a pizza on the lower oven rack and bake for 8 minutes. Rotate the pizza to the upper rack, place the second pizza in the oven on the lower rack, and continue baking for 8 minutes. Then, finish baking the first pizza by sliding it off the pan directly onto the lower oven rack. Rotate the second pizza to the upper rack. Bake the pizza on the lower rack for 4 to 8 minutes to crisp the bottom until well browned. Finish baking the second and third pizzas in the same manner.

Immediately after removing each pizza from the oven, brush the remaining garlic oil onto the rim. Garnish with the parsley.

Potato Pizza

This pizza is adapted from a traditional Italian-Jewish recipe in which thinly sliced potatoes are roasted and layered with Gruyère cheese. This is a big favorite with all of us in wintertime, when there are few fresh vegetables. We use very thinly sliced roasted Yukon Gold potatoes. The potatoes, caramelized onions, and rosemary oil can all be prepared earlier in the day, while the pizza dough rises. To make a Halloween pizza, substitute an orange sweet potato or yam for one of the potatoes.

MAKES THREE 10-INCH PIZZAS
Preparation time: 1¾ hours
(not including making the pizza dough)

2 Yukon Gold potatoes, thinly sliced

8 tablespoons extra-virgin olive oil

⅛ teaspoon kosher salt

½ teaspoon freshly ground black pepper

2 yellow onions, thinly sliced

1 sprig rosemary

1 recipe Sourdough Pizza Dough (page 198) or
 Yeasted Pizza Dough (page 201)

Fine yellow cornmeal or flour for sprinkling

2½ cups (10 ounces) shredded Mozzarella cheese

1 cup (4 ounces) shredded Swiss Gruyère cheese

½ cup loosely packed fresh flat-leaf parsley, coarsely
 chopped

Arrange the oven racks in the upper and lower thirds of the oven. Preheat the oven to 450°F. If using a baking stone, place it on the floor of the oven and preheat the oven for 45 minutes.

Line a baking sheet with parchment paper. Toss the potatoes with 2 tablespoons of the oil, the salt, and pepper. Arrange the potatoes on the prepared pan. Bake for 15 to 20 minutes, or until the slices are almost completely cooked through. Let cool.

Meanwhile, combine the onions and 2 tablespoons of the olive oil in a heavy medium skillet. Cook, stirring occasion-ally, over medium-low heat for 10 to 12 minutes, or until the onions are soft and golden brown. Set aside to cool.

To make the rosemary oil, combine the remaining 4 tablespoons olive oil and the rosemary sprig in a small saucepan. Cook over low heat for 5 minutes, taking care that the oil doesn't bubble. Turn off the heat and let the oil cool in the pan.

To shape the pizzas, transfer the dough to a lightly floured surface and divide it into 3 pieces. Gently form each piece into a loose round (see page 26) and cover with a floured kitchen towel. Let rest for 20 minutes. Scatter cornmeal over 3 inverted baking sheets. Shape each round into a 10-inch disk (see page 197).

Mix the cheeses together. Line up the 3 pizzas for assembly. Sprinkle half of the mixed cheeses over the 3 pizzas, leaving a ½-inch rim. Scatter the caramelized onions on top of the cheese and layer the potato slices on top of the onions, spacing them at least ½ inch apart. Sprinkle with the remaining cheese.

If using a baking stone, place a baking sheet with a pizza on the lower oven rack and bake for 8 minutes. Rotate the pizza to the upper rack, place the second pizza in the oven on the lower rack, and continue baking for 8 minutes. Then, finish baking the first pizza by sliding it off the pan directly onto the baking stone. Rotate the second pizza to the upper rack and put the third pizza in the oven. Bake the pizza on the stone for 4 to 8 minutes to crisp the bottom until well browned. Finish baking the second and third pizzas in the same manner.

If using baking sheets only, place a baking sheet with a pizza on the lower oven rack and bake for 8 minutes. Rotate the pizza to the upper rack, place the second pizza in the oven on the lower rack, and continue baking for 8 minutes. Then, finish baking the first pizza by sliding it off the pan directly onto the lower oven rack. Rotate the second pizza to the upper rack. Bake the pizza on the lower rack for 4 to 8 minutes to crisp the bottom until well browned. Finish baking the second and third pizzas in the same manner.

Immediately after removing each pizza from the oven, brush the rosemary oil on the rim and drizzle it over the rest of the pizza. Garnish with the parsley.

Years ago, we made a potato pizza and it was delicious—we were in a cold month and all the produce was expensive, so we were kind of checking out the root vegetables. We had some really nice carrots and some sage, so we said, let's make a carrot pizza, and it wasn't very good! So we never made another one.

—PAM

Roasted garlic
$ 1.25 each.

Red Cabbage Pizza with Gorgonzola and Nuts

When fresh vegetables are scarce in the in-between months of January and February, we feature this pizza. The ingredient list seems like it's wandered out of the salad section of a cookbook. This recipe is the subject of a lot of debate among pizza collective members, because people either love it or loathe it. The cabbage is a surprisingly sweet counterpoint to the sharpness of the blue cheese.

MAKES THREE 10-INCH PIZZAS
Preparation time: 1³/₄ hours
(not including making the pizza dough)

1 clove garlic, minced

6 tablespoons extra-virgin olive oil

1¹/₂ yellow onions, thinly sliced

1 recipe Sourdough Pizza Dough (page 198) or
    Yeasted Pizza Dough (page 201)

Fine yellow cornmeal or flour for sprinkling

¹/₃ small red cabbage, finely sliced (about 3 cups)

2 tablespoons balsamic vinegar

¹/₄ teaspoon kosher salt

Pinch of freshly ground black pepper

4 cups (1 pound) shredded Mozzarella cheese

¹/₄ pound Gorgonzola cheese, crumbled (about 1 cup)

¹/₃ cup walnuts, coarsely chopped, or pine nuts

¹/₂ cup loosely packed fresh flat-leaf parsley, coarsely
    chopped

Arrange the oven racks in the upper and lower thirds of the oven. Preheat the oven to 450°F. If using a baking stone, place it on the floor of the oven and preheat the oven for 45 minutes.

In a small bowl, combine the garlic and 2 tablespoons of the olive oil. Set aside.

In a heavy medium skillet, combine the onions and 2 tablespoons of the olive oil. Cook, stirring occasionally, over medium-low heat for 10 to 12 minutes, or until the onions are soft and golden brown. Let cool.

To shape the pizzas, transfer the dough to a lightly floured surface and divide it into 3 pieces. Gently form each piece into a loose round (see page 26) and cover with a floured kitchen towel. Let rest for 20 minutes. Scatter cornmeal over 3 inverted baking sheets. Shape each round into a 10-inch disk (see page 197).

In a medium bowl, toss the cabbage with remaining 2 tablespoons olive oil, the balsamic vinegar, salt, and pepper. Divide the Mozzarella into 2 piles, one about two-thirds the total amount and the other one-third.

Line up the 3 pizzas for assembly. Scatter the larger amount of Mozzarella over the 3 pizzas, leaving a ¹/₂-inch rim. Scatter the onions on top of the cheese and place the cabbage over the onions. Sprinkle the remaining Mozzarella on top of the onions. Dot the top of the pizzas with the crumbled Gorgonzola. Scatter the nuts over the pizzas.

If using a baking stone, place a baking sheet with a pizza on the lower oven rack and bake for 10 minutes. Rotate the pizza to the upper rack, place the second pizza in the oven on the lower rack, and continue baking for 10 minutes. Then, finish baking the first pizza by sliding it off the pan directly onto the baking stone. Rotate the second pizza to the upper rack and put the third pizza in the oven on the lower rack. Bake the pizza on the stone for 4 to 8 minutes to crisp the bottom until well browned. Finish baking the second and third pizzas in the same manner.

If using baking sheets only, place a baking sheet with a pizza on the lower oven rack and bake for 10 minutes. Rotate the pizza to the upper rack, place second pizza in the oven on the lower rack, and continue baking for 10 minutes. Then, finish baking the first pizza by sliding it off the pan directly onto the lower oven rack. Rotate the second pizza to the upper rack. Bake the pizza on the lower rack for 4 to 8 minutes to crisp the bottom until well browned. Finish baking the second and third pizzas in the same manner.

Immediately after removing each pizza from the oven, brush the garlic oil onto the rim. Garnish with the parsley.

Roasted Wild Mushroom Pizza with Goat Cheese

Once a year, the Cheese Board Pizzeria makes this pizza using a mixture of wild mushrooms. Roasting mushrooms concentrates their flavor, and because the mushrooms are precooked, they release less moisture than fresh ones would, which makes the baker's job easier.

MAKES THREE 10-INCH PIZZAS
Preparation time: 1³/₄ hours
(not including making the pizza dough)

2 cloves garlic, minced

2 tablespoons extra-virgin olive oil

1 pound mushrooms, sliced (white, portobellos, chanterelles, shiitakes, or a mixture)

¹/₈ teaspoon freshly ground black pepper

Pinch of finely ground red pepper flakes

1 recipe Sourdough Pizza Dough (page 198) or Yeasted Pizza Dough (page 201)

Fine yellow cornmeal or flour for sprinkling

4 cups (1 pound) shredded Mozzarella cheese

¹/₂ red onion, thinly sliced

4 ounces fresh goat cheese

¹/₂ cup loosely packed fresh flat-leaf parsley, minced

Arrange the oven racks in the upper and lower thirds of the oven. Preheat the oven to 450°F. If using a baking stone, place it on the floor of the oven and preheat the oven for 45 minutes.

In a small bowl, combine half of the garlic with the olive oil. Set aside.

Toss the sliced mushrooms with the black pepper, red pepper, and the remaining garlic. Line a baking sheet with parchment paper. Scatter the mushrooms over the paper and bake for 10 minutes, or until the mushrooms are soft and have released their liquid. Remove from the oven, pour off any liquid, and set aside to cool.

To shape the pizzas, transfer the dough to a lightly floured surface and divide it into 3 pieces. Gently form each piece into a loose round (see page 26) and cover with a floured kitchen towel. Let rest for 20 minutes. Scatter cornmeal over 3 inverted baking sheets. Shape each round into a 10-inch disk (see page 197).

Line up the 3 pizzas for assembly. Scatter half of the Mozzarella over the 3 pizzas, leaving a ¹/₂-inch rim. Scatter the onion on top of the cheese. Scatter the mushrooms over the cheese. Sprinkle the remaining Mozzarella on top of the mushrooms. Crumble the goat cheese into almond-sized pieces and distribute it evenly over the pizzas.

If using a baking stone, place a baking sheet with a pizza on the lower oven rack and bake for 8 minutes. Rotate the pizza to the upper rack, place the second pizza in the oven on the lower rack, and continue baking for 8 minutes. Then, finish baking the first pizza by sliding it off the pan directly onto the baking stone. Rotate the second pizza to the upper rack and put the third pizza in the oven on the lower rack. Bake the pizza on the stone for 4 to 8 minutes to crisp the bottom until well browned. Finish baking the second and third pizzas in the same manner.

If using baking sheets only, place a baking sheet with a pizza on the lower oven rack and bake for 8 minutes. Rotate the pizza to the upper rack, place the second pizza in the oven on the lower rack, and continue baking for 8 minutes. Then, finish baking the first pizza by sliding it off the pan directly onto the lower oven rack. Rotate the second pizza to the upper rack. Bake the pizza on the lower rack for 4 to 8 minutes to crisp the bottom until well browned. Finish baking the second and third pizzas in the same manner.

Immediately after removing each pizza from the oven, brush the garlic oil onto the rim. Garnish with the parsley.

My fantasy is that as the customers are preparing for Thanksgiving, they are eating a slice of wild mushroom pizza with a glass of Veuve Clicquot while they bake their pumpkins and pies, and prepare the stuffing the night before.

—PAM

THE CHEESE BOARD: COLLECTIVE WORKS

Sauce Pie

This sauce pie is unusual for a couple of reasons. None of our other pizza recipes use tomato sauce, and we don't actually make this pizza to sell. It is the simplest pizza to make, and also particularly popular with Cheese Board kids, who prefer a simple pizza without any vegetables. Make the sauce while the pizza dough is rising in the bowl.

MAKES THREE 10-INCH PIZZAS
Preparation time: 1³/₄ hours
(not including making the pizza dough)

1 clove garlic, minced
2 tablespoons extra-virgin olive oil

Sauce
1 yellow onion, minced
1 clove garlic, minced
2 tablespoons olive oil
1 can (14 ounces) tomato purée or 1¹/₂ cups favorite
    pasta sauce

1 recipe Sourdough Pizza Dough (page 198) or
    Yeasted Pizza Dough (page 201)
Fine yellow cornmeal or flour for sprinkling
3 cups (12 ounces) shredded Mozzarella cheese
¹/₂ cup loosely packed fresh flat-leaf parsley, coarsely
    chopped

Arrange the oven racks in the upper and lower thirds of the oven. Preheat the oven to 450°F. If using a baking stone, place it on the floor of the oven and preheat the oven for 45 minutes.

In a small bowl, combine the garlic and the 2 tablespoons olive oil. Set aside.

To make the sauce, sauté the onion and garlic in the 2 tablespoons olive oil in heavy medium skillet over medium heat until translucent, about 7 minutes. Add the tomato purée and cook for 10 minutes. Set aside to cool.

To shape the pizzas, transfer the dough to a lightly floured surface and divide it into 3 pieces. Gently form each piece into a loose round (see page 26) and cover with a floured kitchen towel. Let rest for 20 minutes. Scatter cornmeal over 3 inverted baking sheets. Shape each round into a 10-inch disk (see page 197).

Line up the 3 pizzas for assembly. With a rubber spatula, spread enough sauce over each pizza to just cover the dough. Scatter the Mozzarella over the pizzas, leaving a ¹/₂-inch rim.

If using a baking stone, place a baking sheet with a pizza on the lower oven rack and bake for 10 minutes. Rotate the pizza to the upper rack, place the second pizza in the oven on the lower rack, and continue baking for 10 minutes. Then, finish baking the first pizza by sliding it off the pan directly onto the baking stone. Rotate the second pizza to the upper rack and put the third pizza in the oven on the lower rack. Bake the pizza on the stone for 4 to 8 minutes to crisp the bottom until well browned. Finish baking the second and third pizzas in the same manner.

If using baking sheets only, place a baking sheet with a pizza on the lower oven rack and bake for 10 minutes. Rotate the pizza to the upper rack, place the second pizza in the oven on the lower rack, and continue baking for 10 minutes. Then, finish baking the first pizza by sliding it off the pan directly onto the lower oven rack. Rotate the second pizza to the upper rack. Bake the pizza on the lower rack for 4 to 8 minutes to crisp the bottom until well browned. Finish baking the second and third pizzas in the same manner.

Immediately after removing each pizza from the oven, brush the garlic oil onto the rim. Garnish with the parsley.

We have lots of regulars. We often know their names, and they ask us about our vacations. I'll be at the register and look down the line, and I'll know that *he* gets one on paper only and *she* gets two for here. The next one gets a whole pizza, but he likes them on the crisp side, and the baker has already checked the line and is baking one a little longer.

—PAM

Calzone

Cheese wrapped in bread: the perfect Cheese Board food. This particular recipe is still waiting its place in line to make an appearance at the store. It is made very occasionally at the bakery for in-store consumption and more frequently at home by Cheese Boarders. Light, crusty, and deeply satisfying, a calzone is also good the next day for a bag lunch or a hiking snack. Cooking the vegetables while the pizza dough is rising will allow time for them to cool before handling.

MAKES 8 CALZONES

Preparation time: 1 hour

(not including making the pizza dough)

---

3 cloves garlic, minced

5 tablespoons extra-virgin olive oil

1/2 yellow onion, finely chopped

1/3 pound mushrooms, sliced

1/4 teaspoon kosher salt

Pinch of freshly ground black pepper

10 ounces baby spinach, washed

1 recipe Sourdough Pizza Dough (page 198) or
  Yeasted Pizza Dough (page 201)

Fine yellow cornmeal or flour for sprinkling

2 cups (8 ounces) shredded Mozzarella cheese

4 ounces fresh goat cheese

1/4 cup loosely packed basil leaves, coarsely
  chopped (optional)

Arrange the oven racks in the upper and lower thirds of the oven. Preheat the oven to 450°F. If using a baking stone, place it on the floor of the oven and preheat the oven for 45 minutes.

In a small bowl, combine one-third of the garlic with 3 tablespoons of the olive oil. Set aside.

In a heavy medium skillet, combine the onion and the remaining garlic with the remaining 2 tablespoons olive oil and cook over medium heat for 5 minutes, or until lightly browned. Add the mushrooms, salt, and pepper and cook for 5 to 10 minutes, or until the mushrooms are soft. Let cool.

Put the spinach in large saucepan, cover, and cook on low heat for 5 minutes, or just long enough to wilt the spinach. Drain any excess liquid. Let cool.

Transfer the dough to a lightly floured surface and divide it into 8 pieces. Gently form each piece into a loose round (see page 26) and cover with a floured kitchen towel. Let rest for 20 minutes. Sprinkle 2 baking sheets with cornmeal. Pull and pat the dough into 8 disks, each about 7 inches in diameter (see page 197).

Evenly divide the onion mixture, spinach, Mozzarella, and goat cheese among the 8 rounds, filling only one side of each round and leaving a 1/2-inch rim. With a pastry brush, lightly paint the rim of each round with water. Fold the round in half, turn the bottom lip over the top lip, and pinch the edges together. Brush the top of the calzones with 2 tablespoons of the garlic oil. Place 4 calzones on each baking sheet.

Using a single-edge razor, slash each calzone once with a short diagonal slash. Bake the calzones for 10 minutes. Rotate the pans front to back and trade their rack positions. Bake 10 minutes longer, or until golden brown with a firm bottom.

Remove from the oven and brush with the remaining garlic oil. Garnish with the basil.

Source List

Here are a few sources for hard to find ingredients and equipment. (Restaurant supply shops are also good places to look.)

Giusto's Speciality Foods

344 Littlefield Avenue, South San Francisco, CA 94080
Tel: 888-873-6566, 650-873-6566; Fax: 650-873-2826
www.giustos.com

Mills organic flours and sells a range of baking ingredients.

The King Arthur Flour Company

Norwich, VT 05055
Tel: 800-827-6836
www.kingarthurflour.com

Flours, baking supplies, information, and an array of useful and esoteric equipment.

Maytag Dairy Farms

P.O. Box 806, Newton, IA 50208
Tel: 800-247-2458, 641-792-1133; Fax: 641-792-1567

Glass cheese keepers and excellent raw-milk blue cheese.

TMB Baking

390 Swift Avenue, No. 13, South San Francisco, CA 94080
Tel: 650-589-5724; Fax: 650-589-5729
www.tmbbaking.com

Baskets and tools.

www.fromages.com

An online cheese catalogue that specializes in French cheeses. Check out the Gazette section for good cheese information.

www.cheese.com

A great website with an encyclopedia of cheeses by name, country of origin, and type of milk (check out the camel's-milk cheese), and lots of other cheese facts, with good links to other websites.

www.cheesenet.info

A somewhat goofy but informative site with links.

www.efr.hw.ac.uk/SDA/cheese2.html

A very thorough description of how cheese is made, from the Scottish Dairy Association.

Bibliography

CHEESE

Battistotti, Bruno, et al. *Cheese: A Guide to the World of Cheese and Cheesemaking*. New York: Facts on File Publications, 1983.

Courtine, Robert. *Dictionnaire des Fromages*. Paris: Librairie Larousse, 1972.

Eekhof-Stork, Nancy. *The Great International Cheese Board*. New York: Paddington Press, 1979.

Ensrud, Barbara. *The Pocket Guide to Cheese*. New York; Perigee Books, 1981.

Harbutt, Juliet, and Roz Denny (contributor). *A Cook's Guide to Cheese*. New York: Hermes House, 2000.

Jenkins, Steve. *The Cheese Primer*. New York: Workman Publishing, 1996.

Lowe, Alfonso. *The Barrier and the Bridge: Historic Sicily*. New York: W. W. Norton, 1972.

Masui, Kazuko, and Tomoko Yamada. *French Cheeses*. New York: DK Publishing, 1996.

McCalman, Max, and David Gibbons. *The Cheese Plate*. New York: Clarkson Potter, 2002.

Ridgway, Judy. *The Cheese Companion*. Philadelphia: Running Press, 1999.

Slow Food editors. *Italian Cheeses*. Bra(Cuneo), Italy: Slow Food Arcigola Editore, 2000.

BREAD

Beard, James. *Beard on Bread*. New York: Alfred A. Knopf, 1984.

Cunningham, Marion. *The Fannie Farmer Cookbook*. New York: Alfred A. Knopf, 1984.

David, Elizabeth. *English Bread and Yeast Cookery*. Newton, Mass.: Biscuit Books, 1994.

Field, Carol. *The Italian Baker*. New York: Harper & Row, 1985.

Glazer, Maggie. *Artisan Baking across America*. New York: Artisan, 2000.

Greenstein, George. *Secrets of a Jewish Baker: Authentic Jewish Rye and Other Breads*. Freedom, Calif.: The Crossing Press, 1993.

Leader, Daniel, and Judith Blahnik. *Bread Alone*. New York: Morrow and Co., 1993.

Ortiz, Joe. *The Village Baker*. Berkeley, Calif.: Ten Speed Press, 1993.

Reinhart, Peter. *The Bread Baker's Apprentice*. Berkeley, Calif.: Ten Speed Press, 2001.

———. *Crust and Crumb*. Berkeley, Calif.: Ten Speed Press, 1998.

Rombauer, Irma S., and Marion Rombauer Becker. *The Joy of Cooking*. New York: Bobbs-Merrill, 1975.

Steingarten, Jeffrey. *The Man Who Ate Everything*. New York: Alfred A. Knopf, 1998.

Wood, Ed. *World Sourdoughs from Antiquity*. Berkeley, Calif.: Ten Speed Press, 1996.

COOPERATIVES AND COLLECTIVES

Adams, Frank T., and Gary B. Hansen. *Putting Democracy to Work: A Practical Guide for Starting and Managing Worker-Owned Businesses*. Revised ed. San Francisco: Berrett-Koehler, 1992.

Honigsberg, Peter Jan; Bernard Kamoroff; and Jim Beatty. *We Own It: Starting and Managing Cooperatives & Employee-Owned Ventures*. Revised ed. Laytonville, Calif.: Bell Springs Publishers, 1991.

Jackall, Robert. "Paradoxes of Collective Work: A Study of the Cheese Board, Berkeley, California." Williams College, 1977. (Later published in *Worker Cooperatives in America*. Robert Jackall and Henry M. Levin, eds. Berkeley, Calif.: University of California Press, 1984.)

Directory of Cooperative/ Collective Organizations

Association of Arizmendi Cooperatives

733 Baker Street, San Francisco, CA 94115

Tel: 415-346-5779

A mutually supporting association of cooperative bakeries.

Center for Democratic Solutions

733 Baker Street, San Francisco, CA 94115

Tel: 415-346-5779

Email: wie@sbcglobal.net

Educational, legal, and consulting services for worker cooperatives, primarily those in the San Francisco Bay Area. Maintains a lending library of publications, videos, and other information related to worker cooperatives.

CooperationWorks

P.O. Box 527, Dayton, WY 82836

Tel: 307-655-9162; Fax: 307-655-3785

Email: cw@vcn.com

Training for cooperative developers and people wishing to become cooperative developers.

The International Cooperative Alliance

15, Route des Morillons, 1218 Grand-Saconnex
Geneva, Switzerland

Tel: (+41) 022 929 88 88; Fax: (+41) 022 798 41 22

Email: ica@coop.org; www.coop.org

An international organization that promotes workers' democracy and provides information and links to other sites.

Mondragon Corporacion Cooperativa

www.mondragon.mcc.es

A website that will introduce you to the world of the Mondragón Cooperative, with information about its history.

The National Center for Employee Ownership (NCEO)

1736 Franklin Street, 8th Floor, Oakland, CA 94612

Tel: 510-208-1300; Fax: 510-272-9510

Email: nceo@nceo.org; www.nceo.org

A national organization devoted to employee ownership. It provides information on employee stock ownership plans, publishes articles, holds conferences, and provides links to other sites.

National Cooperative Business Association/ Cooperative Development Foundation

1401 New York Avenue NW, Suite 1100
Washington, DC 20005

Tel: 202-638-6222; www.ncba.coop/index.cfm

A national cooperative trade association and foundation serving a range of cooperatives, including worker cooperatives.

The Network of Bay Area Worker Collectives (NOBAWC)

Tel: 510-549-1514

Email: nobawc@igc.org; www.bapd.org/gne-es-1.html

A website with links to many cooperative organizations.

University of California Center for Cooperatives

University of California, One Shields Avenue
Davis, CA 95616

Tel: 530-752-2408; Fax: 530-752-5451

Email: centerforcoops@ucdavis.edu

www.cooperatives.ucdavis.edu

An informative educational site about cooperatives, with research publications for sale, newsletters, events, and links.

Western Worker Cooperative Conference

733 Baker Street, San Francisco, CA 94115

Tel: 415-775-0124

An annual conference for worker-owned businesses.

Index

A

Abbaye de Tamié, 172
Affidelices au Chablis, 171
Almonds
    Stollen, 142–43
    Sunday Bread, 76–78
Amalthée, 159
American Cheese Plate, 165
AOC Cheese Plate, 169, 171
AOC system, 168–69
Apples
    Apple Apricot Muffins, 53
    Apple Walnut Scones, 41
Apricots
    Apple Apricot Muffins, 53
    Holiday Challah, 76
    Wolverines, 114
Asiago
    appearance of, 153
    Asiago Bread, 182–83
    Cheese Rolls, 111, 113
Association of Arizmendi Cooperatives, 13
Avedisian, Elizabeth and Sahag, 2–4
Azeitão, 172

B

Baguettes
    Bastille Day Baguettes, 94
    introduction of, 6, 8
    popularity of, 95
    Sourdough Baguettes, 93–94
Baita Friuli, 156
Baker's cheese, 190
Baking, 33
Baking powder, 21
Baking soda, 21
Baking stones, 17, 88
Bananas
    Banana Mocha Chocolate Chip
        Muffins, 56
    Banana Walnut Muffins, 56–57
Bastille Day Baguettes, 94

Bâtard, 28
Beaufort, 169, 171
Beerkaese, 175
Beer Rye, Sourdough, 124
Bell peppers
    Roasted Bell Pepper Pizza with Feta and
        Olive Tapenade, 204
    Roasted Eggplant Pizza with
        Red Peppers and Feta Cheese, 213
    Tomatillo Salsa, 50
Bellwether Farms Sheep Ricotta, 165
Berkeley Buns, 180–81
Berkswell, 163
Bialys, 100–101
Bleu d'Auvergne, 169
Bleu de Termignon, 172
Blueberry Scones, Lemon, 40
Bonne-Bouche, 165
Boursin, Mock, 190
Braiding, 29
Bran
    Bran Muffins, 52
    Multigrain Bread, 84–85
Breads. *See* Quick breads; Sourdough;
        Yeasted breads
Brie
    appearance of, 152
    ripening, at home, 157
    texture of, 153
Brillat-Savarin, 173
Brin d'Amour, 172
Brioches
    Cranberry Brioches, 61
    master recipe, 60–61
    tips for, 35–36
Buns
    Berkeley Buns, 180–81
    Chocolate Things, 62
    Hot Cross Buns, 130
    Sticky Buns, 65
    Zampanos, 99–100
Butter, 21

C

Cabbage Pizza, Red, with Gorgonzola
        and Nuts, 216
Cabrales, 179
Cacio di Fossa, 159
Cakes
    Deep Dark Chocolate Loaves, 129
    Fruitcake, 133–34
California Cheese Plate, 166
California Crottin, 167
California Goat Cheese Plate, 166–67
Calzone, 220
Camellia, 166
Camembert, 176
    appearance of, 152
    Nancy's Hudson Valley, 165
    ripening, at home, 157
    texture of, 153
Capricious, 167
Caramel color, 21
Challah
    Holiday Challah, 76
    master recipe, 75
Cheddar
    Cheese Balls, 139
    Cheese Scones, 48–49
    Cheesy Muffins, 98–99
    Corn Onion Cheddar Bread, 184–85
    Experimental Bread No. 7, 186–87
    Fiscalini Bandage Wrapped, 166
    Hot Cheddar Spread, 191
    ripening, at home, 157
Cheese. *See also individual cheeses*
    American, 164–67
    AOC system, 168–69
    for camping, 176, 178
    Cheese Balls, 139
    Cheese Onion Curry Bread, 180–81
    Cheese Rolls, 111, 113
    Cheese Scones, 48–49
    Cheesy Muffins, 98–99
    choosing, 152–53

Cheese, *continued*
  cutting, 154–55, 156
  facts or fiction, 159
  graters, 17
  making, 148–52
  Mexican-style, 178
  planes, 154–55
  raw-milk, 161–63
  rinds, 164
  ripening, at home, 156–57
  sourdough and, 170
  storing, 155–56
  substituting, 21
  tasting, 177
  Three-Onion, Four-Herb, and
    Four-Cheese Pizza, 210–11
Cheese Board
  history of, 2–12
  hours of operation, 37
  interns, 59
  meetings and decision making, 1, 51, 70, 80
  music, 64
  neighbors of, 6, 11, 14
  opening shift, 42, 193
  pizzeria, 2, 9–10, 195
Cheese plates
  American Cheese Plate, 165
  AOC Cheese Plate, 169, 171
  California Cheese Plate, 166
  California Goat Cheese Plate, 166–67
  Intimate Picnic Plate, 176
  New Year's Eve Cheese Plate, 173
  Raw-Milk Cheese Plate, 163
  Stinky-Cheese Plate, 174
  Super Bowl Cheese Plate, 175
  tips for, 160–61
  Wednesday-Morning Cheese Plate,
    171, 173
Cherries
  Corn Cherry Scones, 46
  Wolverines, 114
Chiles
  Experimental Bread No. 7, 186–87
  Hot Cheddar Spread, 191
  Roasted Tomato Salsa, 50
  Tomatillo Salsa, 50
Chocolate, 22
  Banana Mocha Chocolate Chip
    Muffins, 56
  Chocolate Chip Scones, 42
  Chocolate-Drizzled Stars, Trees, or
    Hearts, 70
  Chocolate Things, 62

Deep Dark Chocolate Loaves, 129
Florentines, 137–38
  melting, 17–18
City Bread, 97
Coconut
  Fruitcake, 133–34
  Killer Granola, 66
  Killer Granola Cookies, 66–67
Coffee
  Banana Mocha Chocolate Chip
    Muffins, 56
  Deep Dark Chocolate Loaves, 129
Collectives and cooperatives
  directory of, 224
  sister, 13
Cookies
  Chocolate-Drizzled Stars, Trees, or
    Hearts, 70
  Florentines, 137–38
  Ginger Shortbread, 68
  Hazelnut Shortbread, 69
  Killer Granola Cookies, 66–67
  Lemon Shortbread, 69–70
  Shortbread, 67
Cooking spray, 22
Coriander Wheat Bread, 83–84
Corn
  Corn Onion Cheddar Bread, 184–85
  Corn Zucchini Pizza with Lime and
    Cilantro, 208
Cornmeal
  Corn Cherry Scones, 46
  Corn Oat Molasses Bread, 80–81
  Corn Onion Cheddar Bread, 184–85
  Sourdough Beer Rye, 124
Cotswold, 175
Coulommiers, 157
Cranberry Brioches, 61
Cream cheese
  Cheese Balls, 139
  Date Spread, 139
  Mock Boursin, 190
  Salmon Spread, 191
Crottin, 167
Crumb, 33
Currants
  Currant Scones, 39
  Holiday Challah, 76
  Hot Cross Buns, 130
  Oat Scones, 47–48
  Saffron Bread, 140
  Stollen, 142–43

D
Dairy products, substituting, 22
Dark Rye, 119
Date Spread, 139
Day of the Dead Bread, 134–35
Deep Dark Chocolate Loaves, 129
Double boilers, 17–18
Dry Jack, 176

E
Edam, 157
Eggplant Pizza, Roasted, with Red
  Peppers and Feta Cheese, 213
Eggs
  size of, 22
  wash, 31
Emmental, 163
  appearance of, 153
  Fondue, 190
English Muffins, 98
English wire cheese cutters, 155
Epoisses de Bourgogne, 171
Equipment, 17–20, 154–55
Experimental Bread No. 7, 186–87
Extracts, 22

F
Farmer's cheese, 191
Feta cheese
  Corn Zucchini Pizza with Lime and
    Cilantro, 208
  Roasted Bell Pepper Pizza with Feta and
    Olive Tapenade, 204
  Roasted Eggplant Pizza with Red Pep-
    pers and Feta Cheese, 213
  Tomato Pizza with Lemon Zest, 201–2
  Zucchini and Feta Cheese Pizza with Sun-
    Dried Tomato Pesto, 203
Fiscalini Bandage Wrapped Cheddar, 166
Florentines, 137–38
Flour, 22
Focaccia
  Pesto Focaccia, 106
  Ricotta Salata, Lemon Zest, and Cilantro
    Focaccia, 107–8
  Rosemary Focaccia, 104–5
  Small Olive Focaccia Rounds, 101–2
  Sun-Dried Tomato Focaccia, 105
  Tomato, Caper, and Olive Focaccia,
    102, 104
Fondue, 190
Fontal, 210–11
Fontina d'Aosta, 174

Fournols, 152–53
Fresh Mushroom Pizza with Sun-Dried
    Tomato Pesto, 211–12
Fruit, dried, 22. *See also individual fruits*
    Fruitcake, 133–34
    Holiday Challah, 76
    Stollen, 142–43
    Wolverines, 114

G

Géromé, 174
Ginger
    buying, 68
    Gingerbread, 141
    Ginger Shortbread, 68
Gluten, 25
Goat cheese
    California Goat Cheese Plate, 166–67
    Calzone, 220
    Fresh Mushroom Pizza with Sun-Dried
        Tomato Pesto, 211–12
    Heirloom Tomato Pizza with Goat
        Cheese and Fresh Herbs, 209
    ripening, at home, 157
    Roasted Wild Mushroom Pizza with
        Goat Cheese, 217
    Tomato Pizza with Fresh Greens and
        Goat Cheese, 206
Gorgonzola, 174
    Red Cabbage Pizza with Gorgonzola and
        Nuts, 216
    Three-Onion, Four-Herb, and
        Four-Cheese Pizza, 210–11
Gouda
    appearance of, 153
    ripening, at home, 157
    Roomano, 175
Grand Cru, 165
Granola
    Killer Granola, 66
    Killer Granola Cookies, 66–67
Greek Shepherd's Bread, 181–82
Greens, Fresh, Tomato Pizza with Goat
    Cheese and, 206
Gruyère
    appearance of, 153
    Cheese Rolls, 111, 113
    Fondue, 190
    making, 148–49
    Potato Pizza, 214
Gubbeen, 175

H

Halloween pizza, 214
Hazelnuts
    Florentines, 137–38
    Hazelnut Shortbread, 69
Heirloom Tomato Pizza with Goat Cheese
    and Fresh Herbs, 209
Hobrot (Cheese Onion Curry Bread), 180–81
Hoch Ybrig, 172
Holiday foods
    Bastille Day Baguettes, 94
    Cheese Balls, 139
    Chocolate-Drizzled Stars, Trees, or
        Hearts, 70
    Cranberry Brioches, 61
    Date Spread, 139
    Day of the Dead Bread, 134–35
    Deep Dark Chocolate Loaves, 129
    Florentines, 137–138
    Fruitcake, 133–34
    Gingerbread, 141
    Halloween pizza, 214
    Holiday Challah, 76
    Holiday Loaves, 138
    Hot Cross Buns, 130
    Irish Soda Scones, 132
    Saffron Bread, 140
    Stollen, 142–43
    Stuffing Bread, 136
Hot Cheddar Spread, 191
Hot Cross Buns, 130
Humboldt Fog, 166

I, J

Intimate Picnic Plate, 176
Irish Soda Scones, 132
Jelly roll, 29
Just Lemon Scones, 43

K, L

Kefalograviera cheese, 181–82
Killer Granola, 66
Killer Granola Cookies, 66–67
Kneading, 24–26
Langres, 173
Laura Chenel Taupinière, 167
Lemons
    Just Lemon Scones, 43
    Lemon Blueberry Scones, 40
    Lemon Poppy Seed Muffins, 54
    Lemon Shortbread, 69–70
    Ricotta Salata, Lemon Zest, and Cilantro
        Focaccia, 107–8

Stollen, 142–43
    Tomato Pizza with Lemon Zest, 201–2
Light Rye, 120
Limburger, 157
Lincolnshire Poacher, 173
Le Lingot du Quercy, 171

M

Manchego, 178
Maple Pecan Scones, 45
Marble Rye, 122–23
Le Maréchal, 173
Maroilles, 159
Master Sourdough, 92
Maytag Blue, 165, 172
Measuring, 18, 24
Millet
    Millet Pecan Muffins, 54–55
    Multigrain Bread, 84–85
Mixers, 18
Mixing
    bowls, 18
    loaf breads, 24
    quick breads, 24
Mock Boursin, 190
Molasses, 22–23
Mozzarella
    Calzone, 220
    Corn Zucchini Pizza with Lime and
        Cilantro, 208
    Fresh Mushroom Pizza with Sun-Dried
        Tomato Pesto, 211–12
    Heirloom Tomato Pizza with Goat
        Cheese and Fresh Herbs, 209
    on pizzas, 197–98
    Potato Pizza, 214
    Red Cabbage Pizza with Gorgonzola and
        Nuts, 216
    Roasted Bell Pepper Pizza with Feta and
        Olive Tapenade, 204
    Roasted Eggplant Pizza with
        Red Peppers and Feta Cheese, 213
    Roasted Wild Mushroom Pizza with
        Goat Cheese, 217
    Sauce Pie, 219
    Three-Onion, Four-Herb, and Four-
        Cheese Pizza, 210–11
    Tomato Pizza with Fresh Greens and
        Goat Cheese, 206
    Tomato Pizza with Lemon Zest, 201–2
    Zucchini and Feta Cheese Pizza with
        Sun-Dried Tomato Pesto, 203

Muffins
    Apple Apricot Muffins, 53
    Banana Mocha Chocolate Chip
        Muffins, 56
    Banana Walnut Muffins, 56–57
    Bran Muffins, 52
    Cheesy Muffins, 98–99
    crumb, 33
    English Muffins, 98
    Lemon Poppy Seed Muffins, 54
    Millet Pecan Muffins, 54–55
    Pecan Pear Muffins, 58
    Raspberry Orange Muffins, 58–59
    sweet loaves from dough for, 138
    tips for, 35
Multigrain Bread, 84–85
Munster, 174
Mushrooms
    Calzone, 220
    Fresh Mushroom Pizza with Sun-Dried
        Tomato Pesto, 211–12
    Roasted Wild Mushroom Pizza with
        Goat Cheese, 217

N, O

Nancy's Hudson Valley Camembert, 165
New Year's Eve Cheese Plate, 173
Nuts. *See also individual nuts*
    choosing, 23
    Fruitcake, 133–34
    Red Cabbage Pizza with Gorgonzola and
        Nuts, 216
    toasting, 23
Oats
    Apple Apricot Muffins, 53
    Coriander Wheat Bread, 83–84
    Corn Oat Molasses Bread, 80–81
    Irish Soda Scones, 132
    Killer Granola, 66
    Killer Granola Cookies, 66–67
    Multigrain Bread, 84–85
    Oat Scones, 47–48
    Sourdough Beer Rye, 124
Oils, 23
Olives, 23
    Greek Shepherd's Bread, 181–82
    Provolone Olive Bread, 187–88
    Roasted Bell Pepper Pizza with Feta and
        Olive Tapenade, 204
    Small Olive Focaccia Rounds, 101–2
    Tomato, Caper, and Olive Focaccia,
        102, 104

Onions
    Asiago Bread, 182–83
    Bialys, 100–101
    Cheese Onion Curry Bread, 180–81
    Corn Onion Cheddar Bread, 184–85
    Provolone Olive Bread, 187–88
    Stuffing Bread, 136
    Three-Onion, Four-Herb, and Four-
        Cheese Pizza, 210–11
Oranges
    Day of the Dead Bread, 134–35
    Florentines, 137–38
    Raspberry Orange Muffins, 58–59
    Stollen, 142–43
Ossau-Iraty, 169

P

Pans, 18
Parchment paper, 18
Parmigiano-Reggiano, 170, 176
    appearance of, 153
    Pesto Focaccia, 106
    Sun-Dried Tomato Focaccia, 105
    Three-Onion, Four-Herb, and Four-
        Cheese Pizza, 210–11
    Zampanos, 99–100
Pastry brushes, 18
Pastry cutters, 18
Pear Muffins, Pecan, 58
Pecans
    Killer Granola, 66
    Killer Granola Cookies, 66–67
    Maple Pecan Scones, 45
    Millet Pecan Muffins, 54–55
    Pecan Pear Muffins, 58
    Pecan Rolls, 63
    Wolverines, 114
Pecorino Toscano Riserva, 178
Pesto, 106
    Fresh Mushroom Pizza with Sun-Dried
        Tomato Pesto, 211–12
    Pesto Focaccia, 106
    Sun-Dried Tomato Pesto, 105
    Zucchini and Feta Cheese Pizza with Sun-
        Dried Tomato Pesto, 203
Petit Agour, 157, 176
Picandou, 176
Picon, 179
Pizzas
    Corn Zucchini Pizza with Lime and
        Cilantro, 208
    Fresh Mushroom Pizza with Sun-Dried
        Tomato Pesto, 211–12

    Halloween pizza, 214
    Heirloom Tomato Pizza with Goat
        Cheese and Fresh Herbs, 209
    Potato Pizza, 214
    Red Cabbage Pizza with Gorgonzola and
        Nuts, 216
    Roasted Bell Pepper Pizza with Feta and
        Olive Tapenade, 204
    Roasted Eggplant Pizza with Red Pep-
        pers and Feta Cheese, 213
    Roasted Wild Mushroom Pizza with
        Goat Cheese, 217
    Sauce Pie, 219
    Sourdough Pizza Dough, 198–99
    Three-Onion, Four-Herb, and Four-
        Cheese Pizza, 210–11
    tips for, 197–98
    Tomato Pizza with Fresh Greens and
        Goat Cheese, 206
    Tomato Pizza with Lemon Zest, 201–2
    Yeasted Pizza Dough, 201
    Zucchini and Feta Cheese Pizza with Sun-
        Dried Tomato Pesto, 203
Plain and Simple Bread, 82–83
Point Reyes Original Blue, 166, 172
Pont l'Evêque, 157
Poppy Seed Muffins, Lemon, 54
Potatoes
    Potato Bread, 78–79
    Potato Pizza, 214
    Raclette, 189–90
Proofing, 31
    baskets, 19
    chamber, 19
Provolone Olive Bread, 187–88
Pumpernickel, 121
Pumpkin Scones, 44

Q, R

Queso Cotija, 178
Queso Doble Crema, 178
Queso Fresco, 178
Queso Panela, 178
Quick breads. *See also* Muffins; Scones
    Deep Dark Chocolate Loaves, 129
    Gingerbread, 141
    Holiday Loaves, 138
    mixing, 24
Raclette, 189–90
Raisins
    Apple Walnut Scones, 41
    Bran Muffins, 52
    Brioches, 60–61

Holiday Challah, 76
Irish Soda Scones, 132
Millet Pecan Muffins, 54–55
Stollen, 142–43
Sunday Bread, 76–78
Wolverines, 114
Raspberry Orange Muffins, 58–59
Razor blades, 19
Reblochon, 153, 163
Red Cabbage Pizza with Gorgonzola
and Nuts, 216
Red Hawk, 166
Retarding, 26
Ricotta
Bellwether Farms Sheep, 165
Experimental Bread No. 7, 186–87
Hot Cross Buns, 130
Ricotta Salata, Lemon Zest, and Cilantro
Focaccia, 107–8
Rising period, 26
Roasted Bell Pepper Pizza with Feta and
Olive Tapenade, 204
Roasted Eggplant Pizza with Red Peppers
and Feta Cheese, 213
Roasted Tomato Salsa, 50
Roasted Wild Mushroom Pizza with Goat
Cheese, 217
Rolling pins, 19
Rolls
Cheese Rolls, 111, 113
Experimental Bread No. 7, 186–87
Pecan Rolls, 63
Wolverines, 114
Roomano Gouda, 175
Roquefort, 159
Cheese Balls, 139
making, 150–51
Rosemary Focaccia, 104–5
Rustichella, 179
Rye breads
Dark Rye, 119
Light Rye, 120
Marble Rye, 122–23
Pumpernickel, 121
shaping, 117
Sourdough Beer Rye, 124
tips for, 117

S
Saffron Bread, 140
Saint-Agur, 173
St. George, 166
Salmon Spread, 191
Salsas
Roasted Tomato Salsa, 50
Tomatillo Salsa, 50
Salt, 23
Salzbrot (Cheese Onion Curry Bread),
180–81
Sauce Pie, 219
Sbrinz, 159, 178
Scales, 19
Scones
Apple Walnut Scones, 41
Cheese Scones, 48–49
Chocolate Chip Scones, 42
Corn Cherry Scones, 46
crumb, 33
Currant Scones, 39
Irish Soda Scones, 132
Just Lemon Scones, 43
Lemon Blueberry Scones, 40
Maple Pecan Scones, 45
Oat Scones, 47–48
Pumpkin Scones, 44
tips for, 35
Scrapers, 19
Seeds, 23. See also individual varieties
Selles-sur-Cher, 163
Sesame seeds
Killer Granola, 66
Killer Granola Cookies, 66–67
Multigrain Bread, 84–85
Sesame Sunflower Bread, 81–82
Shaping, 26–30
Shortbread
Chocolate-Drizzled Stars, Trees, or
Hearts, 70
Ginger Shortbread, 68
Hazelnut Shortbread, 69
Lemon Shortbread, 69–70
master recipe, 67
tips for, 36
Sifters, 20
Silicone baking mats, 18
Slashing, 31, 33
Small Olive Focaccia Rounds, 101–2
Sourdough. See also Starters
baking, 33
Bastille Day Baguettes, 94
Bialys, 100–101

cheese and, 170
Cheese Rolls, 111, 113
Cheesy Muffins, 98–99
City Bread, 97
crumb, 33
English Muffins, 98
Light Rye, 120
Marble Rye, 122–23
Master Sourdough, 92
mixing and kneading, 24–26
Pesto Focaccia, 106
proofing, 19, 31
Pumpernickel, 121
retarding, 26
Ricotta Salata, Lemon Zest, and Cilantro
Focaccia, 107–8
rising period for, 26
Rosemary Focaccia, 104–5
shaping, 26–30
slashing, 31, 33
Small Olive Focaccia Rounds, 101–2
Sourdough Baguettes, 93–94
Sourdough Beer Rye, 124
Sourdough Pizza Dough, 198–99
Suburban Bread, 109–10
Sun-Dried Tomato Focaccia, 105
tips for, 87–88
Tomato, Caper, and Olive Focaccia,
102, 104
Wolverines, 114
Zampanos, 99–100
Spatulas, 20
Spice grinders, 20
Spinach
Calzone, 220
Tomato Pizza with Fresh Greens and
Goat Cheese, 206
Sprayers, 20
Spreads
Date Spread, 139
Hot Cheddar Spread, 191
Mock Boursin, 190
Salmon Spread, 191
Starters
condition of, 88, 91
maintaining, 91
reinvigorating, for baking, 91
Sourdough Starter, 90–91
Steaming, 20, 33
Sticky Buns, 65
Stilton, 157, 179
Stinky-Cheese Plate, 174
Stollen, 142–43

Stuffing Bread, 136
Suburban Bread, 109–10
   Cheese Rolls, 111, 113
   Wolverines, 114
Sunday Bread, 76–78
Sun-Dried Tomato Focaccia, 105
Sun-Dried Tomato Pesto, 105
Sunflower seeds
   Coriander Wheat Bread, 83–84
   Killer Granola, 66
   Killer Granola Cookies, 66–67
   Sesame Sunflower Bread, 81–82
Super Bowl Cheese Plate, 175
Swallow Restaurant Collective, 13
Sweeteners, 23
Sweet potatoes
   Halloween pizza, 214
Swiss cheese, 157

T

Taleggio, 151–52, 159, 175
Tête de Moine, 157
Tétoun de Santa Agata, 159
Thermometer, oven, 20
Three-Onion, Four-Herb, and Four-Cheese
   Pizza, 210–11
Timers, 20
Tomatillo Salsa, 50
Tomatoes
   Fresh Mushroom Pizza with Sun-Dried
     Tomato Pesto, 211–12
   Heirloom Tomato Pizza with Goat
     Cheese and Fresh Herbs, 209
   Roasted Tomato Salsa, 50
   Sauce Pie, 219
   Sun-Dried Tomato Focaccia, 105
   Sun-Dried Tomato Pesto, 105
   Tomato, Caper, and Olive Focaccia,
     102, 104
   Tomato Pizza with Fresh Greens and
     Goat Cheese, 206

Tomato Pizza with Lemon Zest, 201–2
Zucchini and Feta Cheese Pizza with
   Sun-Dried Tomato Pesto, 203
Tomme de Savoie, 152, 163
Tomme du Lévezou, 171
Tumelo Tomme, 165
Turban, 30
Turkey Bread (Stuffing Bread), 136

V, W

Vacherin du Haut-Doubs/Mont d'Or, 159,
   179
Valdeon, 179
Valençay, 159, 169
Vegetables. *See also individual vegetables*
   for pizzas, 198
   Raclette, 189–90
Vento d'Estate, 171
Walnuts
   Apple Walnut Scones, 41
   Banana Walnut Muffins, 56–57
   Bran Muffins, 52
   Cheese Balls, 139
   Red Cabbage Pizza with Gorgonzola and
     Nuts, 216
   Sticky Buns, 65
   Sunday Bread, 76–78
Water temperature, 23
Wednesday-Morning Cheese Plate,
   171, 173
Whisks, 20
Whole-wheat flour
   Coriander Wheat Bread, 83–84
   Corn Oat Molasses Bread, 80–81
   Dark Rye, 119
   Multigrain Bread, 84–85
   Plain and Simple Bread, 82–83
   Sesame Sunflower Bread, 81–82
   Suburban Bread, 109–10
Windowpane test, 25
Wire racks, 20
Wolverines, 114
Work surface, 20

X, Y

X Bread (Experimental Bread No. 7),
   186–87
Yeast, 23
Yeasted breads
   Asiago Bread, 182–83
   baking, 33
   Challah, 75
   Cheese Onion Curry Bread, 180–81
   Coriander Wheat Bread, 83–84
   Corn Oat Molasses Bread, 80–81
   Corn Onion Cheddar Bread, 184–85
   crumb, 33
   Dark Rye, 119
   Day of the Dead Bread, 134–35
   Experimental Bread No. 7, 186–187
   Greek Shepherd's Bread, 181–82
   Holiday Challah, 76
   mixing and kneading, 24–26
   Multigrain Bread, 84–85
   Plain and Simple Bread, 82–83
   Potato Bread, 78–79
   proofing, 31
   Provolone Olive Bread, 187–88
   rising period for, 26
   Saffron Bread, 140
   Sesame Sunflower Bread, 81–82
   shaping, 26–30, 73
   slashing, 31, 33
   Stollen, 142–43
   Stuffing Bread, 136
   Sunday Bread, 76–78
   tips for, 73
Yeasted Pizza Dough, 201

Z

Zampanos, 99–100
Zesting, 20, 22
Zucchini
   Corn Zucchini Pizza with Lime and
     Cilantro, 208
   Zucchini and Feta Cheese Pizza with
     Sun-Dried Tomato Pesto, 203